Russell Coutts

COURSE TO VICTORY

ISBN 1-86958-346-9

Published in 1996 by Hodder Moa Beckett Publishers Limited
[a member of the Hodder Headline Group]
4 Whetu Place, Mairangi Bay, Auckland, New Zealand

Printed by Wright & Carman (NZ) Ltd, Upper Hutt, New Zealand

Russell Coutts

COURSE TO VICTORY

AS TOLD TO PAUL LARSEN

Hodder Moa Beckett

A 17th Man's View

I've always been big, and now I'm fully grown – 2.0 metres tall (6 feet 5 inches) and 110 kilograms wide (17 stone). Being big has its advantages – for uninterrupted views at the movies, for winning the ball in lineouts, and for a degree of stability in a Wellington gale. But it also has its downsides – cramped seats in aeroplanes, head butts from door fames and being last man chosen for piggy back races.

But when I went to San Diego to support Team New Zealand in early 1995 I found out a new benefit of being big – and it provided me with an experience I'll never forget.

Under the new America's Cup rules the competing boats have a crew of 16 with the option of carrying a 17th man or 'owner's representative'. Carrying a large 17th man in heavy conditions actually helped boat speed and to provide a pool of 17th man candidates a "Big Boys Club" had been established by the biggest of all Team New Zealand members, Aaron Hansen – the qualification was to be at least 6 foot 4 inches tall, or to weigh more than 100 kilograms. I also had no problems fulfilling the ruling that the 17th man had to be 'technically incompetent'.

And so it came to pass on a windy day in San Diego that Russell invited me on board *NZL32* in the Louis Vuitton semi-finals and I had the thrill of my life as Team New Zealand spent 75 percent of the race behind *One Australia* only to sail past the Aussies on the last upwind leg. It was a honour and a privilege to sail with 16 talented New Zealanders and I was happy to retire at the peak of my 17th man career.

But on another windy day just before the start of the third race in the finals of the Louis Vuitton Cup Peter Blake arrived and told me Tony Rae was replacing him as mainsheet trimmer for the day and that I was welcome to have another turn as 17th man. Of course I didn't need to be asked twice.

To cut a long story short this was the only race that Team New Zealand lost at San Diego and it unleashed a multitude of misguided accusations about who was to blame. My fellow sponsors had no hesitation on blaming me, despite the prohibition on me doing anything while on board. Tony Rae was also unfairly blamed (it was the only race where Peter was not the mainsheet trimmer).

Fortunately, however, we were both saved by TVNZ when they identified the real problem as being the absence of Peter's lucky red socks. This in turn launched a new national craze that saw nearly every New Zealander wearing red socks – effectively keeping *Black Magic* free of losses for the rest of the regatta.

Bob Fields, Managing Director – Toyota

Contents

Acknowledgements

Thanks to Team New Zealand and all those people who contributed to the stories and successes so far.

Russell Coutts

Foreword
by Sir Michael Fay

In *Course to Victory*, Russell Coutts tells the story of how the America's Cup became New Zealand's Cup. While the name of this oldest trophy in all of sports will never change, in 1995 its home did, thanks to Russell and all the members of Team New Zealand. Their victory was one of the most thrilling moments in my life, and I dare say many of my countrymen and women join me in that sentiment.

This book is much more than a simple tack-by-tack description of what happened on the waters off San Diego, California. It is instead the yachting history of one man and one nation, and how the two intersected in time to produce a team of dedicated individuals that surprised the world by their achievement. It is the inside story of how the tiny island nation of New Zealand, population 3.5 million, mounted a team to go against some of the richest and most technically advanced countries in the world and accomplish the most decisive victory ever in the America's Cup.

Russell has been in the forefront of New Zealand, and international, yachting for more than 20 years and his emergence as the world's number one ranked match racing skipper parallels his country's emergence as a sailing superpower. After learning to sail in the strong winds off Wellington, he began winning dozens of championships that brought him to the attention of first Olympic organisers (he won a gold medal in 1984) and then America's Cup hopefuls.

I met Russell in 1984 when I became involved in the first of my three New Zealand challenges for sailing's "Holy Grail". He was fresh from his Olympic victory and in his quiet, methodical way, he was looking for greater challenges in the sport he loves. But I also sensed a certain intellectual restlessness that later compelled him to leave our campaign in Fremantle, Australia to return to university. Although disappointed at the time, I recognised Russell's strength of commitment to unfinished business, a commitment that has served him so well in his pursuit of yachting excellence.

He tells the story in the book of a phone call he made to me on the eve of the 1987 challenger trials' final series in which the New Zealand Challenge was matched against Dennis Conner's *Stars & Stripes* team. At first baffled and a bit angry that he would call me at home the night before the big race and ask to use our workshop because his mast needed repair so he could sail in an 18-foot skiff regatta, I later realised just how focused an individual Russell Coutts is. And it is just that focus, that singular commitment to winning, that is the hallmark of Team New Zealand, not just the man behind the wheel, but everyone who helped bring glory to our country.

If *Course to Victory* is part history book, it is also a delightful read. I'm not sure I really wanted some of the stories told in these pages to be made public but, nevertheless, they are true and, to be honest, I enjoyed reliving them. As well, the light-hearted approach the author takes perhaps best describes him as a sailor and a person.

I once told Russell that you don't learn much from winning an America's Cup, but you learn a great deal from losing them. On that score, I feel I've learned more than if I'd received three degrees from Harvard, but after reading this book, I think I'd better amend the statement. Russell obviously learned a great deal in his personal course to victory, and the reader is better off for it.

The approach of the man is evident throughout. He is quick to give credit to his teammates, his competitors, and to many who came before him, yet I know how important he was to the 1995 campaign. Russell did much more than just drive the boat, as he'd have you believe. There is absolutely no doubt from where I sit that the way Russell attacked the America's Cup puzzle from the front end, by acting on all he has learned over time to select the team of designers and sailors he did, is the major reason the Cup now resides in Auckland. He is not the type of person to promote himself and his book emphasises the team approach, but I would like it known that it's my opinion that, without Russell Coutts, Team New Zealand probably wouldn't have accomplished what they did. That's not to say he was the single reason for the victory, but it is to give him credit for bringing in Tom Schnackenberg and Laurie Davidson, who, along with Peter Blake, probably were the reasons for victory.

The America's Cup is a design contest, first and foremost. Yet New Zealand didn't put a man on the moon, America did. Countries like Japan and France have strong backgrounds in art, automobile and aircraft design and engineering. None of that exists in this country. But, at the end of the day, a bunch of Kiwi sailors outdesigned the world.

Hopefully those lessons aren't lost on young people here and they become part of the confidence, part of the psyche of our people as we grow. The symbol that we can do remarkable things is found in the Blakes and Couttses of the world and hopefully the average Kiwi can learn from their story about what goes into achieving great things – the focus, the commitment, the sacrifice needed to reach the goal.

What the yachties have done over the years is market this country in a very positive way. They have put our flag up against much bigger countries and proved their dominance. The America's Cup to me is not the quest for the trophy but a test of what we can do ourselves.

Sir Edmund Hillary climbing Everest represents the daring, adventurous, self-reliant Kiwi of the 1950s. I'm interested in the Kiwi of the year 2000, someone who is conversant with the Internet, whose skills in design and communication and management are world class, who can get educated here and get a job anywhere in the world. I think that *Black Magic* and the Team New Zealand win is the strongest example that those qualities exist in our country and are obtainable by anyone who puts forth the effort. Bringing the America's Cup to New Zealand will hopefully do more good for Kiwis under 25 than for those over 55, because the future will be built by the young people. Their dream of success now has a base in reality.

Michael Jay

1

Ghosts of Challenges Past

It was like an ice skating rink on board the boat that day. Everyone from the afterguard to amidships had to hold on to something throughout the entire race. The hydraulic system had sprung a leak and oil was spurting all over the cockpit floor. None of us felt any better about the situation as more than 20 tons of high-tech machinery in the name of *oneAustralia* bore down on our racing yacht at 10 knots, heading right for our starboard side.

We'd expected their aggressiveness, knew they'd try to get a penalty on us, or at least try to gain a significant advantage at the start. And they knew we had to avoid a penalty or a collision at all costs because it was perhaps the only way *oneAustralia* could win. After four long months of racing, two more losses to us would send the Aussies home without the reason they had come to San Diego – to capture the America's Cup. They hadn't found a way to beat our black boats since January and now, in mid-April, they were prepared to employ more aggressive tactics and strategies to get that first victory. Attempting to win a foul on us was perfectly legal and, in truth, it's exactly what we would have done had the situation been reversed.

I needed to change course and needed to do it quickly. They had right of way which meant we had to move our boat away from theirs. It was still several minutes before the starting gun, but they were already dictating the terms of the action. Things certainly weren't going our way. It was just one more situation during that day that was rare, if not unique.

The day didn't seem all that different in the beginning. I'd woken at 6am and was running on the beach 20 minutes later. It was my usual routine to start the day next to the waters we'd be racing on in just a few hours. It gave me an opportunity to study the early conditions and assess how close they were to the predictions made by Bob Rice, our meteorologist, the night before.

It was April 5, 1995, and in just over five hours Team New Zealand would take the boat we called *Black Magic* out into the Pacific Ocean off San Diego, California for the fourth race of the America's Cup Challenger finals. As in the last three races, we were up against 16 Australians who were looking to carve our heart out with a boat that was just beginning to come into its own. But that was a task easier said than done, as *Black Magic*, officially known as *NZL-32*, was sailing faster than she had during the past eight months since she was launched in Auckland.

We'd been second-guessed more than once about our decision to use *NZL-32* in the Louis Vuitton Cup semi-finals and finals. She was the older of the two boats built to challenge for yacht racing's most coveted trophy, and conventional wisdom had it that newer boats were usually the faster boats. We'd used our newer yacht, *NZL-38*, in each of the four round robins that began back in January while using *NZL-32* as our test boat. It had been our intention to exchange the two boats after the first round, then the second, then the third, because we always knew *32* was faster. She had been the first day the two raced and still was, even after a thousand changes to both boats.

But *38* was no dog either, despite the rumours that swirled around us since the day the boats were put in the water. Competitors and press heard the two black boats Team New Zealand built couldn't get out of their own way; couldn't even beat the old red boat, *NZL-20*, late of the 1992 America's Cup. Dogs they were called. Dennis Conner termed them "the Black Labradors". The Aussies referred to them in even less complimentary terms. David Barnes, the Kiwi who was now working for oneAustralia, was known to be suggesting that the boats would go backwards in a seaway. We howled when we heard that and Brad Butterworth suggested we send David a team shirt for his contributions to our effort.

All this, of course, was music to our ears because those rumours had come full circle. We knew when and where they started. We knew, you see, because we were the ones who started the rumour!

With three America's Cup challenges behind New Zealand, we knew the battle ashore is often as fierce as the war on the water. And we had learned that misinformation is a key tool in deceiving the opposition – besides, we decided to have a few laughs. So that day in the Loaded Hog pub, when a member of the Team New Zealand afterguard pulled a well-chosen target aside and whispered that our designers had tried a radical approach that had failed miserably, was the beginning of a ground attack that was a planned strategy. Phase two was a call to one of the major paint suppliers, whom we asked if they had enough black paint to cover *NZL-20*, the 1992 America's Cup warrior. Their curiosity earned them a "confidential" briefing that *20* was routinely beating the new boats. The third call went to one of our own suppliers who we knew was a bit of a town crier.

Not more than two hours later the word had spread throughout Auckland. Soon thereafter I received a call from Jane Dent of TVNZ, who asked me to substantiate the rumour. I used the party line, "It's still early in the game, lots of changes to come. And remember, *NZL-20* has had the benefit of several years of tuning." Jane's too good and too knowledgeable to buy that, so I levelled with her. Well, not exactly, but with a wink and a laugh I got the point across. Not long after that TVNZ broadcast throughout the nation a hilarious piece with dogs barking in the background about our "slow" boats.

We knew the first day we sailed *32* that the designers and builders were spot on and that it was necessary to protect some of the features on the boat from prying eyes. After 1992, one of the main design questions every Cup syndicate faced was how narrow the boat should be. The 1992 winner, *America³*, was the most narrow boat by far. Had that yacht achieved the limit or could that philosophy be taken further?

We'd experimented with even more narrow designs and *Black Magic* was actually built considerably narrower than the American boat. At first we were concerned that we may have exceeded the limit, but once we trialled her, our doubts evaporated as her performance increased. We knew every other team was pondering the how-narrow question, so if our boats were rumoured to be dogs, then it might make others nervous about stretching the limit.

If the opposition knew the boat's true performance, we'd be followed and spied and photographed and interrogated. We also knew that nothing travels along the waterfronts of the world faster than a good America's Cup rumour. In no time at all our competitors were quietly laughing at the poor Kiwis who just couldn't get it right.

The strategy worked. We were pretty much left alone. What could be gained from learning any secrets about a couple of dogs? The press, always quick to believe what they hear, discounted us and went in search of other stories. There was the possibility of a rematch between Australia's John Bertrand and America's Dennis Conner, the two combatants in the historic 1983 match that resulted in the America's Cup leaving the United States for the first time in 132 years. Bertrand was back with his team oneAustralia and the press had it that they were the favourites on the challenger side. What they were really saying is that a Bertrand/Conner rematch would make great copy.

The other story the media loved to tell was about the formation of an all-women's team by Bill Koch and his America³ group. As a first in America's Cup history, the group had attracted worldwide attention, which was both good for the sport and great for Team New Zealand. The more the spotlight was shown on others the better we liked it.

So throughout late 1994, with all of Team New Zealand selected and anxious to begin our challenge and concentrate on the long hours of training and testing, we operated in relative obscurity. But that all began to change on January 14, 1995, when *NZL-38* finished her first race of the first round robin with a

10:53 victory over Spain. By the end of the round, when we had beaten each of our opponents (we'd led at every mark in every race), our competitors and the press began to realise maybe you shouldn't believe everything you hear.

We had a pretty good idea that the two boats Laurie Davidson, Doug Peterson, Tom Schnackenberg, and the team had designed were a match for any challenger in San Diego. We thought that, but until we raced them all over the span of three months and went up against all the changes that made their yachts faster we couldn't prove it. The one thing I did know was that I was confident the team had taken the right approach in designing the two black boats.

Some of the designers are named above and included among them is "the team". The contributions from the structural designers, mast designers, sail designers, boat builders and sail makers in detailing all the various components that went into *Black Magic* is the real secret to the yacht's superior performance.

It was established that the sailors were the clients of the design team and that they were to be included in all major design considerations. Their ideas were continuously solicited and constantly analysed. While Peterson, Davidson and Schnackenberg were widely praised for drawing the hull lines, devising the tank and wind tunnel tests, for running the velocity prediction programmes, and for supervising the actual construction, each one of us knew the boats were the product of the entire team.

No, neither *32* nor *38* was a dog. But neither boat was ever faster than on the last day she was sailed. That was the story of Team New Zealand in the 1995 America's Cup. We tested and trialled and tested and then tested some more. The boats got faster. The sailors got better. Our focus became keener.

I thought about all that as I ran the beach at Coronado that sunny spring morning. Bob Rice, one of the few non-New Zealanders in our camp, had told me the night before to expect some lumps and strong breeze. Already early this morning the wind was up and there was perhaps two metres of swell on the ocean. We'd come to trust every word from Bob and his team of weathermen. They had devised a programme that took a month or so to work out the flaws, but their estimates of conditions, especially wind strength and direction, over the past two months had been so accurate they were almost telling us the precise time of day the wind would shift and where it was going. Their words were key to the tactics we employed.

I had chosen to live in Coronado, the small island off San Diego where we had established "Kiwinado" in 1991–92. Where each of us was to live in 1994–95 had been a question when the team was first organised. This was the fourth America's Cup New Zealand had entered, and living quarters had been prescribed in the three previous challenges. This time, we decided that everyone should have the freedom to choose his or her own place. It was only one of many rules we changed from the past, but in many ways it was the most important. It said to the team that management trusted each individual's judgment and wasn't concerned with our lives outside the compound or off the boat. There was really only one thing each of us was to concentrate on. Winning the America's Cup. Not just winning the Louis Vuitton Cup, awarded to the winner of the challenger trials. Not just being in the America's Cup. But winning it. Three times we had come and three times we had gone home empty-handed. Each of us knew that if we didn't win this time, there probably wouldn't be another time for many, many years.

So my mind was on the race later that day against Bertrand and his boys. It would be the fourth race of the challenger finals, the thirty-seventh time we had started a Cup race in 1995. Our record was pretty good; in fact, almost perfect. We hadn't lost a race on the water since we'd started against Spain three months earlier. In truth, we were already planning changes for the Cup match against the American defender. Such plans could be construed as overconfidence, but with only two victories needed to make it to the Cup match and a boat-building schedule to organise, it was a necessary strategy.

What we did concentrate on that morning was scheduling the testing programme for the three weeks between the challenger finals and the Cup match. We had a new keel we needed to analyse. There were new wings, new sails, modifications to the rudder, and a few new ideas on how to mode our boat relative to the performance of the defenders that all needed to be tested. The schedule for these changes to the boat had to be finalised that night.

So instead of our usual 8am meeting that started with the weather report and led into a tactical analysis of our opponent and what had worked for us and what had not, we abandoned the chalk talk and our usual preparations in favour of some long-range planning.

While many of the rules and regulations of past challenges had been scrapped or greatly modified, one constant from the days of Michael Fay remained. I remember the first team talk he gave to us as we began New Zealand's very first challenge for the America's Cup.

"I'm a banker," he told us, "not a sailor. I might not know a lot about how to make these boats go, but I do know when they'll go. If you have a plane scheduled to leave for New York City at 9am, you'd better not get to the gate at 9.05. These boats will leave the dock at 9am no matter who is on board and who is not."

He meant it and he kept his word. It was just one element of a fairly militaristic-style management, but it was a discipline we found useful almost 10 years later. Each day the dock-off time was posted and each day everyone was on board. It was never a question. The programme was never delayed. Except for the morning of April 15. *Black Magic* left the dock without her genoa trimmer and helmsman. Simon Daubney and I were busy scheduling the tests we needed to perform.

So what seemed like a routine day just a few hours earlier was off track already. I didn't feel comfortable hurtling in our small inflatable through the San Diego slop, the mixture of nature's waves and spectators' wake left by a thousand boats all headed for the America's Cup starting line. The first doubts of preparedness momentarily unsettled me. In about an hour we would take on my counterpart on *oneAustralia*, Rod Davis, who just the day before told the press, "Our whole goal is to take a race off them." Were we ready for this race? There was no doubt in my mind the Aussies were plenty ready for us.

As the inflatable tore through disturbed water, I saw the boat being towed and the crew mostly relaxing. My comfort level rose as I realised I'd known and sailed with and against most of these guys for more than 25 years. Some of us had learned to sail and raced each other in Wellington. Others had shared at least one, and in some cases several, Whitbread Round-the-World Races, and most of us had competed on the international match-race circuit or in one or more of the previous Kiwi attempts to bring the America's Cup home. I always had every confidence each one would bring every bit of his experience to the battle at hand. No one had done anything less since the first day we had all sailed together as members of the team. Each man on board was a star in his own right, but we'd all agreed from the beginning that the team could be the only star.

When we were less than 20 metres off *Black Magic*'s starboard quarter, I watched the racing yacht as she rode the waves. I'd been with her since she was conceived on a computer and I'd been party to all the changes made to the yacht. She had performed as close to perfection in all variety of conditions as any boat I'd ever raced. Only in the last dozen contests had she developed something of a manoeuvring problem that forced us into a few stalls at critical moments in the always tense pre-start battle for position. But her raw speed had compensated for that as well as any and every other problem we had encountered.

The inflatable came alongside the racing yacht and as I boarded *Black Magic* I remembered Peter Blake wasn't sailing with us today. It was the only race he had missed since we began competition and it felt odd to be sailing without him. In many ways the reason the 16 of us were on the race course was because of Peter. In the beginning he'd staked us to the Team New Zealand programme with his own money. It was his approach that had given complete freedom to the team to make all decisions concerning the design and sailing of the yacht. And, of course, he was the architect of the good luck red socks phenomenon that swept New Zealand. Today, no one on board *Black Magic* wore red socks.

In Blakie's place was Tony Rae. We lost neither skill nor experience with Tony on board. He was the mainsail trimmer on *KZ-7*, the first New Zealand challenger. He'd sailed with Blake in two Whitbreads and he'd won a handful of championships in small boats through the years. Like the other back-ups, he was good enough to retain a permanent position on board.

When I took my position in the back of the 75-foot yacht my mind was still pre-occupied with the new testing programme. I wanted to discuss it with some of the crew who would schedule the tests, but I recognised the mood on board wasn't conducive to anything serious at the moment. The guys were as loose as usual. In fact, I began to wonder if we were too relaxed, too casual. I remembered back to an early round when one of the sponsors was on board and he later commented he wondered if we'd ever get serious. Those sentiments were echoed by my father who one day accompanied us as the 17th man. He told me it was hard to believe the team knew we were in the America's Cup.

But that was our way. It had been from day one and I never thought to discourage the stay-loose approach. We all knew each other extremely well, we had spent almost every day for more than eight months together, most of the time at close quarters on the boat, and when we raced we were intense. So during the tow out to the race course, if the jokes were flying and the attitude seemed indifferent, no harm was done.

"Hey Meaty," Joe Allen called to Andrew Taylor, who also answered to the nickname "Raw Meat" because of his size and the pleasure he derives from eating. "I'm feeling a bit flat. How about giving us a lift?"

Meaty was our best cheerleader. His pep talks never failed to entertain and even served to inspire every now and then.

"Okay, as a matter of fact I do have something to say to all you slackers. I prepared a little poem especially for today."

This was met with anticipatory laughter.

"Shut up you guys and listen up. It's time to get serious. Here are the words of wisdom for today:
We've battled hard
We've battled long
But now it's time to march on!"

A stunned silence followed. I can't remember who started to laugh first but it was infectious and in just a matter of seconds a roar of laughter spread out across Point Loma.

Joe looked at the huge grinder and, with thumb up, said, "Thanks Meaty, that really worked. I'm pumped up now." More laughter followed, but it was the last laugh of the day on board *Black Magic*.

Soon the crew began to take their positions. Barry MacKay, our diver, went under the hull and checked for damage and seaweed. When all was clear, we raised the mainsail. Robbie Naismith tailed the halyard as the powerhouse team of Matthew Mason, Jeremy Scantlebury, Meaty and Craig Monk hoisted the huge sail. Then the towlines were cast off and Nick Heron, our "sacrificial bowman" – so named as he was sent to the top of the mast, thus preventing anyone sailing in the race from becoming seasick or risking injury – locked off the main before jumping onto the tender. Jeremy checked the halyards and made sure none of the lines were fouled. Warwick Fleury cleated the mainsheet, leaving it somewhat slack. We were under sail.

It was now less than an hour before the start and the afterguard began to collect as much weather intelligence as they could. Murray Jones and Richard Dodson were on their VHF radios to Mike Drummond, Bob Rice, Mike Quilter, Jamie Gale and Kevin Shoebridge in the weather boats. On race days the meteorology team sent out three small tenders, packed with all types of instruments, to the outer perimeters of the course. They set current buoys to examine strength and direction, as well as letting off weather balloons and charting their flight at various altitudes. They studied their daily records, searching for like statistics or telltale elements that would help them advise us where to position *Black Magic* for the first leg. Like Indian scouts reading the trail, our weather gang kept a sharp eye on the wind, waves, clouds, barometric pressure, humidity and all ambient factors that might affect race course conditions over the next three to four hours. In a language all their own, they relayed data and analysis to our boat.

We now had raised our jib and Simon began trimming the headsail, playing it in and out, seeking the optimal setting for today's wind and the angle of sail. We gradually loaded the boat up and headed upwind, changing tacks so that Schnack could check the wind sheer and calibrate the instruments. This is where we had an advantage over every other team in San Diego. Schnack is a master at programming the instruments to give us exact measurements of critical information such as true wind speed and true wind direction. While many people think the instruments do all the work, it isn't exactly like that. Computers and electronic instruments are only as good as the programs and calibrations that are fed into them.

A good case in point is the phenomenon of wind gradient and sheer. A mast on an IACC boat is more than 100 feet in length. The wind that fills against the sail at the top of the mast is usually stronger and from a slightly different direction than the wind that hits the bottom of the sail. The uneven force in the strength of the breeze causes an additional apparent wind twist when the boat is moving. Instruments read only the wind at the top of the mast, often giving a false true wind speed and direction. They measure only the apparent wind at one point on the yacht, or the wind that is felt by the boat due to the boat's speed coupled with whatever breeze is blowing at the time.

So the actual true wind speed and direction has to be calculated. This is partly handled by the software in the instrumentation package, but the software can't handle what it can't "see" and that's when the skills of a good navigator pay their biggest dividends. The true wind direction is a critical factor that must be accounted for in any tactical analysis. When the tactician makes a call as to whether the yacht should tack or gybe, he often bases that call on what the true wind direction is at the time. This is where Schnack may have outperformed many, because he was able to calibrate the instruments continuously, giving us a great deal of confidence in most of the tactical battles.

As usual, it was very quiet on board. Everyone knew his job, could perform it in his sleep, so it was rare when instructions were called or voices were raised for any reason. The only noise at the moment was the static from the VHFs, the soft voices of Murray and Rick as they shared information with each other and with me, and the ever-present creaks and groans of a somewhat fragile yacht under tremendous loads as more than 8000 square feet of sail caught the wind.

I liked this time of the race day. The guys began to whip into action, bringing their boat-handling skills to the fore, setting up *Black Magic* for her best performance in the conditions. As we got closer to the start, I once again regained the feel of the yacht and began to visualise the pre-start manoeuvres.

Now the VHFs buzzed with more information. Rick and Murray began to create the tactical scenario they would ask me to follow. Depending on the wind strength and direction, on the current, on any probable windshifts, and on what they believed our opponent would plan, my two old competitors from Wellington P-Class days would tell me which side of the course was favoured, where to place *Black Magic* in relation to *oneAustralia*, and which tack was preferred coming off the line.

By this time I had such total confidence in Murray, Rick and the weathermen that I never questioned their calls. If I saw the wind was dead out of the north two minutes before the start and they told me at start time it would be dead out of the south, I'd believe every word of it. We'd won more than one race over the past four months counting on their predicted shifts and I wasn't about to dispute their forecasts or tactics at this point.

It was during the pre-start manoeuvres, too late to request a break-down postponement, that all hell broke loose. Over the years each of us on board the black boat had collectively sailed perhaps more than 2000 boats. Each of us will tell you that the majority of them broke down at one time or another. Most of us had experienced everything from frozen winches to dismastings, so gear breakage didn't come as a big surprise.

But that was one of the things that was so extraordinary about the Team New Zealand campaign. Very little had gone wrong with the equipment through the round robins and the semi-finals. There were several reasons for this. Our maintenance programme and diligence of the shore team was no doubt chiefly responsible. Secondly, I think the boat's speed was also a major factor. Throughout the campaign we had repeatedly been able to quickly get ahead of our opponent and stay ahead. I believe that the fact that so many members of the sailing team had raced in the Whitbread Round-the-World, where boat preservation was often equated to person preservation, played a key role in keeping *Black Magic* sound. When we got a lead the guys would instinctively ease up just a bit.

I don't even remember what went first, our hydraulic system or our electronic instruments. What I do remember is that the boat was wounded going into the start, oil started to leak out all around Warwick, who controlled the hydraulics, and suddenly we were sailing by the seat of our pants. Without the instruments we were essentially sailing by feel. True wind speed and angle were now a matter of calculation by imperial means and guessing. Same with the boat's speed, range, bearing, and time to the next mark. Most of our navigating equipment was out. All weather recording information was lost, and the laser range finder measuring the performance difference between the two race boats was not functioning. Other information lost was such sail-control measurements as the load on the headstay which determines the sail depth and shape of the headsail.

I remember thinking that the situation presented a challenge to us. This was going to be a test for our afterguard and a chance to get back to the fundamentals of sailing and the basics of match racing. It also presented to our opponent the opportunity to seek any advantage possible and prey on any weakness they exposed. That's what match-race sailing is all about, and when the stakes are as high as those in the America's Cup, no quarter is ever given.

This is especially so in any match between Kiwis and Aussies. For as long as I can remember, there has always been an intense rivalry in sports between our two nations, more from our side than Australia's. We're the smaller country by far and I suppose we've always tried to prove our equality, if not our superiority, to our trans-Tasman competitors.

The competition is fierce in yachting. The sport has a large and enthusiastic following in both countries, no doubt due to the fact we're both islands and our people have relatively easy access to the sea. As well, Kiwis and Aussies understand yacht racing. They appreciate the intellectual challenge of the sport and the more subtle nuances lost on the casual observer.

So even though we were racing in another hemisphere, halfway around the world, our rivalry was attracting huge television audiences from Auckland to Sydney. The America's Cup, the oldest trophy in sports, had taken on increasing importance in New Zealand. In some ways a victory in this technological and sporting challenge would help place the tiny nation on the world's stage, no matter for how brief a moment, as a country that can excel in competitions against larger and more advanced nations. It was a sports version of *The Mouse That Roared*.

This vision, this belief held by so many Kiwis that we are equal to the big guys, no doubt found its origin in our neighbours to the west. For it was the six Australian challenges, starting way back in 1962 when *Gretel* lost to America's *Weatherly*, that showed us it could be done. And then in 1983, syndicate head Alan Bond and designer Ben Lexcen put *Australia II* with its famous winged keel in the hands of John Bertrand, the same John Bertrand who now looked across the 1995 race course at me and nodded a greeting. It was Bertrand who drove the boat and his crew back from 3–1 down to wrest the Cup from America where it had been perched in the New York Yacht Club for 132 years. And it was Bertrand who was quietly revered by every Kiwi yachtie who ever raced a boat, for his magnificent accomplishment became proof and incentive to New Zealanders that we, too, could do this. Wasn't it the unwritten rule of our trans-Tasman rivalry that whatever the Aussies can do, we can do better?

And there, behind the wheel of *oneAustralia*, was Rod Davis, the same Rod Davis who had been behind the wheel of the New Zealand challenge for most of the 1992 America's Cup. An American who is generally considered one of the great helmsmen of our day, he'd done himself no favours with many New Zealanders by agreeing to drive for the Aussies. Kiwis can understand sailors leaving their nation for greater rewards on a foreign boat, but after the bitter defeat of 1992, Davis' leap to Australia was seen by many as an unnecessary defection.

For my part, I really wasn't too concerned who was behind the wheel of any of our competitors. I didn't see this as a race between me and Rod or me and Kiwi John Cutler (sailing for the Japanese), or me and Frenchman Marc Pajot, or me and Kiwi Chris Dickson (sailing for the other New Zealand challenger). I saw it as Team New Zealand versus all of them. Our boat against theirs. Our 16 sailors battling their 16 sailors. Our design team opposing their design teams. Our shore team clashing with their shore teams.

So there we were on the Pacific Ocean at 1.08pm on April 15, 1995, skidding around an oiled cockpit with no electronic instruments, two minutes from the starting gun against a starving-for-victory boat perhaps already sensing we were wounded.

"Two minutes, Russell," Brad says to me in his usual, calm voice. "At least my stopwatch works," he informs me with a grin.

Murray and Richard had established that the right side of the course was favoured and the start line was heavily biased towards the starboard end. This was probably the most difficult set of pre-start conditions we could face and it wasn't really what I wanted to hear.

Murray let me know that the boat was a minute and 15 seconds from the start line. "We're close to the starboard tack layline and just under the favoured port tack layline."

The situation wasn't good. The Australians had clearly out-manoeuvred us and I now had little chance of winning the favoured right-hand side of the line or the course. Both boats were on port tack and *oneAustralia* was to windward and close enough to prevent us from tacking back to lay the start line.

Murray, observing that the situation wasn't great, suggested "just be close to the line. They'll try to hold us outside the starboard end, but that's not too bad."

Not too bad! That was fine for him to say, but here I was facing one of the most embarrassing situations in racing – being closed out of the start. Two thoughts went through my mind. One was to take Murray's advice of taking the conservative approach of starting close behind, giving them the start, but putting ourselves in a position to overtake them if the opportunity arose. The other thought was to execute one more gybe and hope they would follow us. If they did so, we could manoeuvre so that neither boat would make it to the favoured end of the start line. Murray's advice proved to be good. I should have followed it.

We knew oneAustralia had made massive modifications to their yacht between the semi-final and final rounds. The changes included lengthening the hull by perhaps as much as two feet, changing the boat's weight and reducing sail area, and altering the size of the rudder. Presumably, the rudder modification was done in the hope of out-manoeuvring us in the pre-start and then, by grabbing the lead, they could negate our speed advantage by forcing us into downspeed tacks. It seemed a reasonable strategy, perhaps one of the few left to them after losing to us in the 10 races we'd already contested.

But a team has to pay for such massive changes and the price was the time needed to tune and learn the "new" boat, to get in sync with how she performed in different conditions. Unfortunately for them, that time could only be found on the race course in a best-of-nine format. Race one of the finals started in 13 knots of wind with maybe a one-metre swell. We won by the largest margin, five seconds shy of five minutes, of any of the races we'd had against them. Race two started in 6 knots and ended in 13, and they had cut our winning delta to 1:57. Race three was on a cold, grey day with the wind never blowing much more than 10 knots. Final margin to us: 2:26.

Just looking at the numbers doesn't tell the story. We recognised that *oneAustralia* was now faster upwind and that she didn't seem to give up much speed downwind. But we also knew that *Black Magic* had improved her speed. We, too, had made changes between the rounds and they had been successful. Except for one thing. We had not completely solved our manoeuvring problem which compromised our pre-start tactics at slow speed. Throughout the regatta, we had continually de-emphasised the importance of winning the start. While this went against normal match-race strategy, we had repeatedly put the emphasis on our speed that could make up for being second over the line. As in so many facets of life, compromise is often the name of the game in yacht racing. When we were confronted with the design choice of speed versus manoeuvrability, speed won out every time.

In each of the three finals races we'd had, the Australians may have crossed the starting line first, but we were always positioned to take advantage of the favoured side of the course that our weather programme predicted and to use our speed to get there.

On the first leg we had reached the first mark in the lead by times of 0:48, 0:26 and 1:01. Yet getting to that position wasn't always easy, and in some of the semi-final races, when the boat was even more difficult to handle at low speeds, I was often frustrated when my timing or positioning was off. I also knew Rod and John and their team, if not the whole country, recognised my weakness and had made plans to exploit it.

Despite Murray's good advice, I went for my second option.

"Gybing," I called.

I swung the wheel and *Black Magic* turned away from the wind, changing direction and momentarily evading our pursuers. But after the gybe, our boat was slow to accelerate and *oneAustralia* had not been suckered into following us. I made an instant situation analysis and knew that where we were was a long way from where we wanted to be.

"Well, this isn't ideal," said Brad, with his expert analysis of the obvious, "but we'll get back to them. If you can get close enough to Rod, maybe I can talk him out of his lead." Brad liked joking about Rod's susceptibility to mind games and our tactician was a master at playing on this vulnerability.

Now we were back to speed, but the Australians were totally in control. All the tacking, gybing and circling common to the pre-start of any America's Cup race is done in an effort to secure an advantage by positioning your yacht relative to your opponent, to the wind, to the start line, and to the direction you think the wind will shift. All of those things can be done if you first establish control.

Brad was calling the time. Murray and Rick were already working on the best way out of this mess and looking for an opportunity to gain a favourable position or find a windshift later in the leg.

Then Rick announced "the right-hand shift we expected is early. We'll start with the course biased to the right."

The news just given me was one more nail in the coffin. In a match race where the two boats race first into the wind, then turn and go downwind, then repeat the same for four more legs, the race committee does everything possible to lay out the course so the first windward mark is directly upwind from the starting line. In other words, they try to set the mark so there is equidistance to the right and left sides of the course from the middle. While there are no out-of-bounds parameters to the course, sailing beyond a layline results in having to sail more distance.

Since a yacht cannot sail directly into the wind, it has to go up that first leg in a series of tacks, changing its direction from right to left and vice versa, tacking through about 70 to 90 degrees. But if there is a windshift of 15 to 20 degrees, the course becomes skewed, or biased, to one side or the other, making one of the tacks much longer than the other. In such a case, the boat in the lead has an even greater advantage because it can push the trailing boat to beyond the layline, making it sail a longer distance. This is done by tacking on the wind of the opponent when they are on the long tack, thus forcing them onto the short tack to clear their air. The short tack therefore becomes shorter and shorter the more the opponent is forced to sail on it, until, eventually, there is no more room left on the short tack.

We were now a little more than 20 seconds from the start and *oneAustralia* had us exactly where they wanted us.

"They're on us again, Russell. We'll have to tack."

I had chosen the wrong option. What I should have done was minimise the loss, take the conservative approach to the line and focus on staying as close behind as possible. Instead I went for the high-risk move of an immediate gybe which just made an already bad situation worse.

We were late to the line and we'd been caught in the worst possible start with *oneAustralia* in phase, on top of us at the gun. They crossed the line 12 seconds ahead, the biggest lead at the start any boat had had on us in the entire regatta.

I looked at Brad and said, "That start won't get me on the ESPN Dream Team." Gary Jobson and the ESPN commentators had previously announced their version of an America's Cup "Dream Team". Brad and I were overlooked, but we considered that somewhat of an honour as we felt their version of what was happening on the course and what we were experiencing often had little in common. So Brad and I had selected our own "Nightmare Team". I told Brad today's start should firmly establish myself as the helmsman of that team.

"It's like the third race in the semis," I remember saying to the afterguard. "You guys worked our way out of it then, just do the same today!"

In that race, *oneAustralia* had a six-second lead at the start which she stretched into 1:04 at the first mark. Then in each of the next five legs we closed the gap until we passed them on the third windward beat.

The conditions on this day, 12 knots of wind and choppy seas, were to their liking and they played to their strengths throughout the race. Our only option on the first leg was to try to shake their cover by tacking, but they'd set their boat up to force us onto the wrong tack and we would never be able to settle down and use our straight-line speed.

The course was biased to the right and we were to the left of *oneAustralia*. Time and time again we attacked, throwing 33 tacks at them, but each time we were repelled from slipping by as the Aussies guarded their favoured position. Meaty and Craig Monk suffered the brunt of our situation, but they pounded away on the coffee-grinders without complaint.

The Australian boat caught a nice shift near the top mark which pulled them around the mark 14 seconds in the lead. We'd been racing for 30 minutes since the gun and *oneAustralia* had gained just two seconds. Every man on board knew we were in the tightest race of the regatta.

Then we saw our first opportunity. As they rounded the mark and tried to set their chute, their spinnaker halyard slipped about 30 feet, giving us the opportunity we'd been seeking. Davis had to steer *oneAustralia* higher than he would have liked to avoid running over their spinnaker. I turned *Black Magic* to starboard and as we rounded the mark we dived down on the inside of them. But then Robbie Naismith, better known as "Battler", our starboard trimmer, tangled the spinnaker sheet with the brace preventing him from grinding the brace back. We had had a late tack coming into the mark and the jib sheet became caught in the same winch as the brace or after-guy, the line that controls the spinnaker pole's movement forward and aft. We couldn't fill our spinnaker until Battler cleared the fouled sheet. Opportunity found. Big opportunity lost.

On the next windward leg we pulled a fake tack on the Australians which enabled us to split tacks, but unfortunately we ended up on the short tack heading to the left side of the course. When we tacked across to meet them again, we had made no gain. There was no doubt about it, the crew on *oneAustralia* was sailing very, very well. As well, we had never seen their boat perform better. After a series of further tacks, a shift went our way and we were approaching them on port tack and needed to dip behind them.

Dino went to the bow to signal the dip. In a dipping situation like this, the helmsman loses sight of the other yacht, obscured behind the headsail for a few nervous seconds. He must rely on the bowman's signals to communicate the boat's position relative to the opponent. As our bow approached the stern of *oneAustralia*, Rod Davis spun the wheel and tacked, forcing us to tack away. It was a conservative dip by Dino's standards – we missed by about 10 feet. The same situation repeated itself several times with the boats getting closer and closer, missing by between two to five feet.

Even if we couldn't get past *oneAustralia* on this leg, we had closed the game up to the point now that we would really be able to put some heat on Rod and the boys downwind. In other words the trick now was to remain patient, stay close and set up for the attack downwind where we could position ourselves to force them the wrong way and take their wind.

As we closed on the top mark, the two boats approached each other once more, the Aussies on starboard and the good guys on port. Just before I lost sight of *oneAustralia*, I thought this was going to be very close, but Dino had signalled to hold course. Then, as we were about to go nose to nose, they tacked and Dino indicated we'd better do the same and do it rapidly if we were going to miss their stern. The old saying a collision at sea can ruin your day crossed my mind as I realised not only would be puncture both hulls, but if our bow hooked one of their running backstays mounted near the stern of their yacht, it would bring their whole mast system down. Now, considering they are Australians, that option wasn't immediately repellent, but then I had to consider what might happen if their mast fell on us. All things considered, it was best to avoid them.

I decided it was too close to tack (in fact I had no doubt we would have hit) and I reversed the turn. This meant *oneAustralia*, after completing her tack, was firmly on our wind, on the same tack as us and we were pinned below them.

This was obviously an expensive error and one that I'm sure the grinders didn't appreciate. After all their work grinding *oneAustralia* down we would now round the mark almost 20 seconds behind, instead of right on their hammer! Frustration arose again and I let loose a few descriptives at Dino for a few seconds to vent my thoughts, as the Australians would be just a bit too far ahead to really attack them downwind.

No, it wasn't our day. We made a couple of position errors around the rest of the course, and we traded gains on the remaining windward and leeward legs until they crossed the finish line 15 seconds in front. We raced for two hours and 23 minutes and, in the end, they gained three seconds on us after the start.

The start. It was all-important this day. Our failure wasn't the result of leaking hydraulic fluid or failed instruments or position errors by the afterguard or gear breakage or any other reason. Our failure in the start was the result of human error and I was the human who made the error.

As we crossed the finish line, I remember being disappointed that we were no longer undefeated. We had a chance to set a record in the America's Cup, but it wasn't to be. I looked around the boat and saw the disappointment in the faces of my friends, but nothing was said.

As we made our way back to the dock, I really don't think anyone read much more into the loss than the fact that we weren't as focused as usual and a lot of things didn't go our way.

On the other hand, I'm not so sure each of us wasn't visited by the ghosts of past New Zealand America's Cup challenges. We'd all lived through three of them, either directly involved or from an immediate distance.

1987 – *KZ-7* established an incredible first-time record of 37–1 before she was handily beaten by Dennis Conner's *Stars & Stripes* in the challenger finals.

1988 – The big boat debacle produced losses on the water to Conner's catamaran . . . and on land in the PR and courtroom battles.

1992 – *NZL-20* was 4–1 against Italy in the challenger finals and needed just one more victory to advance to the America's Cup match when the bowsprit controversy went to the international jury and the fourth victory was declared null and void. We never won another race.

Was our loss today yet another turn towards ultimate defeat? Had the ghosts of challenges past been in hiding, waiting for our most vulnerable moment to make their cruel visit?

As *Black Magic* was towed to dock, I thought back on how we as a team, and how I as a sailor, had come to this point in New Zealand's sailing history.

2

The Early Days

Sailing is in my blood. My grandmother, Priscilla Johnson, was winning yacht races back in the 1920s and '30s. My grandfather, whom I always called Onzo, used to sail as well. One of my favourite stories about him is he once won a bath full of beer and was drunk for days afterwards. A true sailor!

My father, Alan, met my mother, Beverly, at the Napier Sailing Club. He has always been good at building things, he comes from a construction background, and he's always been interested in sailing. When my oldest brother, Robin, was a kid and began sailing, my father built him the first of a series of P-Class dinghies that spanned the Coutts brothers' junior sailing efforts. My other brother, Grant, was the next in line and I was the last.

People tell me they remember when I was just five and six years old I'd go to regattas and watch my brothers race. Then I'd go home and re-enact the races with model boats. I was thinking about racing strategies and tactics before I even knew how to sail.

Robin competed in the 1979 Laser World Championships in Perth, Western Australia. Grant was a lot more laid back than Robin and me, but the competition between the three of us went a bit beyond sibling rivalry. We earned something of a reputation as a feisty lot when the three of us were all sailing Lasers on Otago Harbour in the late 1970s. A few punch-ups between us brought some amusement and entertainment to the locals more than once.

Robin and I were very serious and trained hard. Grant was another story.

He'd turn up to a race late, usually tired from the previous night's activities, and then, more often than not, sail off in the lead leaving Robin and I arguing. I recall one time a local television station was filming a story on what a nice, clean, friendly sport sailing is. The cameraman caught the Coutts brothers, Robin and Russell, at the bottom mark just as we began a dispute over who had buoy room. The skippers got angrier and angrier until they found it necessary to board each other's boats with arms flailing. The television story aired about the fun sport of sailing, but the footage of the two Coutts was mercifully left on the editing floor.

I was seven years old when Robin took me in my first race, in a Z-Class. I don't remember how we did, but I do remember being thrilled. Twenty-seven years later, I still feel the same excitement when I step on a yacht.

I learned to sail on Paremata Harbour, to the north of Wellington, where all the local kids sailed. It is a perfect place to learn. There's a little tidal lagoon with a channel that has current and leads to a bay without much current. There are also sandbars to negotiate and lots of hills surrounding the area which create windshifts. All these variables add up to a lot of different conditions to test and build your skills.

I guess I just learned by doing, although my brothers and father had a hand in it. There's a narrow channel there that causes a good deal of current to flow in and out and the sailing is pretty tricky. I can remember that by age nine or so I had learned all there was to know about the sport and I used to convey that knowledge, in the loudest terms, to my opponents on the race course. I was always right, of course, except for my first race when I got mixed up between port and starboard and couldn't figure out why the other boats weren't getting out of my way. Since that bit of learning is perhaps the most critical part of knowing right-of-way situations, I never understood why someone hadn't straightened out the other kids.

And then there were the collisions. I guess there must have been a dozen or so, all preceded by my yelling "STARBOARD" at the top of my lungs. They left me wondering why these guys wouldn't give way. It's not something I repeat too often these days, but I will confess I earned a bit of a reputation as "Crash Coutts" before I realised I'd better get it straight.

It is fun to laugh at those days now, but there is no doubt they left a huge impression on me. And aside from the impressions I left in the port (or was it starboard?) sides of a few of my mates' boats, I learned a great many lessons that have stayed with me through a thousand races. The most valuable lesson learned is you can never stop learning. Once my nine-year-old arrogance gave way to a bit of humility, if not humiliation, as a result of being on the wrong end of the penalty flag, I decided to study the sport, both on and off the water. Since then I've made a practice of reading everything I can on tactics, design, improving speed, boat handling, steering and so on. And over the years I've kept note books in which I write about my mistakes, draw tactical and rules situations, doodle designs and make notes on things I think are important to remember.

My first boat was a P-Class: the national youth boat and an amazing little craft. It is seven feet long and until recently was usually home-built out of plywood. It has one sail, a short mast, a long boom, a low aspect sail plan and it has the mast stepped well forward. The cockpit has no self-draining system and you have to bai[1] the water out continuously when sailing in strong winds. They are much more demanding boats to sail than the Optimist or Sabot and they are one of the most difficult boats to sail downwind in strong winds because they frequently nose-dive.

I look back at all the technology involved and the thinking behind it and it's such a complicated boat in terms of balance, sail shapes, and tuning that there's no doubt that if you can master it you can sail almost any boat. It's a great training boat because it's difficult to sail correctly, especially in windy conditions.

I have six nephews, two each from Robin and Grant and two from my sister Linda. They all have been involved in sailing P-Class boats and it seems that every time I see them their understanding of sailing and racing has improved immensely, due, I'm sure, to their early years in that boat. This great little boat is a big reason that New Zealand has produced so many good sailors who have done so well internationally.

I can remember stories about sailors like Mark Patterson who went to the Olympics in 1976 and just missed winning. When he sailed P-Class, he would rig at the opposite end of the beach to everyone else. You can imagine these young kids in the psychological wars that go on in these junior boats, but that was the environment in which I was brought up. I took it very seriously and I guess it went a long way to building my competitive edge.

In some ways the difficulty of the boat and the psychological stuff is too intense and drives some kids away. On the other hand, so many of the top Kiwi sailors of today went through this type of programme, so I guess you can't ignore the success. But I wonder if the intensity was a little less keen we might not lose kids who with a couple more years of maturity would decide to stay with the sport for a lifetime.

When I was growing up yacht racing was just coming of age in New Zealand. Rugby has always been the most popular sport, but sailing began to create its own heroes and generate more interest at the end of the 1950s and in the early '60s. When Peter Mander and Jack Cropp brought home a gold medal from the 1956 Olympics, Kiwis began to take notice. I wasn't born then, but when Chris Bouzaid won the One Ton Cup in 1969, I do remember joining a lot of my fellow countrymen in thinking of him as a real hero.

As international competition grew, so did the national contests in small boats. P-Class championships became increasingly important, especially to me. I wasn't even close to that class of sailor, but I lived, ate and breathed dinghy racing at the time. In 1968 I went to a talk given to the Wellington P-Class sailors by 1964 Olympic gold medallist in the Flying Dutchman class, Helmer Pedersen. At that time the top Kiwi sailors were based in Auckland and they had always dominated the P-Class national championships. There was no doubt the prevalent thought among the Wellington P-Classers was that they couldn't beat the Aucklanders.

But Pedersen's talk was all about how the Wellington sailors could not only compete on a national level, but also on an international level. He told us hard work, desire and focus were the ingredients of a winner, not the size of the city or country we were from. I remember to this day his message came down to one simple thought: you can win if you really want to. It was a message that I carried with me to San Diego some 30 years later.

It was also a message that was proven true on the national level when David Barnes won the P-Class nationals in 1974 and again the next year when Gavin Auld won. And again in 1979 when Crash Coutts had learned the difference between port and starboard.

When I was 11 my family moved from Wellington to Dunedin. In Wellington, I had had to rely on my parents to transport me and the boat and all the gear to the water. In Dunedin we had a boat shed close to the water and I could go sailing whenever I wanted. I was no longer dependent on someone else to get me to the sea. I quickly met others who were interested in the same things I was and we used to have a bit of fun on the water, just mucking about in all kinds of boats. That was the key difference between Wellington and Dunedin. Up north I was pretty much limited to sailing on the weekends; almost exclusively racing. It got to be fairly intense and, although it gave me a good understanding of the sport, I'm not sure how much fun I had. In Dunedin, I got to sail all the time and I learned the pure joy of being on the water, having the time to discover how the wind and waves affect the boat and the sails, how positioning the boom and trimming the mainsail changed the speed and modes of sailing.

The great Danish sailor Paul Elvstrom once suggested that sailing in the cold waters of his homeland during the winters taught him to sail around the larger, steeper waves rather than through them. While this tactic was employed to avoid repetitive cold showers, it also taught him this was the path of least resistance for the boat to sail. The same could be said of my experience in the winter waters of Dunedin, where the spray from the waves would numb my face, even with a woollen balaclava on.

One of my sailing partners was John Irvine, who went on to become a World Youth Champion in 1984 and a member of the 1992 New Zealand challenge for the America's Cup. My other regular partner was Alan Garbutt, who competed with me in all the junior championships including the national Starling Class regatta in 1978. He was never short of new ideas and theories, including his conclusion that a pair of five-dollar gumboots were as good as or better than 40-dollar sailing boots, especially when he drilled holes in the soles to let the water out! I never figured out how he planned to keep the water from coming in, but at least he'd solved half the equation.

Alan and I became close friends and during the America's Cup of 1995 I called him back in New Zealand just to keep in touch and see if he'd come up with any new inventions I could use to keep my feet dry or otherwise aid my sailing. Not only did those early days produce good friends like Alan and John, but they also taught me the true value of a good training partner with whom you can share information, discuss strategies and compare notes on other competitors. Of course, when we'd meet in a race the gloves would come off and it was every man for himself.

None of the happenings in Dunedin were by design. My family didn't move so little Russell could spend every day training to become a professional helmsman. It was just a lucky circumstance and it was key to my love of the sport and to my development as a sailor.

While sailing was growing in profile and popularity when I was in my teens, it still had a long way to go to achieve the status of the major sports. It seemed the three Rs of New Zealand schools' curriculum were Reading, Writing and Rugby. I used to play a bit of rugby. Not very well I must add, but I used to play. Like most kids in New Zealand, I got involved in a lot of sports from time to time and there was a period when golf became a real passion and I seriously considered concentrating on that as my main sport. That consideration didn't last for long, but the passion for the game still remains, although I've lost the skills that allowed me to achieve a handicap of 13 some 20 years ago.

One day in high school a teacher asked me what I wanted to do. I said I liked yachting and maybe I'd pursue that. This guy was very surprised and said, "Why would you want to go yachting? There aren't any opportunities in that."

I also remember in another class we all had to get up and say what our ambition was. In front of all the students I said someday I'd like to go to the America's Cup. This was met with laughter all around. At that time, the early 1970s, no one in New Zealand talked about the America's Cup. For our country to sail in that event was roughly equivalent to us putting a man on the moon.

When the laughter died, the teacher told me that was perhaps too ambitious and she suggested I might lower my expectations. I never understood why I should and I never did.

But that shows how the sport of yachting was viewed by most people when I was growing up. The nation's few international successes hadn't made much of an impression on the population at large – but to those involved in the sport, they had opened up the world.

In Wellington I attended Brentwood School and Fergusson Intermediate. When we moved to Dunedin I went to Tahuna Intermediate and Otago Boys' High School. In my early years at primary school, art was my major interest. I also was reasonably comfortable in maths, which led me to study engineering at university. One day a bunch of us were sitting around at a Team New Zealand dinner in Auckland and I asked my fellow scholars what they'd got for School Certificate mathematics. I'd thought I'd done pretty well with a 93. Tom Schnackenberg, after suggesting that I really wouldn't want to know, replied he got a 99. David Eagan told me he got the same. Mike Drummond got 97. Several others were above 95. That quickly put me in my place!

It's interesting how an affinity with maths translates into an attraction to sailing. So much of the sport deals with mathematical concepts and calculations. The process of designing a boat is steeped in algebra, geometry and physics. The more sophisticated disciplines of computational fluid dynamics, scale modelling and velocity prediction programmes are maths-based as well. Once the boat is on the water, racing it becomes a matter of angles and timing and numbers. Surrounded by these maths geniuses, it's no wonder I became the driver. All I had to do was point the boat in the direction they told me to.

There's a story about my academic ability that puts things into perspective. Another one of the lucky coincidences in my life placed me in a class that went through high school together and generally performed brilliantly. Teachers used to talk about the class and how we exceeded everyone's expectations in School Certificate. They would tell classes behind us that ours was the standard to which to aspire.

John Irvine was a year or two behind me. He lived in the same area and followed along the same classes as I did in high school. One day one of his teachers was telling him about how well our class had done and he asked, "Wasn't that the class Russell Coutts was in?"

The teacher paused for a moment, searched his memory, and said, "Well, I don't know about Coutts, but I do know there were others who were smart."

If my high school career was less than memorable, my university years set some kind of record. I had the sailing bug bad by now and was spending almost all my time either racing or preparing for races. At Otago Boys' High I would sit in class and draw race situations in my exercise books. I'd be thinking about starting tactics while the teacher was talking about literature.

But I realised that a university education was essential if I was going to make a living, because at that point I didn't see how I'd ever earn a crust pushing a yacht around a set of buoys. When I applied to the school of engineering at the University of Auckland, I requested an interview with the dean, Professor Meyers. It went something like this:

"You're the sailor, aren't you?"

"Well, yes sir, I like to sail."

"Like to sail, eh. You seem to be on the water more than you're in school."

"Well, that's been the case up to now."

"So why should I let you in university? Won't it be just a waste of our time and yours?"

"Oh, no sir, I intend to concentrate on my studies. I'll put them first. I won't be sailing."

"Well, you've got a pretty good foundation in mathematics. I have no doubt you can be successful if you spend some time on campus rather than at sea. Are you willing to promise you won't go off yachting?"

"Yes, I'll definitely put my studies first."

"Well then," he said with a glint in his eye and offering me his hand, "Good luck."

In a lucky circumstance, the dean's daughter was married to Jock Bilger, a top sailor. In the 1970s he and Murray Ross were runners-up in more than one

Flying Dutchman World Championships. I wasn't fooling my academic mentor for a second.

I actually did buckle down in the first semester and received two As and a B. In the second semester I somehow found myself at the pre-Olympic championships and other practice regattas most of the time and I barely scraped through at university. The dean turned a blind eye to my continuing absences, particularly in 1984 when I devoted most of the year to the Los Angeles Olympics. I'd entered the University of Auckland in 1979 and then went off to a succession of regattas: the New Zealand Youth Championships; the World Youth Championships, first in Italy and then in the US; the New Zealand Laser Nationals; the pre-Olympics and the Olympics. I'd try to make it back to university as much as I could, but it took me a while to finish my studies. I received my degree in 1986, some seven years after I'd entered. It stood as a record until another student took eight years to finish. I can't believe the university put up with his behaviour. He wasn't even a sailor!

My father played an important part in the Coutts boys' early sailing careers, taking a real interest in our participation and being very supportive. Because he has a real talent at building, he would make boats for us. Actually, we all became involved in the process and it was one of the most enjoyable periods of my life. We used to discuss different theories on shape and foils and think up new details and then try to build in various developments. Some of the boats were narrow and others had more beam or there were variations in the centres of buoyancy. My specialty was making the rudders and centreboards.

In 1978, we built two identical boats and told no one. We'd race one boat one weekend, then test both boats, changing a few things around, then show up with the other the next weekend. I don't imagine it gave us any advantage, but it was a favourite topic of conversation within the family. Shades of the two-boat America's Cup programme Dennis Conner made famous a few years later.

I started racing about the same time I was learning to sail. My first race was as a nine year old and I crossed the finish line first. It was the lowest division at the Paremata Boat Club, but it was a thrill. Two years later I won the Wellington P-Class Fresh-Water Championships. I was becoming more and more competitive and I began to set goals, one of which was to race at the Olympic Games.

Long before I got there, I needed to race in local championships, then national championships, and then on to international competition. I held as heroes the few Kiwis who had been successful in previous Olympics and world-class regattas. I was inspired by two local guys in particular, Barry Thom and Clive Roberts. Thom came second in the 1976 Laser World Championships and was runner-up in the 1977 OK Dinghy Worlds held in Auckland. Roberts had won the OK Dinghy Worlds when they were held in England a couple of years earlier. Peter Lester won the 1977 OK Dinghy Worlds which was highly publicised and actively followed by yachties and fans throughout New Zealand. Their successes had proven to me that New Zealand sailors could match the world's best and I was determined to try my hand.

Throughout my sailing career there has been one fellow countryman who has provided me with more competition, both on the water and off, than anyone else. He's probably received more press than any other Kiwi sailor – for that matter, perhaps as much as any sports figure in the country. He's outspoken, he's something of a rebel, and he hasn't always had the nicest things to say about me. But I doubt I'll meet many more competitive sailors on the race course and I still admire his skills. His name: Chris Dickson.

Chris and I first met in 1977 when we were both racing in the national Junior Championships. We met on the beach one day and decided to train together. I'd never heard of him before, but it was immediately apparent that this guy was a good sailor. He went on to win the regatta and I was second. For the next two or three years I always seemed to be just a little behind him. He went off to the World Youth Championships and qualified the year before I did. I won the P-Class championships the year after he did. It seemed every major regatta that I wanted to win, Chris had been there the year before.

At that stage, the major issue for a New Zealand sailor was to get funding for the Olympics. No one even thought about the America's Cup because our country had never fielded a team, the United States seemed a million miles away, no non-American team had won the Cup, we were far behind in technology and, logistically, the event seemed too big to be run in New Zealand if we ever should win the right to host it. It may have been the Holy Grail of yacht racing, but no one paid it much attention in New Zealand. So we were all gunning for the Olympics, with funding and qualifying the major issues on our mind. We knew that whoever won the most races leading up to the Olympic trials would get the major funding and the recognition and the support needed to wage an Olympic campaign.

This was still the early days of New Zealand yachting, when big boat sailing was mainly an excuse to work up a thirst. But things were changing. Yachting was beginning to get increasing media coverage and the public was becoming more knowledgeable about the sport. My first World Youth Championships were in 1979 in Livorno, Italy. Dickson was there defending the double-handed title he had won the previous year with another hot Kiwi sailor named Hamish Wilcox. I was competing in a Laser in the single-handed division in which I thought, if I sailed as well as I could, I might have a chance at winning. I actually sailed above myself and even after being unable to race on one of the days because of sickness, the championship came down to the last day between me and Luis Doreste from Spain. I remember looking at this guy and thinking I would need to do something exceptional to beat him (since then he has gone on to become one of the top sailors in the world, winning two Olympic gold medals and several world championships). I was ahead of him through most of the final race, but he outsailed me on the downwind reaching legs and I ended up second. What I learned from that regatta, and from my early skirmishes with Dickson, was that if I wanted to win, if I wanted to get to the Olympics, the answer was very simple. I had to get better.

So for the next year I trained pretty hard and went into the World Youth Championships in Texas thinking I would be very competitive. I came in fourth. On the water I had sailed well enough to win by beating a very good Australian sailor named Larry Kleist, only to have the championship taken away on a protest. The American sailor, Russ Silvestri, claimed I hit a mark. To this day, I swear I did not. We went into the protest room and I had a witness, a Danish sailor, who saw the incident and said I didn't hit the mark. Tom Ehman, who later became a major player in the America's Cup, filmed the incident and he agreed the mark was untouched. But the video was shown to the judges and the angle was such that it was inconclusive. So Silvestri argued that we couldn't really tell from the film and that when the boat went around the mark, its wake moved the mark and it could be construed that I hit the mark at that point. The jury bought his argument and I went home empty-handed again.

When I thought about that protest hearing, I realised my presentation of the facts was poor. The degree of hurt from the loss was so great that I resolved immediately to improve my performance not only on the water but also, and especially, in the jury room. The experience was significant as I later used what I had learned in more serious events such as the Olympics.

In 1983, while preparing for the Olympics in Los Angeles, I met up with Silvestri in a bar in Long Beach, California. He'd already had a few when he introduced me to his girlfriend. He said, "This is the guy I chucked out of the World Youth Championships in 1980 . . . and he really should have won." A friend I was with asked me how I could just stand there silently and take his insults. He'd screwed me out of a championship and here he was bragging about it. I said, "I'll get even, sooner or later. It may take me 10 years, but these things have a way of evening out."

A year later, just days before the Los Angeles Games, Silvestri was in a bitter protest, which actually went to a court of law, with his fellow American John Bertrand. The outcome would determine who would represent their country in the Finn class. When Silvestri lost I went up to him and said, "Russ, you know how upset I am about you not making the Olympics. You probably feel the way I did in Texas." It many ways, I've considered us even ever since.

While losing the championship in 1980 on a jury call was devastating to me, it taught me that even races as important as the World Youth Championships aren't always won and lost on the water. New Zealand America's Cup sailors were taught the same lesson repeatedly between 1987 and '92. In the months following my defeat in Texas, I realised that if I was going to continue in yacht racing, continue attempting to achieve the highest levels, I needed to become well versed in all aspects of the sport. It wasn't enough just to know how to sail.

I quickly became interested in the rules angle and I remember that Paul Elvstrom, four-time Olympic champion, once wrote that he couldn't understand why his long-time opponent Helmer Pedersen was never too concerned about the rules. Elvstrom's point was that while Pedersen was a great sailor, he left himself vulnerable because he neglected a fundamental part of the sport. After Texas, I understood exactly what he meant.

I often think I should have studied law because I came to be very interested in presenting legal arguments. The whole protest system in sailing lends itself to that sort of presentation. So there was a whole period in my sailing career when I concentrated on studying the rules carefully and used them to gain every advantage possible. Perhaps I upset some of the other sailors along the way as I never had any hesitancy at calling for a penalty, but I came to look at protests and the subsequent presentation to the jury as no different from knowing how to roll tack or set a spinnaker. It is all part of the game and world class sailors are proficient in the jury room as well as on the race course. So, for me, this became an important aspect of winning big regattas.

There was the psychological game to consider as well and I recall an important Finn race just before the New Zealand Olympic trials leading up to the 1984 Games. Rick Dodson, one of the Wellington boys and a teammate years later in our 1995 America's Cup group, and I were racing against each other and the pressure was on. These were the days when all New Zealand sailors our age were pretty intense and operated under the theory that anything and everything was fair in love and war. Actually, since sailing consumed our entire lives, make that everything was fair in war.

When I had unloaded my new boat from a container before this race, I'd discovered the cleats had been removed. Rumour had it that Rick Dodson was responsible. I silently vowed to get even.

In the race we were battling for position coming into a mark when he called for buoy room, which meant I needed to give him enough room to round the mark. I thought it was a judgment call at best and, besides, I didn't feel like giving in to him. He surfed inside me anyway, between my boat and the mark, and when he gybed at very close quarters my boom went straight through his sail. When that happened I pulled hard on the mainsheet which ripped the clew out of his sail, ending the race for him.

Back on shore heated words were exchanged and we almost came to blows, but I reminded him about the missing cleats incident. We laugh about it today, but the point is that at that time I believed in using the rules to any advantage, even if it meant stretching them a bit. I was determined not to show any weakness.

As time went on, I became less and less interested in the technicality of rules situations and more interested in the science of sailing. What intrigues me now is hearing some of the expert designers and scientists discuss the physics of the sport. I still dream up new strategies from the point of view of new tactics and using the rules, but not with the same intensity that I once put into it.

The removal of the cleats from my boat and the boom through the sail may sound more like bitter guerrilla warfare than a sporting endeavour, but they serve as examples of just how serious we took our racing. Remember, too, we were teenage rivals who weren't about to demonstrate any vulnerability if at all possible.

This is best illustrated by the psychological games we played. While some people might think sailing is a non-athletic recreation, just sitting in a boat and letting the wind push you along, yacht racing is a totally different story – especially in small boats and especially in single-handed small boats. Showing just how fit we were became something of a game among those of us competing in the Finns back in the early 1980s. We'd be on the water most of the day, fighting wind and waves as well as each other, and common sense would dictate at the end of the day we should have sailed back to shore in a leisurely manner and then pretty much collapsed. But, oh no. We couldn't hint at being tired, much less complete exhaustion. So we'd race back to shore, sailing as hard and fast as we had all day. Then it was an exercise of how fast we could pack up the boat. Everything was done to create an image that you weren't the slightest bit tired and you could easily go again. It all sounds pretty silly now, but I must admit I look back on those days with a great deal of fondness. You're only young once, and you can be excused for not knowing any better!

After the emotional gutting I received in the Texas Youth Worlds, there followed a period when I seriously considered giving up racing. Chris Dickson won his third youth title at the same regatta and I began to wonder if I was ever going to be able to win at international level. I'm not sure I was comparing myself to Chris, but during those years he always seemed to be a step or two ahead of me. He's only a year older, but his victories seemed to come easy for him and his reputation was growing with every win.

While I may have given thought to quitting, I was also as determined as I was discouraged. I consoled myself with the fact that I had won on the water in Texas and if I sorted out the rules part of the game, I could come home with the championship. So I buckled down, trained hard, and in 1981 I finally reached my goal. That year the World Youth Championships were held in Portugal. My father and long time youth sailing coach Harold Bennett continued to be very supportive, as was my whole family. With rule book in one hand and the Laser tiller in the other, I sailed well and won what to me was the most important international regatta I had entered.

The championship not only kept me in the sport, it energised me to seek greater goals. I began thinking about the possibilities of an Olympic attempt through the rest of 1981, but it was difficult to imagine making a go of it. The time and money needed to put together a successful Olympic campaign are staggering, and officially, if not in practice, I was still a university student. Although Dean Meyers used to tell me I found it easier to find my way to Europe or the US than to the university, I did want to obtain my engineering degree. With encouragement about the Olympics from my father, who sincerely believed I could perform well enough to get among the medals, in 1982 I decided to make a run at it. I chose to race in the Finn class, a 16-foot, displacement dinghy. The biggest challenge was raising enough funds to buy and equip a boat and then get it and its sailor halfway around the world. With cap in hand I began knocking on New Zealand corporate doors, one of which was a relatively unknown company called Fay, Richwhite. I'd been sent there by a gentleman named Irvine Sibbald at property developer Riddiford Holdings. He had written me a cheque and said, "Go see my friend Mike Fay. I'll set it up for you."

When I showed up for the appointment I was told Mr Fay would not be available, but a Mr Peter Debreceny – later to play a critical role in the Fay America's Cup challenges – would see me. I went through my song and dance about Olympic sponsorship and Peter was very intent, but I quickly realised I wasn't getting anywhere with him. I got the distinct impression he was looking at me and thinking, "This guy is nuts. There's no way sponsoring him would get us any kind of a return."

So I left the offices with the old "Don't call us, we'll call you" type of send off. As I walked out I thought that's the last time I'll ever see that guy and I never will meet this Mike Fay character. How wrong I was.

Despite this and many other rejections, I found supporters. Peter Menzies and John Roy of Mainzeal Corporation put forward the bulk of the funds needed. This was backed up by the New Zealand Sports Foundation, Auckland clothing company owner Ray Barker, Tim Bailey of Continental Cars and by my parents, who topped up the balance needed to get the campaign under way.

To be honest, I didn't believe I would get to Los Angeles because there were too many top sailors in New Zealand who had more experience and had been through this type of thing before. Rick Dodson is a case in point. Like Dickson, he'd reached championship calibre a few years ahead of me. He'd also been sailing a Finn since 1980 when he was runner-up in the National Championships and the Olympic trials. In 1982 he won the OK National and World Championships as well as the New Zealand Finn Class Olympic Sail regatta, which he won again in 1983. Bruce Deegan was the other favourite, having won the British Finn Championships and placing well at other top European events as well as winning the New Zealand Finn Championships in 1984, just before the Olympic trials.

There was no doubt that one of those two guys was heavily favoured to win the trials and I would have to beat both if I wanted a ticket to California. Even before the regatta started, I was fighting anything and everything to the point of protesting technicalities about Dodson and Deegan's life jackets and clothing, more to try to unsettle them than because I thought I really had a good case.

At the start of the series, just before heading out on the water to race, I was approached by Peter Montgomery, New Zealand's foremost yachting commentator. I was doing everything possible to psyche myself up for the competition and was extremely intense at the time. I believed that in order to get anywhere in the Olympics I had to stay focused every minute of every day. Anyone interrupting my concentration was met with what can only be termed immature disdain.

Peter asked me for an interview. Anyone who knows him will tell you he's one of the nicest, most affable and enthusiastic guys you'll ever meet. He was just trying to do his job, but I took his request as an imposition, something that would break my concentration.

I said, "If you don't mind Peter I've got to get going."

He said, "So you want me to piss off", to which I said "Basically, yes."

A couple of months later he came back and pulled me aside. He said, "You know, Russell, in my job I've had the opportunity to interview many of the world's most famous athletes. I've had top All Blacks in front of the camera, I've talked to the best tennis players and golfers. I even interviewed Muhammad Ali. No one has ever told me to 'piss off'!"

I think Peter understood I meant no disrespect and I have always appreciated his giving me a little lesson in humility. With age and a little maturity, I think I've lost some of the edge my intensity caused in the early days of my sailing career, although I'm told I still have the "tunnel vision" focus I believe is necessary to succeed in any endeavour one takes on. Peter and his wife Claudia have been special friends to me and my family for many years. And any history of yachting in New Zealand has to include the significant influence that Peter has had on it. The first event I remember him covering was the OK Dinghy Championships in 1977 in Auckland. Since then he has brought, almost single-handedly, the sport to the people of New Zealand. His broadcasting of yacht racing from local regattas to the America's Cup has taken listeners and viewers behind the scenes and provided them with a knowledgeable, interesting explanation of the sport. During the past 17 years I've sailed all over the world and I can say without hesitation that no one explains yachting more diligently than Peter Montgomery.

The New Zealand Olympic trials were held in Auckland in March 1984 and, sure enough, it came down to Deegan, Dodson and Coutts. The advantage changed several times early in the regatta. Dodson was clearly better than I was at sailing downwind, although I believed his technique was bordering on being illegal. In the second half of the competition, his downwind edge began to play a significant part and he took the lead. I issued a protest, supported by Deegan and others, based on a technical interpretation of his downwind sailing. Although the protest was unsuccessful, it served as a warning and the jury watched him very closely for the remainder of the regatta. Richard, aware his technique was borderline and he was under scrutiny by the jury, began to fall off the pace slightly. Fortunes changed and I put together a strong finish to win the series in very tight competition.

After something of an upset in the trials, I was far from being favoured to win at the Olympics. I wasn't even considered to have a chance to do well. The New Zealand selectors were considering whether or not to send me and I was hearing there was a strong negative vote. But I got there, mostly thanks to the support of my father. Ralph Roberts, the Olympic yachting manager, said: "Look, Russell, why don't you just try to enjoy the Olympics; don't go into the racing with any expectations, because you may end up disappointed at the end of it." He explained that the English Flying Dutchman representative Keith Musto was expected to win gold in a previous Olympics, but won silver instead and was extremely downcast when he should have been pleased with himself for doing as well as he did. I thought, stuff that, I think I can win. Even though I hadn't performed well in international competition, I just had the feeling that if I got boatspeed, which I'd never really had in the Finn class, I could win.

I trained off Long Beach and continuously improved, especially with boatspeed. My two tuning partners, Bruce Deegan and Mark Page, had trialled against some of the competition just a few days before the Olympics and had reported being extremely competitive. Since I'd been matching them, my confidence was at a peak going into the Games.

Ironically, in my first race I had an incident with John Bertrand, the guy who had won the court case against Silvestri and most people's prediction to win. He had achieved almost legendary status after winning two world Laser titles and was favoured to win a gold medal in 1980 until the boycott intervened. I got a great start and Bertrand was just to leeward of me. The right side of the course was heavily favoured and the first boat to tack and cross would probably win the race. I had Wolfgang Gertz, a very good German sailor, just to windward of me and I might have been able to tack and narrowly cross him, but I considered it too risky a manoeuvre at that moment. I planned to wait just a little longer and tack when Gertz tacked.

All of a sudden, Bertrand tacked and tried to cross me. I couldn't believe he was trying to cross me on the first tack in the first race of the Olympics! I was on starboard with the right of way and he was on port, which meant he had to give way. I couldn't tack because Gertz was on my hip, restricting my manoeuvrability, so I continued on starboard, held a straight course and hit Bertrand, hit him hard. At that time, sailors couldn't absolve themselves from fouls by taking penalty turns, so we kept racing. Bertrand got to the right of the course first and won the race. I came in second, and the rules were such that if you had a collision you had to protest. But no one would come forward as a witness for me because this was the very first race and no one wanted to be the bad guy.

When we got into the protest room, and with the advice of team coach Brett de Their, I turned to Bertrand and said, "John, can you look me in the eye and honestly say we didn't collide?" He couldn't. He immediately looked away, then looked back at me and said, "Well, to the best of my knowledge, we didn't hit." John was no doubt conscious of the fact that if he denied the incident and the jury saw it, he could be retired from the entire series. The protest was won right there and Bertrand was disqualified from the race.

But he came back strong and was clearly in contention after race four. Although I was now leading, I was still not expected to win and very little press attention was paid to me. I heard an interview with Bertrand, however, and when asked who he thought his major competition was for the remainder of the series, he replied, "There's a guy by the name of Coutts going pretty well."

I didn't help my situation when I was over the starting line in race five, had to return to re-start and finished well back in 21st. Premature starts are a common hazard to racing sailors, especially to those who race aggressively. I knew if I was to beat the best in the world, I'd have to take some risks, but that knowledge did little to cheer my mood after my error.

That evening I was asked by a New Zealand reporter if I still felt I could win a medal, to which I responded, "I didn't come here to just win a medal. I came to win the gold." It was the kind of remark that I regretted almost immediately and, regardless of that bold statement, I knew that it was going to take a very big effort in the last few races to beat Bertrand. Coupled with that, I was beginning to have serious problems with salt water boils that were spreading down the backs of my legs and all over my behind.

When you hike out in a Finn dinghy, with about 15 kilograms of weight in the form of water bottles on your shoulders, the backs of your legs bear the brunt of that load. It's a little like doing half sit-ups for about two hours while sitting with the back of your legs on a fence. It's not the most comfortable occupation in the best of times, and the boils only made the situation worse.

Good Finn sailors, much like rugby props, are not always rated for their intelligence, but they usually have the ability to block out pain and get on with the job. In a typical heavy-air race, it is not unusual for your legs to go numb about halfway up the first leg of the course, which is actually a bonus because you can no longer feel the pain. That is, it's a bonus until it comes time to tack. Imagine moving from one side of the boat to the other with no feeling in your lower legs. All this is going on while you're trying to think about windshifts, tactics, sail trim, the opposition and getting to the finish line as fast as possible. The more you can take your mind off the pain, the better the decisions you'll make about the rest of the game.

There was no doubt that my affliction was not helping matters, although I remember suggesting to one of my competitors that it actually encouraged me to hike out further, thus taking the weight off the boils, though in retrospect this was a very weak rationalisation at best.

At this stage, I was hearing all kinds of helpful suggestions from some of the team. Most are unprintable, but one of them actually made a little bit of sense. I was advised that on the laydays, I should get some sun to dry the area and help draw out the infection. It might have worked had I not overdone it, resulting in a sunburnt arse on top of the boils!

While the agony lingered, my teammates continued to find great amusement in my predicament. I believe it was Murray Jones, backed up by a few others in the team, who sent the cleaning lady up to the third floor sunning balcony, as a matter of urgency, to clean up the "horrible mess". Her screams could be heard for miles.

Ralph Roberts, realising my ailment may have required a more skilled opinion, contacted the team doctor, Dave Gerrard. Roberts had hoped to procure a prescription for some medication which would work its wonders in the briefest of time, but Dr Gerrard advised that the best drugs available to treat the infection were banned substances under the Olympic rules.

When the good doctor appeared at the team house to gauge the level of the problem, he suggested that the only way to get some relief would be to lance the boils, but because of the anti-drug rules, it would have to be done without anaesthetic. I'm sure this provided a similar level of discomfort as the earth must feel before a volcanic eruption, but I was in considerably better shape after Dr Gerrard's slick knifework, although I was shaking for about 15 minutes afterwards.

Race six was in heavy air and Canadian Terry Neilson, a former World Laser Champion, won with Spaniard Mario Blanco narrowly beating me out of second. Bertrand was out of the placings. As a result of his good performances in races five and six, Neilson had sailed himself into contention and it was essentially a three-way tie at the top of the ladder. Bertrand, Neilson and Coutts would decide the gold, silver and bronze by virtue of who beat who in the final race. I remember thinking before that race that I didn't want to have to come back to the Olympics and go through this hell again in the Finn class, so I'd better make sure that I gave this everything.

Kiwis Rex Sellers and Chris Timms had already won the Tornado gold medal with a race to spare. They were the most unlikely looking pair of Olympic gold medallists. Sellers, a fisherman, and Timms, an industrial chemist, appeared as though someone had dragged them off a South Island high country sheep farm to come and sail at the Olympics. They, too, were not rated coming into the regatta, but had blitzed a fleet that included the greatest sailor of all time, Paul Elvstrom. I recall Timms saying to me that he was at a loss for words when Elvstrom approached him and Sellers asking for their advice. They were so dominant, they made it look easy.

In contrast, I seem to have a habit of making things difficult for myself and I knew the last race in the Finn Class would be a real battle. Deegan and Page went down to the boatyard particularly early that morning to check the weight of my clothing which, under the rules, was not allowed to weigh more than 20 kilograms when wet. The strictly enforced rule is a safety measure, brought in after one of the top sailors in Europe wore too much weight and paralysed himself from the waist down. In strong winds there is no doubt that the more weight you can support on your shoulders the faster you can make the Finn go.

We were concerned about the clothing weight limit because in the previous race I had traded off one water bottle and worn baby nappies as additional padding to try to help the boil situation. Nappies? By that stage I was willing to endure humiliation if it would help reduce the pain.

For the final race, though, I would sail with all four water bottles and no additional padding as the forecast was again for strong winds and I needed all the weight on your shoulders that I could carry. Deegan also checked the boat over thoroughly and re-tied all my knots as he didn't trust my ability in that area.

Peter Montgomery apparently went into graphic detail on the Radio New Zealand breakfast show that morning describing the state of the boils on my backside, including the procedure employed by Dave Gerrard to remove the pus. PJ can no doubt be credited for reducing the national cholesterol intake derived from the consumption of bacon and eggs that morning.

As the Finns headed out to the final start, I was still probably considered a long shot to win as Bertrand and Neilson had both won major senior regattas and, by comparison, all I had to show was a World Youth title. Before the start I remember observing that those two guys were watching each other pretty closely and not really paying much attention to me.

I got a reasonable start and led them around the first mark, but they both blew past me on the reach. I can remember recalling the loss to Doreste in 1979. Would this be a similar result? Third place, bronze medal, I started thinking.

This was fleet racing with a lot of boats, but it only mattered how the three of us finished as far as the gold medal was concerned. I got ahead of John on the next windward leg, but Terry still had a nice lead on me. On the downwind leg I caught up with him and was encouraged at the start of the next leg when I was closing on him. Toward the top of that leg I remember feeling filled with energy and using that sensation to put absolutely everything I had into the end of the race. Finally, I passed Neilson near the top mark and then held him off on the reaches. We had a tacking duel up the final windward beat to the finish, and I stayed in front, finishing fifth in the race but in front of Neilson and Bertrand. The gold medal was mine! Even though I believed it could be done, I was probably as surprised as anyone. It was the first international Finn regatta I'd ever won. And since I considered myself lucky, it was the last Finn regatta in which I would ever compete.

As fortune would have it, fifth place was the position that had been pre-chosen for a weight check. After being informed of this, I headed towards the shore and was passed by a boat full of Kiwis, my mother and father among them, very vocal and yelling out congratulations – obviously helped along with a considerable head start in the celebration proceedings.

Peter Montgomery met me at the dock and I told him, "It won't be any problem Pete, just a formality, because we checked the clothing on the same scales this morning."

Most of the New Zealand team were still expecting me to arrive at the beach as they had not been advised I'd gone straight to the weigh-in tent. On the first weigh, the clothing was over by a kilogram. "This is impossible," I advised the committee. "The same gear was checked on the same scales earlier this morning."

Some of the committee members were aware of the morning check, so they decided to re-weigh the gear. This time it actually weighed less but was still over the limit. The committee advised that they would have to inform the jury. The jury would have only one course of action and that would be to disqualify me from the race, meaning the gold would turn to bronze.

Montgomery, who had been thrown out of the tent before the second weigh-in because his journalistic status was not considered official enough, sensed that this was now not just a formality. He ran off to find Ralph Roberts, who arrived just as I was completing my argument with the committee. Ralph proceeded to start joking around with the measurers, either not sensing the building tension or trying to diffuse it.

I must admit to thinking that Ralph was not helping the cause but, in a strange way, and whether it was planned or not, it served to delay the proceedings just long enough for one of the committee members to suggest that we weigh the clothes individually. It was suggested that I did have the right under the rules to weigh the clothes one last time but, if that failed, they would have to report their findings to the jury.

We carefully wet each piece of clothing and arranged it on the scales. As we were doing it, both Ralph and I realised that as we pulled the clothing out of the water, the longer we took to arrange it, the longer it would have to drain. Also, when the clothing was weighed as a bunch, the individual articles were not as free-draining.

When the weights were totalled, we were slightly under the limit. The measurers didn't believe such a different result, so they checked it again. Again it weighed under, and finally the gold medal was secure. Ralph looked at me, winked and said, "Let's get the hell out of here."

As soon as I left the tent, Deegan and Page grabbed the gear and took the clothes away for a ceremonial burning. They would never be re-checked! Nor would I have any use for my hiking pants, weight jacket or hiking boots ever again.

The fact was, that was the last time I would ever set foot in the Finn dinghy.

Peter Montgomery approached with a TVNZ camera crew in tow and a microphone at the ready. Suddenly we were on live television, being broadcast to the whole of New Zealand. I thought I had managed to hide the boil problem reasonably well up until this time and had no idea Pete had already broken the news to the radio audience that morning. I suppose in reality it was a bit like trying to hide an elephant in your bed and it was obvious that walking was uncomfortable, sitting down impossible.

"Russell Coutts," said Peter in his most professional tones, "you've just won the gold medal in the Finn Class after overcoming what I understand was a serious affliction that almost knocked you out of the competition. Can you show us the extent of the problem?"

With that, Peter reached over and pulled my pants halfway down my hip as the camera zoomed in.

"I can't show you them Peter," I managed to mumble as articulation failed me. "They're on my bum."

I knew the gold medal might increase my profile as a sailor, but this wasn't exactly the type of exposure I anticipated.

It had been a tremendously successful Olympics for the New Zealand team. Bruce Kendall had also won bronze in the boardsailing. In the three classes in which we won medals, we had not been expected to win. Similarly, in all three classes, most of the pre-contest favourites from the top yachting nations had not come close to winning.

That night, the whole team celebrated with passion. Chris Timms stood up on a table in a local restaurant to deliver a speech which he had obviously spent considerable time preparing. He was starting to sound like a politician, thanking anyone and everyone who had even the slightest involvement with the Olympics, so one of the guys sneaked up behind him and lowered his trousers. Timms, still concentrating heavily on his delivery, didn't immediately realise what had happened. He was in the closing stages of his speech and it wasn't until the laughter completely drowned out his monotone that he rectified his appearance. His political career was over before it started.

The best preparation for the Olympics were the World Youth Championships. I'd done three of them before Los Angeles and I felt I knew what type of competition and what type of a regatta the Olympics would present. Both regattas demand total dedication to the goal of performing at your peak. Long hours in the gym and on the water, building endurance and preparing mentally and physically for anything you might encounter are prerequisites to success.

The format of the Olympics was very similar to that of the WYC, especially in the Finn class where competitors had to draw for boats.

The value of the World Youth Championships was proved by results at the 1984 Olympics. I won the gold medal in Finns, Luis Doreste won the gold medal in 470s and Carl Buchan won the gold in the Flying Dutchman. All three of us had won World Single-handed Youth Championships.

Far from being awed by the opening ceremonies in Los Angeles, I remember being more concerned that here I was spending time at the parade rather than doing something to help me win the gold medal.

Our team travelled to the US about five weeks before the Games began. We opted to stay not in the Olympic Village but in a house owned by an American, Bill Kingsley. It had been severely damaged by fire several months before we arrived, but with typical Kiwi spirit none of us seemed to mind. In fact, most of the team helped Bill rebuild the house, even adding extensions for more room for all of us.

With the Finn being such a physical boat and with the sea breeze off Los Angeles fairly strong, I had realised that, to do well, I had to be fired up. So here we were in living conditions that made it seem just like home, like this regatta was nothing more than a weekend sail. I'd never performed well if my mindset was "just another Sunday sail" so I went into the competition telling myself that this was the most important regatta I'd ever been in or ever would be in. I purposely put as much pressure on myself as possible. I didn't want to wait four years to have another go.

That approach worked well for me, but I recognise it doesn't work for everyone, or even for the majority of sailors. The Finns are single-handed boats so I didn't have to worry about how the pressurised approach would affect my crew, but in later years when I began sailing more and more in crewed boats, I had to learn to change my approach entirely. Then it became, "It's just another regatta, no big deal, you've been through hundreds of these, treat it just like practice."

When I returned home from the Olympics, I was further honoured by my country when I was presented the MBE. It is an honour I regard with great appreciation.

Talk had begun to circulate about New Zealand possibly organising an America's Cup team for the 1986/87 event to be held off Fremantle, Western Australia. The Alan Bond/John Bertrand victory in 1983 had finally broken the New York Yacht Club's hold on the trophy and had proven to the world that someone other than the Yanks could win. For the first time, Kiwis began to take our participation seriously.

And since my gold medal had established me as one of the higher profile sailors in the country, I thought if I continued to sail well, especially in match-racing events, I might be considered for the team. How quickly that perception changed when I entered my first international match race.

3

The First Challenge

On reflection, it was probably a bit foolhardy of me to think I had much of a chance in the 1985 Citizen Cup match-racing regatta in Auckland. First and foremost, I'd never been in an international match race before. Every major competition I'd ever entered had been a fleet race. The two formats are very different, especially considering strategies and tactics. In a fleet-race regatta, you're racing every boat on the water, and as you go along through a number of races, your position in the standings dictates which boats you have to beat and which ones have no bearing on where you finish. In a match race, you're racing just one opponent and every manoeuvre from pre-start to the finish line is influenced by what your competitor does and where you are on the course in relation to the other boat. The two disciplines demand two different mindsets.

Two other factors argued against my success in this event. One was that I was used to sailing small boats and the yachts used in the Citizen Cup that year were 34 feet long. Secondly, I'd just been through an Olympic campaign in a single-handed boat. The Stuart 34s to be raced in Auckland were sailed with a crew of seven. The differences between single-handed sailing and racing with a crew are as great as the differences between fleet and match racing. Put all of these factors together and there's little doubt I was like a fish out of water in this particular regatta.

I should have known something was amiss when, on the first day of practice, I had a bit of an argument with the Auckland Harbour Bridge. The bridge won. It seems it never had any intention of getting out of my way.

While it was a minor collision, it illustrated how much I had to learn. The whole experience was so new to me I felt like I did in those first days on Paremata Harbour in the P-Class. I was learning all over again.

Unfortunately, I couldn't learn fast enough. In the first real contest of the first match-race regatta I'd ever sailed, the luck of the draw placed me against Rod Davis. I can imagine his glee at discovering he was up against the greenest rookie in the field in his initial battle. Rod not only had considerable match-racing experience, he had been sailing big boats for a number of years. Also, he'd already been in three America's Cups – in 1977 as Lowell North's bowman aboard *Enterprise,* in 1980 as a coach for Australia I and sailed on Tom Blackaller's yacht *Defender* in the 1983 trials. I think it's fair to say I was over-matched.

I didn't know much about match racing but I did know getting a good start was critically important. I also felt that to do so meant you had to be very aggressive. Despite this approach, Rod had no trouble establishing the controlling position immediately and within the first two minutes of my first match race, I was squarely behind the eight-ball. Even worse, in the final few seconds before the start, I was headed straight for the committee boat, anchored on station as one end of the starting line.

It's a favourite tactic of many skippers to achieve the controlling position in the pre-start and then drive the opponent outside the committee boat. This usually prevents the other boat from establishing the windward position, and as it has to duck below the committee boat, the opponent is forced into the wind shadow of the controlling boat, thus losing boatspeed. Davis was all over me and as we both raced at full speed towards *Titianui* he executed a perfect tack just centimetres from the stationary craft. His yacht changed direction in a split second and the sails filled with wind. He was now off to the starting line on starboard tack with full rights, leaving me on port tack at ram speed, with no brakes, a few metres from the committee boat.

I, too, tried a nifty manoeuvre, attempting to duck into the gap between Rod and the committee boat. It failed. My bow slammed into the committee boat's bow, splitting the planks down three-quarters of the *Titianui* on the opposite side of impact – $35,000 worth of damage. It was so bad, some members of the race committee had to stay on board throughout the entire four days of the regatta, pumping out the ocean that threatened to sink the beautiful old boat.

"Crash Coutts" had returned. Did someone say something about a gold medal?

Whatever profile I might have raised in Los Angeles was quickly lowered by my performance on Auckland Harbour. If there was talk about a challenge by New Zealand for the America's Cup, strictly a match-race regatta since 1870, I doubt the name of Coutts was spoken in the same sentence after the Citizen's Cup. The name that did begin to get some play was that of the Citizen Cup winner that year: who else but Chris Dickson.

Chris had still been a step ahead of me over the past few years, but I

Brentwood Primary School, eight or nine years old.

My mother and father have been big supporters over the years. They were at the Olympics, our first win in the match race worlds and the America's Cup, all raced off the coast of California.

Heavy air P-Class training on Otago harbour.

NZ Herald

Rounding Mark One in Long Beach, California, during the 1984 Olympics. I was happy to have drawn boat number 12, the same number I used at the World Youth Championships in Portugal three years earlier.

Ross Land

After winning the Olympic Gold Medal on the water, there were some tense moments when I thought I might lose it on the weight scales. Team manager Ralph Roberts helps me weigh each item of gear, piece by piece.

Kiwi yachties Rex Sellers and Chris Timms celebrate their Gold Medal victory in the Tornado class at the 1984 Olympics. The great Danish sailor Paul Elvstrom dubbed them 'The Fast Guys'.

Boardsailor Bruce Kendall won the Bronze Medal in Long Beach. He and I roomed together on the top floor of 'The Zoo', Bill Kingsley's house in Alamedos Bay. He and his sister Barbara went on to win gold medals at later Olympics, making them one of the outstanding sporting families in New Zealand's history.

Michael Fay's original design team for the first fibreglass 12-metre yacht ever built. Left to right: Laurie Davidson, Ron Holland, Bruce Farr, and Russell Bowler.

Chris Dickson. He is often a tough competitor.

Michael Fay's interpretation of the America's Cup Deed of Gift was that it outlined rules for a "match race in two like and similar boats". Obviously Dennis Conner and the San Diego Yacht Club had a different interpretation.

During the series of practice regattas we held in 1994, I met up with one of the truly great legends in our sport, Buddy Melges. The charismatic sailor came to Auckland as part of the America[3] team. Buddy was the first sailor to have won both the Olympic Gold Medal and helmed an America's Cup winner.

The team soon after our win in the 1993 World Match Racing Championships in Perth, Western Australia. Daubs refused to leave the yacht club without the trophy.
From left: Simon Daubney, Jeremy Scantlebury, Russell Coutts, Nick Heron and Warwick Fleury. Missing is Australian dinghy legend Glen Bourke who called tactics.

began to think I was pulling level after my Olympic experience. Those same Olympics had been a nightmare for Chris. He had made a run at becoming New Zealand's representative in the hotly contested 470 Class. Competition was intense to say the least, with stories about boats filled with water, missing equipment and sabotaged sails making the rounds almost daily. Few of the stories were based in truth, but there was absolutely no doubt there was no love lost among the 470 sailors.

The kings of the 470 were David Barnes and Hamish Wilcox. The two had mastered this tricky little boat and from 1980 to '83 they had collected enough silver in the class to make Bunker Hunt envious. They were the favourites to win the 470 Worlds in early 1984 and then go on to win the 470 Olympic trials six weeks later.

But there were several other Kiwi teams nipping at their heels. Murray Jones, another of the Wellington guys I'd grown up with, was making a strong showing sailing with Earl Berry. Chris Dickson had also chosen the 470 to provide his ticket to the Olympics.

New Zealand's participation in the 1984 Games must be set against the black clouds of disappointment caused by the boycott of the 1980 Moscow Olympics. For political and, I suppose, moral reasons too complex to rehash here, New Zealand chose not to send an Olympic team to Russia. Eight Kiwis chose to defy the politicians – Prime Minister Robert Muldoon had told the athletes publicly "if you go, you won't get any of my help" – saying they had worked too hard and trained for too long to stay at home. The yachting team was not among them. Canoeist Ian Ferguson did go and was well prepared for 1984, when he won three gold medals to become a New Zealand Olympic great. Just what good the boycott did escapes me.

So by the time the 1984 Games loomed on the horizon, the country's best athletes were more than anxious to perform on the world's stage. This was true of all the sailors; particularly true in the 470 Class.

As predicted, Barnes and Wilcox won a very competitive 470 Worlds that included a stellar field from around the globe. In second place was Dickson, who had Joe Allen aboard. Just three places down the ladder were the new combination of Peter Evans and Sean Reeves. The stage was set for what developed into an extremely hard-fought, and quite bitter, Olympic selection trials.

Dickson had already begun to develop something of a reputation as the bad boy of New Zealand sailing, an image he appeared to encourage and one which later paid benefits in his America's Cup campaigns. While his talent and skills were unmistakable, his "take no prisoners" approach to yacht racing did not sit well with many competitors and observers. Part of this building animosity was the result of jealousy over his ever-growing record of victories, but part of it was also his style on and off the water. Many of those who had sailed with him to capture his championships didn't have much to say about their experience. In New Zealand, their silence spoke volumes.

The trials started badly for Barnes and Wilcox and went from bad to worse. All sailors have had inexplicable bad days and bad regattas. This was one of those. Jones and Berry sailed unevenly, up one day, down the next. Out of nowhere came Peter Evans and Sean Reeves, whom no one thought would do much, but they sailed consistently well.

And then there was Chris. Sailing again with Joe Allen, he had also put together a strong regatta. But it was the year for the underdog, as I proved in the Finn Class, and the Evans/Reeves team won the 470 Olympic trials on the water.

But then Chris issued a protest over a technicality. The issue was fiercely debated and Chris became more and more adamant a rule had been infringed. The jury didn't see it his way, but the argument didn't stop there. He hired a lawyer and threatened to take the New Zealand Yachting Federation to court. The entire affair didn't win Chris many friends.

But the Kiwi public tends to be quite forgiving, especially to its sports heroes, and after Chris won the Citizen Cup his status as one of New Zealand's top sailors was restored. If there had been any preliminary America's Cup talk, and if so it could all be written off as bar chatter, certainly Chris Dickson would have been the top and logical speculation as helmsman.

It could be said that New Zealand's first America's Cup challenge was the result of a controversial beginning followed by a string of rather remarkable coincidences. Many Cup observers believe Michael Fay was the man who began the first challenge, but that wasn't the case. I think it best to let the person most intimately involved with it all tell the story. I recently asked Sir Michael Fay how the America's Cup Challenge of 1986/87 came to be. Here's what he had to say:

"The man who first began the challenge was Marcel Fachler. He was a Belgian businessman who dealt in futures and commodities. He was based in Sydney, but I believe his motive was to promote his business interests in New Zealand. I was living and working in Sydney in 1984 and I remember reading in the papers that New Zealand didn't have an America's Cup challenge and the deadline to issue one was in about three or four days. I spoke to my partner, David Richwhite, and said we should do something about that. But something else came up and we forgot to do anything about the challenge.

"So the idea originated with Fachler and he put it in the name of the Royal New Zealand Yacht Squadron. I believe I'm correct in saying the squadron knew nothing about it and the members spent a few days asking each other who the hell made the challenge. Apparently Fachler did the whole thing by himself, made the challenge, put up the original money, got the whole thing going. But shortly thereafter he suffered a number of business reversals and never played a part in the challenge he had begun. I never met the man and I've never heard from him.

"My only connection to him was pure coincidence that I had a slight guilty conscious because I'd committed in my mind to making sure that New Zealand had a presence in the Cup, but I hadn't followed through.

"So here was the Royal New Zealand Yacht Squadron with an America's Cup challenge on its hands that they knew nothing about and I'm not sure they wanted anything to do with it. But before I became involved, there had obviously been discussion within the squadron and it had been decided to try to make something out of the situation they had inadvertently found themselves in.

"Two of the powers who first became involved were Aussie Malcolm and Tom Clark. Both were great yachties who had played important roles in New Zealand's yachting history. Aussie had been a National Party cabinet minister who had used his persuasive powers to further a number of the squadron's activities. Tom was one of the nation's leading industrialists as owner and chairman of Ceramco. Tom had sponsored the Whitbread yacht *Ceramco New Zealand* in 1981/82, and was a true America's Cup aficionado, who I think had attended every Cup since World War 2.

"I was first approached by Peter Montgomery and Alan Sefton, who explained to me the brief history of the challenge. Ron Holland, who had produced some successful Admiral's Cup boats, had been commissioned to design a boat to race in Australia. But, there hadn't been any organised effort to get the kind of support needed, so the challenge was floundering a bit. Their view was that unless someone got behind it pretty solidly and pretty quickly, it would probably fail.

"I became somewhat interested and several of us met on a number of occasions over three or four months to decide whether we would get involved and support the campaign or not. But, from the beginning, my only interest was as a potential financial supporter, certainly not as a sailor or manager, and most certainly not as a syndicate head. Although as a Kiwi I'd followed Australia's many attempts to win the Cup and was inspired by their spectacular win in 1983, I wondered if New Zealand would ever be able to get it together. Too far, too hard, too expensive. But here was this challenge and I was being asked, 'What are you going to do about it?'

"So I did a lot of walking and talking, looking for advice as to whether or not this thing could be done. We convened a couple of think tanks at our offices, and invited all of the names that I had heard of or was told about. These were the crème de la crème of New Zealand yachting, old and young. I can't recall everyone who came, but some of them were Roy Dickson, Tom Schnackenberg, Tom Clark, Peter Montgomery, Alan Sefton, Aussie Malcolm. I think Chris Dickson came once or twice. There were about 12 or 14 of us at those sessions. And I really approached it as I would any other feasibility study. New Zealand was the smallest country that had ever challenged for the Cup so it was simply a question of can we do this?

"There were four major issues we addressed. The first was did New Zealand have the design capabilities to produce a winner? Next was did we have the construction expertise to build a boat that would be capable of winning at that level of competition? The third was did we have sailors capable of competing at that level? And the fourth question, which was never on the agenda, but Tom Clark put it up, was did we have the money? Would we be able to get all the resources necessary to do it?

"I studied all the bases for about three or four months. In the short term, I told Aussie that we would meet the costs over that period of time to keep the challenge going. If we decided not to become more involved, the money that was funded would be considered a donation. If we decided yes, then we'd come on board, boots and all. That was the end of 1984 and the first month or two of '85.

"What excited me first about the America's Cup was Australia's victory. Not just the racing, but the way they had won, both on and off the water. All the intrigue with the wing keel and the New York Yacht Club and the closest score ever. It was a drama that caught people's imagination here. And I understood the America's Cup is the most exciting thing you could do in yachting. In the end I guess it was mostly a gut reaction. Something inside said you've got to have a go.

"The think tank sessions provided positive answers for all four major issues. Yes, we had the design talent, the construction expertise, the sailors, and, with effort, we could find the money. On the design issue, the names that kept coming up in addition to Ron Holland were Laurie Davidson and Bruce Farr. So I came up with the design team idea. What I said to Aussie Malcolm was it's your job to go and put a design group together and I think three heads are going to be better than one on this project. And that was a condition of our involvement. So the actual design group was put together by Aussie Malcolm.

"For all of my enthusiasm for other sports, I've never seen anything to compete with the America's Cup in terms of its complexity. I think it's fair to say its really got little to do with yachting in a way. It's got to do with your ability to plan, to organise, to pull together the financial resources you need. You must understand the importance of the critical path. I often say to people, I'd rather do the America's Cup than receive an MBA from Harvard."

After Michael Fay came on board, sailors throughout New Zealand began to take the challenge seriously. Michael is a merchant banker who, with David Richwhite, has established a successful and growing business. He had also been involved with a few yachting sponsorships that had drawn him into the game and increased his profile among sailors. When we heard he was supporting the challenge, our confidence level that this was for real rose considerably.

As Michael says, it was a series of coincidences that brought him into the challenge. But perhaps the strangest one of all placed him squarely in charge of it all, a position he was reluctant to take, but one which I believe changed the course of New Zealand's America's Cup participation for the next decade.

During the think tank sessions one subject of discussion was who was best qualified to manage this first-ever challenge. Michael was interested only in helping to set up the framework for the challenge and help with funding. What was needed was a hands-on person, someone to run the campaign on a day-to-day basis.

One name was repeatedly suggested, a sailor who had considerable experience in keel boats and had been project manager for one of the maxi-boat owners. At the time, there were few people in New Zealand who matched this fellow's qualifications. We were a nation mostly of small-boat sailors and there just hadn't been many big boat campaigns for people to manage. But this was a critical position and one that demanded expertise in many different areas.

A meeting was arranged between Michael and the proposed manager. The two got along well and Michael made the guy an offer. It was accepted, providing the guy could join the team in Fremantle in January of 1986. Until then, he was committed to several projects for the maxi-boat owner.

Michael, ever-diligent, wrote out a 14-page, hand-written contract which both men signed. The manager-designate returned to the United States and Michael returned to Sydney. Let's let Michael pick up the story from here:

"When we decided to have a go for the America's Cup, we made a number of critical decisions, two of which had significant impact on the entire campaign. The first was to build the boats in fibreglass, as suggested by a man named Peter Bateman, a mate of Phil Holland, Ron's brother. The other decision was that we would have to have a dummy run at the Cup in the form of the 12-metre World Championships, to be held in Fremantle in February 1986. It was just illogical to think we were going into our first America's Cup and win it without some experience in the boats, against competitors we'd meet on these same waters in the Cup trials. Our approach to this challenge was we weren't doing this as a practice run, as a preliminary to the next America's Cup. We believed we could win and we had every intention to do so.

"I had come back to New Zealand toward the end of '85 when the campaign appeared to be running into management difficulties. It didn't look to me as though we were on track in terms of getting to the world championships. Things were chaotic and we were behind on deadlines on construction timetables. In fact, I can remember Chris McMullen, the builder, begging me not to go because he thought we were just going to embarrass ourselves.

"But we had to go and so I remember pushing quite hard at that time in November/December to get us organised. And, really, there was no one else in a management sense at that stage because the guy we hired wouldn't be available until January. So it was left to me and I thought I'd step in to get us through this rough period and then hand everything over to the manager we had hired.

"There was only one thing wrong with that plan. Our designated manager, the guy we considered absolute key to the challenge, never showed up. To this day, I've never heard a word from him.

"So there I was in Fremantle, waiting for our man to come and realising it wasn't going to happen. I called up David Richwhite and said, 'Listen, old boy, you've got to run the business on your own because I'm stuck. Our man didn't show up and it looks like I've got the job.' And that's why I stayed. Not because I wanted to, but because I had to!"

It's interesting that Michael would mention the use of fibreglass as one of the most important decisions made in the 1986/87 campaign. I remember when I first heard the idea I thought it would be difficult to achieve. No 12-metre yacht had ever been built of fibreglass. Aluminium was the material of the day and every boat that showed up for the 12-metre World Championship was made of it, except for the two identical Kiwi racers that were fronting up for the first time.

The major proponent of using fibreglass in the construction of *KZ-3* and *KZ-5*, the first two boats to arrive in Fremantle, was the Brit Peter Bateman. He'd been brought into the campaign by Ron Holland's brother Phil very early in the game. Bateman pushed Fay to use fibreglass and perhaps because this was an initial challenge without precedents to restrict free thinking, the decision was a go. It was a decision that caused a sensation in Western Australia and rocked the America's Cup world.

While fibreglass had been used in marine construction long before it was used for the New Zealand boats, this was a first in America's Cup yachts. The material had been considered by a number of designers for 12-metres but abandoned for several reasons. One was cost; another was malleability. An aluminium boat can be reshaped, cut, welded and repaired as a boat is optimised during an America's Cup competition. Fibreglass can not. Another perceived problem with fibreglass, central to the controversy that erupted, was that it is difficult to achieve the same weight distribution as an aluminium 12-metre. Uniform weight was a critical rule that had to be complied with.

The theory behind using fibreglass is that it makes the yacht stiffer. As well, because less fairing material is used as a result of the boat being formed in a mould, the boat can also be lighter. Designers were well aware of the prevailing conditions in the Indian Ocean off Fremantle. Lots of wind, lots of waves. When sailing in heavy seas under the huge loads that large yachts generate, an aluminium boat tends to bend and buckle. Not a great deal, almost imperceptibly, but the bow and stern would rise fractionally and the panels between the ring frames would distort. This might cause the forward and aft mast stays, wires that support the mast, to slacken just a bit and the water flowing around the hull to be a little more disturbed. Also, the slackened rig would cause the sails to lose some of their desired shape, disrupting the forces propelling the boat. The result was a loss of boatspeed.

Fibreglass gave benefit to those problems. And while cost was still a factor that had to be dealt with, the ingenuity of the Kiwi design programme was that it employed an approach that mitigated that dilemma. Simply said, it was more economical to build two boats at once using fibreglass than two boats at different times using aluminium. This saving was the result of what may have been the most critical decision made by the design team and supported by syndicate management. It was also a decision that had enormous ramifications in the 1995 campaign. The decision was to build three boats, the first two of which would be formed in identical moulds.

The philosophy of a two-boat programme owes its origins to Dennis Conner. Before he took control of the USA's America's Cup defences in the early 1980s, both challengers and defenders would build one boat and come to the starting line hoping for the best. As the famous American newscaster Walter Cronkite once wrote, "In the years before Conner, challenging for and defending that one hundred guineas worth of Victorian silver was a sometime sport, almost an after-office-hours sort of game . . . Conner's multi-boat program changed the sport forever . . . Those that built a single boat and sent a single crew to Australia never were seriously in the running."

Dennis saw that by using a second boat as a "trial horse" or tuning partner, he could test different concepts, different rigging, different sails, different appendages, all in the quest for more speed. There was only one difficulty in his two-boat programme: the boats started out somewhat different and so performed differently no matter what was done to them. The tests could never be 100 percent accurate.

Recognising this, the Kiwi design team of 1986/87 did Dennis one better. Peter Bateman and the New Zealand Challenge conceived the idea of producing two identical boats, fabricating them from the same mould. Thus, whenever a change was made to one of the boats, such as adding a new keel or reconfiguring the sails, the result was immediately known and considerably more accurate. This eliminated a great deal of guesswork as well as reducing the time necessary to test the different variables.

The New Zealand boats were quickly dubbed the "Plastic Fantastics". They caused quite a stir in the yachting world, and the reaction to them by Conner opened up what is now more than a decade-long love/hate relationship between him and New Zealand sport fans. One night at a press conference during the races, Dennis was asked for probably the thousandth time what he thought about the Kiwi boats being built with fibreglass. This had been an issue with his campaign for several months and his Sail America syndicate had already submitted several official protests and calls for clarification of the measurement rule. On this particular night, Dennis apparently had lost his patience and, many suspect, his sobriety. He then uttered the words that will no doubt live in America's Cup infamy: "The last seventy-eight 12-metres built around the world have been built in aluminum so why would you build one in fibreglass unless you wanted to cheat?"

When the statement was made, the crowd of journalists were stunned and the room went deadly silent for a few moments. Dennis started a weak explanation that he didn't really mean it, but rival American skipper Tom Blackaller quickly took command. "Uh oh," he said, "I wouldn't have said that, but you can't take it back now." Blackaller cemented Dennis' earlier words perfectly. There was no turning back.

A firestorm of criticism aimed at Dennis followed. New Zealanders were insulted because they felt Dennis had called their team, and thus their nation, cheats. Headlines denounced the American skipper, America's Cup officials scrambled to calm the waters, and the issue media pundits labelled "Glassgate" took on a life of its own.

For the New Zealand challenge's part, the outburst solidified support back home and attracted more international attention to their mounting victories. Michael Fay later called Dennis "our greatest public relations asset". For Dennis' part, he later said he regretted his statement as soon as he had said it. He also wrote in his book *Comeback*, "I've eaten my share of leather over the years for things I've said, but there are still times I can't keep my foot out of my mouth."

The fibreglass controversy came to a head after Sail America proposed an amendment to a measuring rule that could very well have disqualified New Zealand from the competition. Lobbying was fierce and emotions at boiling point when 12 of the 13 challengers met to vote on the proposal. It failed by just one vote! Had that one vote gone the other way, I wonder if New Zealand would have ever returned to future America's Cup events.

While the design team was one story, the sailing team was another. Following my ill-fated entry into match-race sailing in the Citizen Cup, I was surprised to receive a call from Michael Fay requesting a meeting. We met in his Auckland offices in December 1985. He told me the challenge was for real, the top Kiwi sailors would be given a chance to make the team and he believed we would win the America's Cup. Then he surprised me again by asking how I thought the campaign should be set up. I thought for a minute, then said we should form two teams which would compete against each other, and may the best team win. A modified version of this approach was used, but not for the reasons I believed would build a strong team. The fact of the matter was that there were very few New Zealand sailors who had big boat experience, and even fewer who had match-racing experience. Those who had match-racing experience in big boats could be counted on the fingers of one hand.

Inexperience was our biggest liability. We believed, however, that if we could sail dinghies well, we could eventually sail 12-metres. I remember the first time I ever stepped foot on a 12-metre yacht, Laurent Esquier, our coach, asked me if I knew how to work the runners.

"Sure," I responded, looking at them, trying to figure out what could be so difficult. Since that day, I've sailed many boats on which the most inexperienced people are put on the running backstays. For our first sail on a 12-metre, this observation was no exception. Actually, this concept is surprising when you consider that it is the runners that hold the rig in the boat when performing a gybe!

The wind was blowing and none of us on board was too sure how to control this bucking bronco of a boat we were on, but none of us was about to show our ignorance.

This was the first time most of us had ever been on a boat larger than 35 feet. A 12-metre, at almost twice that size, seemed to me like an aircraft carrier! It took all of one gybe in 25 knots of wind before we had things so fouled up Laurent must have realised this wasn't the best place to hold the first day of school. He ordered we take down the mainsail, but the halyard had been overhoisted and was jammed. So there we were pounding around in these pretty rugged conditions on this big boat with a stuck mainsail and the wind blowing like stink and the waves crashing all around us. Someone needed to go up the rigging and clear the halyard. Laurent looked around the boat, shook his head, and went up the mast himself. I remember watching him bounce around up there and thinking, "Holy smokes, this is serious stuff."

When he came down, he began swearing like a bullocky in his native French. He blasted each of us, telling me, "I thought you said you knew how to operate the runners. Why didn't you just tell me you don't have a clue?"

Of course he was right, but, on the other hand, what did he expect? Hadn't he heard the recruiting stories that circulated during the formation of the team? It was said that Ralph Roberts would drive through the back country of New Zealand until he'd spot a man up a tree, cutting branches.

He'd get out of his car, stroll up to the tree, and yell to the guy, "You ever been sailing?"

"No, why do you ask?"

"Because you'd make a good bowman. Want to go to the America's Cup?"

This and a dozen stories like it were designed for amusement, but do point to the truth that in 1986 we needed everyone we could find. In most of the think tank sessions held in the Fay, Richwhite offices, Chris Dickson's name continued to surface whenever a helmsman was discussed. Now and then someone suggested I should be considered because of my Olympic experience, and Graeme Woodroffe was also mentioned, along with a few other sailors. But I doubt anyone other than Chris was really seriously considered as he was the one New Zealand sailor who not only was recognised as a champion, but who had big boat, match racing, and match racing in big boats experience. Unlike the majority of us, Chris had actually sailed on a 12-metre!

I joined the team and made the initial trip to Fremantle. This quaint little Victorian city on the west coast of Australia pulsated with hospitality and welcomed the America's Cup with open arms. While a festive atmosphere permeated the city for more than a year, the New Zealand challenge managers chose a more austere, almost military, approach to the event. We were housed as a team in an old Portuguese fishing club that was turned into a barracks for the sailors. Even Michael Fay lived there, in the "chairman's suite" which was much grander – he had his own bathroom. The only problem for him was they forgot to hook up the hot water so he spent three months taking cold showers.

The team was given pretty rigid guidelines as to our off-site behaviour. Given that most of us were quite young at the time – the average age was below 25 – this type of parental control was probably necessary. But the rules didn't sit well with everyone.

The first New Zealand America's Cup challenge occurred during a transitional period in our country's yachting history. We were beginning to emerge from a strictly amateur approach to a more professional one, and a whole new group of sailors were making their way into the sport. While we had had some success in the Olympics dating back as many as 30 years and had shown some strength in One-Ton regattas and Admiral's Cups, we weren't exactly feared on the international scene. Our original team contained a sprinkling of old-style yachties who had established themselves in a number of national regattas, both on the water and in the pubs. They represented an earlier image of the Kiwi sailor, the guy who saw yacht racing as the short prelude to a long post-race party. If their style was a bit antiquated for the mid-1980s, they nevertheless remained heroes in the eyes of the generation which followed.

As the personal style of the individual sailor was changing, so too was the entire approach to the sport. America's Cup campaigns were becoming one-, two-, even three-year affairs. Leaving home for another country, where we would set up camp for more than a year in order to compete in both the 12-metre World Championship and the America's Cup, was something new to all of us.

The first meeting held in Fremantle typifies the changes in attitude and style of both management and athlete. Most of us had just arrived off the plane from Auckland, on which some of the older guys, in keeping with the sailing-as-a-party theme they favoured, had quickly found the bottom of several rum bottles. The younger guys viewed the spartan barracks, the two brand new 12-metre racing boats down at the dock and each other with a mixture of wide-eyed awe, anticipation and fear.

Michael Fay stood before us. Here was the man who had saved the challenge, the man who had put up his own money to give his country a chance to make a statement in front of the world, the man who had been forced to take the reins when the would-be manager never managed to show. Michael introduced himself and gave us the little speech about the 9am plane to New York and if we show up at the dock after the boat has left, we wouldn't sail that day. He made clear he believed discipline was an important part of a winning equation.

When he finished, he asked if anyone had any comments or questions. "Let's get any problems you may have out in the open right at the beginning," said Michael.

The room was quiet for a moment, then one of the rum-filled old salts stood up slowly and said, "Michael, you're a ____." His obscenity, in this setting, shocked everyone. "But you're a good ____."

Dead silence followed. No one knew what to say. This wasn't exactly how Michael Fay, or any of us for that matter, envisioned the first steps in our long journey to capture the Cup. When the shock subsided, someone offered his advice on how to run the campaign. That was followed by someone else's suggestions. Soon the room was on the threshold of chaos. Now everyone had an opinion and everyone was expressing it at the same time.

Then there was a loud whistle and a single shout calling for order. As voices calmed, Joe Allen stood up and faced all of us.

"At this moment, I'm ashamed to call myself a Kiwi," he said in sombre tones. "Everyone in this room represents our nation in our first challenge to win sport's oldest trophy. Michael Fay has put his business reputation on the line for us, not to mention his money. He's the man who is responsible for all of us being here and for those two boats sitting down at the dock. You don't seem to realise what we have here. None of you seem to have figured out that we've got a great chance. I think you're all a pack of whiners!"

The outburst had the immediate effect of calming the waters. A majority of nodding heads greeted Joe's words and the first threads of team unity began to be tied. But it still took a number of weeks before it all shook down.

Laurent Esquier was a man with a mission. He took on the challenge of teaching us how to sail 12-metre yachts. He had only a few weeks to do so before the 12-metre Worlds but, if anyone could, Laurent was the man. He was knowledgeable, organised, worked well with the young guys and liked to run things on time. It was that characteristic that fitted in so well with Fay's overall philosophy. As Michael liked to say, "We can find everything we need for the America's Cup except time. We won't run out of technology or sailors or money, but we will run out of time."

So during the first week or two of the New Zealand challenge in Fremantle, Michael and Laurent were on the dock every morning and they cast off the dock lines at precisely 9am. Most of the sailors were hopeless. We had never operated under such strict discipline and during the first days in camp there was usually a mad scramble to jump on the boats as they began to head out to sea.

Those first few weeks turned into a comedy of errors, at times closer to tragedy. After the fiasco of our first sail on a 12-metre, on the chartered *Challenge 12*, we began sailing our own boats, *KZ-3* and *KZ-5*. The first disaster was a broken mast on *KZ-3*. We borrowed an old mast from the Brits, but it didn't fit. We didn't hook up the check stays to the hydraulics properly and we couldn't figure out why we couldn't shorten the stays to reduce the mast bend. The result was we bent the mast permanently.

We sailed like that for a while, which of course didn't do the boat or the team any good. Then a day or so before we were to race some of the other challengers, we determined we had to fix the mast. We didn't have a spare and we decided we couldn't continue with the bent one. One morning Laurent, Woody, myself and several others were on the dock when Laurent said, "We've got to fix the mast." None of the sailors had a clue how to do so, but Laurent, ever-resourceful and always prepared, walked us through a method of reversing the bend. Then we welded a steel plate on the front of it and stepped it on the yacht. It wasn't ideal for speed, it was like carrying around 100 lbs up the rig, but it got us racing.

Somehow Laurent whipped the guys into shape. He got us up to speed sailing the 12-metres in about two weeks, which I've always thought was a miracle. The military approach was working, although it had started with a few hiccups. Michael Fay tells the story of his first few days in Fremantle:

"I hadn't selected the sailors and I didn't know them personally, other than a few names. I didn't know what some of these fellows were all about, but I wanted to learn, so I would go to dinner with them. We had these big, open glass door refrigerators that were stocked with Steinlager beer, courtesy of one of our sponsors. Before dinner, the refrigerator doors got a real workout as some of these guys would head over and return with five or six bottles of beer under each arm. Of course, by the time dinner got on the table, these guys were as full as bulls.

Each dinner was turning into a monstrous piss-up.

"After three or four nights of this, I'd had enough. I thought this routine had to be broken. So one night I lost my temper and let loose, calling these guys a bunch of drunken bums who had no idea what the America's Cup campaign was all about. I asked them if this was how they were going to operate for the next year, how did they think they were going to win the Cup. Then I asked them if they really wanted to win. Because if they didn't, they could leave now. If they wanted to win, if they wanted to make sacrifices and put forth the effort, they were welcome to stay.

"Afterwards one of the guys approached me and told me I didn't understand Kiwi sailors. He told me this was part of the yachties' lifestyle, that to change them was to break their spirit. I was told to back off. But I kept pushing hard on the discipline front and a great source of inspiration to me was that some of the young guys seemed to respond. They seemed to understand what I was after. They began to buckle down and they began to become quite proficient.

"So two distinct factions developed over the first couple of months. One was led by the old hands, the rum drinkers, the hard arses of the world who couldn't stand the pace, couldn't handle the discipline, couldn't make the changes that were necessary to lift the game. The other included the young, committed guys, the guys who really wanted this thing to happen, were willing to leave the party behind and do whatever it took to turn the campaign into a successful programme. I sincerely believe that if we had gone the traditional route, continued the way it had been and ended up with just one of the average campaigns in Fremantle, we would have come home licking our wounds and I don't think New Zealand would have ever gone into another America's Cup."

Fay's leadership and demand for discipline combined with Esquier's coaching began to have their effects. Yet while their approach brought some positive returns, it also resulted in attrition. An exodus of the old salts trimmed the ranks. And it took some of the guys a while to adjust to the new ways. Two incidents perhaps illustrate this best.

Part of the new regime was an emphasis on physical conditioning. Roy Dickson, father of Chris, was a key player in the New Zealand challenge from back in the Fay think tank days. He was an experienced yachtsman and he was committed to this America's Cup project. Roy suggested bringing physiological expert Jim Blair into the campaign to manage the conditioning programme. A Scotsman, Jim came to New Zealand in the 1960s and made his name in the physical education field as advisor to the great rugby teams Canterbury and Auckland fielded in the early 1980s.

Jim, like the other members of the management team, was pretty strict. He demanded everyone be in the gym each morning at 6.30 for the daily workout. This was difficult duty for most of us, particularly for those guys who spent their nights seeking more entertaining pursuits.

The first incident involves Graeme Woodroffe, who had spent the night partying and had arrived at the compound just minutes before the conditioning exercises were to begin. He had his warm-ups in his car and as he was changing in the back seat, he noticed Blair walking towards the gym. Not only was lateness frowned upon, but if Blair sensed that Woody had been AWOL the night before, his position on the team might be in jeopardy. So Woody thought fast, realised his only option was to get to the gym before Blair and hopped over the compound's perimeter fence and jogged towards the gym. Blair turned, saw Woody apparently completing a run before the conditioning programme, and said, "Good on you, Woody. You'll be in shape in no time."

The other incident happened in the early days of the campaign. One of the old salts who wasn't buying the new approach to yacht racing was having himself a smoke, in one of the offices. He thought he heard Michael Fay approaching down the hall, so he reckoned it best to bail out. He jumped through a window, landed awkwardly on his ankle and broke it. The next day he showed up on the dock with a fresh cast wrapped around the ankle. His explanation was "I must have injured it sailing yesterday."

I had committed myself to making the trip to Fremantle and being a part of the team through the Worlds. I was newly married, I still didn't have my degree from university, and I still believed it was almost impossible to turn a sailing career into a regular pay packet. I suppose a little bit of maturity was catching up with my new responsibilities, but the fact that I was in Fremantle argued against abandoning altogether the sport I loved.

I ended up sailing on the boat which had Graeme Woodroffe at the helm. Chris Dickson had recruited some guys he'd sailed big boats with and as the World Championship approached it became apparent Chris and his guys were considered our number one team. When the first race of the 1986 12-metre World Championships was won by Chris aboard *KZ-5*, to the surprise of everyone, I began to see that my own participation in the America's Cup was highly dubious at best.

The Worlds ended with *KZ-5* in second place, behind Alan Bond's *Australia III. KZ-3*, the boat I raced on, finished seventh, a result that further demonstrated to me that my time might be better spent back in New Zealand. I asked for a meeting with Michael Fay not long after the Worlds finished to tell him my decision. I remember he was very excited about how well we had done, and rightfully so. From the campaign's perspective, we were probably ahead of schedule. But from my personal perspective, I was behind schedule in the game of life. I explained to Michael I thought it best I return to university and finally complete my degree. I think if the positions had been reversed, if I was the guy who had given this kid the chance of a lifetime and he was now telling me thanks, but no thanks, I'd have been ticked off. But his reaction is a measure of Michael Fay's character and an example of why his 1986/87 programme was so successful. He was obviously disappointed, but he looked at me and said if that's what I thought was best for me, that's what I should do. He thanked me for my help, told me he respected my opinion and supported my decision.

I did return to New Zealand and I did complete my engineering degree, no doubt to the great surprise of Dean Meyers, but I've always regretted leaving the team in Fremantle. The experience of sailing big keel boats would have been invaluable, and because I chucked it, I was rarely considered for other keel boat regattas in the next few years. When Chris and the team returned to New Zealand, they were national heroes and a whole new chapter in Kiwi yachting had been written. It was a chapter in which the name Russell Coutts would appear, if at all, only as a footnote. And now a new class of yachtsman had been established, a class from which so many of the top international regattas drew their New Zealand teams. It took me a good five years to re-establish myself in this elite class.

4

A Tarnished Cup

While I was at Auckland University, the first New Zealand challenge was putting together one of the most remarkable winning streaks in the history of the America's Cup. It was rare for a first-time effort to do well. It was unheard of for a first-time effort to win more races than any of the other challengers. The trial races to select a challenger for the 26th running of the America's Cup began on October 5, 1986, off Fremantle. Thirteen teams, representing six nations, sent their new 12-metre yachts into the fray. Chris Dickson, 24 years of age, with tactician Brad Butterworth, 28 years old, and a very young crew would be racing the best sailors the world had to offer. Among them were Marc Pajot with Marc Bouet of France; Harold Cudmore with Chris Law and Eddie Warden-Owen of the UK; my Olympic competitor Terry Neilson with Hans Fogh from Canada; Americans Dennis Conner with Tom Whidden and Peter Isler; Tom Blackaller with Paul Cayard; John Kolius with my other Olympic competitor John Bertrand; Buddy Melges and Rod Davis.

In the first round robin each team raced every other team. New Zealand, which now had *KZ-7* built and tuned for racing, finished the competition with an 11–1 record. The only loss was by 49 seconds to Dennis Conner's *Stars & Stripes*. The second and third round robins were held in November and December. *KZ-7*, now dubbed *Kiwi Magic*, won every race and entered the semi-finals in first place with the unbelievable record of 33–1 (*Courageous IV* had dropped out after the first round). The other semi-finalists were *Stars & Stripes*

(27–7), *USA* (23–11) and *French Kiss* (20–14).

The start of the semi-finals was notable on two counts. One was the record of New Zealand and the other was that for the first time in the history of the America's Cup the New York Yacht Club would no longer be competing in the event. Although their yacht *America II*, helmed by John Kolius, actually had the third greatest number of victories with 26, the points weight of the wins (one point for a first round win, five for a second, and 12 for a third) worked against them. They ended up with 128 points, one less than *French Kiss*.

New Zealand, in first place, raced fourth place *French Kiss*, while the two American boats battled each other. *Kiwi Magic* proved too much for the French, winning all four races with margins greater than two minutes. Conner also disposed of his old nemesis Tom Blackaller in four races.

The weight of the points should have sent a message to the New Zealand challenge. The way the points increased gave a much greater reward for a win in the third round than in the previous two. This signalled that performance improvement between October and December was expected. Changes to the boats were allowed, even encouraged, between rounds.

To my mind, that's where the Kiwis failed. While they had made some changes to *Kiwi Magic*, they were nowhere near as extensive as other teams had made. Their inexperience in the game and their almost undefeated record led them to be too conservative with their boat changes. While this is easily understood – why make changes to a proven winner? – the New Zealanders didn't seem to take stock of what the Americans, particularly Dennis Conner, were doing. *Stars & Stripes* was radically changed throughout the competition. New appendages, new sails and new sail shapes, new spars and something called riblets had all been added before the challenger finals.

KZ-3 and *KZ-5* had served their function well, even better than expected. They had always been considered test boats. The plan had always been to gain as much information from them as possible, information that would be used in the design and building of the third boat. It was the third boat that would be sent into America's Cup battle. The progression of sail numbers, 3 to 5 to 7, was planned as well – Michael Fay's lucky number is 7.

The keel for *KZ-7* owed much of its design to a man called Richard Karn. Compared to the keels on *3* and *5*, it had an aft-sweeping bulb with smaller wings on the back of it. When the new boat was launched, it was apparent it was much faster than the two previously built yachts. And then as she compiled this incredible record, the conventional wisdom within the syndicate was not to mess with her. Apparently the designers were quite sure they could have produced a better keel. This could have been fixed to *KZ-5* and tested before fitting it on the race boat, but the project was rejected.

Larger wings were tested, fitted in only one position, and only used for a very short time before being prematurely discarded. *KZ-7* was not optimised or moded to meet the longer, more heavy-air oriented *Stars & Stripes*. Larger wings, a new keel, perhaps a displacement change and the crew's better knowledge of their heavy-air mainsails may have moved the performance of *KZ-7* more towards *Stars & Stripes* in strong winds while still retaining most of the advantage in light winds.

Kiwi Magic was clearly the better boat in lighter conditions, but *Stars & Stripes* was potentially faster upwind in very heavy air. For *Stars & Stripes* to have an advantage, the breeze needed to be stronger than 20 knots and, as luck would have it, that's exactly what was in store for the Louis Vuitton finals.

One of the more important lessons learned by New Zealand from the Fremantle battles, and later from the 1992 challenge, was that the America's Cup is a contest of continuous change, continuous testing, continuous improvement. The team that best applies this approach and is both bold enough and open-minded enough to test new solutions is the team that will win. Complacency is the biggest enemy of success.

And while the press and public hailed New Zealand's record as proof of how well the Kiwis worked together, the behind-the-scenes story was somewhat different. Not all was brotherly love among the design team nor the afterguard.

While Michael Fay's idea that three heads examining design lines would be better than one seemed to prove itself in the racing record, what he may not have anticipated was that three egos aren't necessarily better than one. Boat designers are creative individuals who bank on new, innovative ideas and the currency they trade in is called "intellectual property". Although the collaborative process was both efficient and effective in producing the three fibreglass yachts, it opened the door to some intra-team disputes over who thought of what. As well, when the team received credit for a particular idea or innovation, it rankled the individual who felt he was responsible for that specific concept.

That there were such problems among the designers in the first New Zealand challenge was kept within the syndicate. It was a well-kept secret that, at one time or another, each of the designers walked out. It's a tribute to both the campaign's management and the designers themselves that such "strikes" were quickly resolved. Some people consider that such friction fuels the creative process, but in the case of *KZ-7*, it seemed to have the opposite effect.

The problems that arose on the sailing team were of a different origin. The designers had jobs. They needed only to perform. The sailors performed to the best of their abilities on a daily basis for more than seven months without any assurance they would have a job during the Cup races. Rivalries formed. Competition at each position grew. Laurent Esquier and Roy Dickson were chiefly responsible for selecting the team, a thankless task. They were damned if they did and damned if they didn't. No matter who they selected, the decision would create a good deal of disappointment.

The method used to select the sailors on the "first team" was a natural evolution from the training Laurent was conducting. Since so many of the sailors were inexperienced in big boats, the coach was constantly fighting time trying to teach necessary techniques and boat-handling skills. And with time becoming more and more elusive, and inexperience considered the biggest potential weakness, the team adopted an approach to training that common sense would normally rule out. An extreme situation was reached one day when the wind was blowing at over 40 knots and a crew trial race had been scheduled. On the tow out, the boats had to be pumped out continuously to prevent them from sinking. None of the other syndicates were out and many of the crew thought it obvious that sailing would be cancelled for the day. A camera crew from Channel Seven Sports got into action to document what they believed might be an impending disaster.

The order came from Roy and Laurent for the race to be started on time, and within minutes of hoisting the sails there was considerable carnage on both boats – battens broke, sails blew out, and fittings strained under the tremendous loads. This was dangerous sailing.

On yet another day, still under pressure to bring the team up to speed, management sent the boys out again in conditions only slightly less extreme. Later, several of the sailors told me that if they had been kept on the race course much longer, they were certain one of the boats would have sunk! There is no denying these episodes tested the boats and the crews to the limit, nor is there any disputing that such exercises put both boats and sailors in harm's way. While it might be argued that pushing the crews in such conditions proved which guys were up to the task, I wonder just how much was learned and if this approach truly helped the team meet its ultimate goal, which was to win the America's Cup. Cup racing was cancelled in any similar conditions.

So while all this was going on, there was little boat development. Internal competition had set up a "race team" and a "tune-up team" and co-operation had stagnated. Ultimately, boatspeed suffered the most.

Every sports team faces similar challenges. Certainly each of the international America's Cup teams over the past 20 years has had to deal with comparable competitive issues. I believe that because these problems had arisen and had been dealt with in a mostly satisfactory way by the three New Zealand challenges that preceded the 1995 team, we were the beneficiary of their experience. We knew what to expect and we made plans to avoid certain pitfalls.

The sailing team also faced a challenge in Chris Dickson. Although nominally there was a competition between Chris and Woody for helmsman, there really wasn't much doubt Chris would end up with the job. I always believed he was the most talented and experienced sailor in the camp. He was also totally committed to the campaign and his leadership qualities were made evident from the first days. On the other hand, his youth and capriciousness signalled dark clouds on the horizon.

Chris' style on board was seen by some as overbearing. As the weeks of training turned into months, Chris may have lost some perspective. About halfway through the campaign, I'd heard he was seen back in Auckland. Rumours abounded that he'd quit and that he'd been fired. Michael Fay has the real story:

"The best way to describe Chris Dickson returning to Auckland, I think, is to use basketball terminology. He needed a 'time out'.

"The pressure that builds during an America's Cup campaign is tremendous. No matter who you are, no matter how good you are, you come to a point where there's an enormous amount of pressure that builds up as you approach the final racing. Remember Chris was very young and none of us had ever been through anything like this before. We'd also been in Fremantle a long time.

"As the pressure built, Chris took a lot of it on himself. He was the helmsman, the skipper, the on-the-water leader. I think he reached a point where the pressure got to him a bit and he needed to take time out. He went back to Auckland and he sat down and took a breather. He needed to look at himself and work certain things out in his own mind. He needed to examine his management style, how he dealt with people, the relationships he had formed within the team.

"He took the time and it was beneficial to both him and the team. I think by getting away, by reducing the pressure, he recognised how intense the Fremantle situation was and how to deal with it."

If Chris had established himself, and then re-established himself, as the on-the-water leader, there was a growing problem of who was calling the shots on land. Michael Fay had more or less been forced into the position of managing the day-to-day affairs of the syndicate, and I believe as he grew more and more comfortable in the role, he began to thrive on the Cup pressure. But not everyone saw it that way.

There was some talk down at the dock that Michael's management style wasn't good for the campaign as far as the day-to-day activities were concerned. He didn't understand the technicalities of sailing, so it was said, why certain things were done and why other things couldn't be done. It was suggested that having to deal with that was holding up the programme. This train of thought spread throughout the team. The issue of who had control and who was receiving the recognition and media attention for the good performance of the team was high on the agenda. So Michael ended up relinquishing his management of that aspect of the campaign.

This was amazing! Michael was the entire reason everyone was there. He was the reason the money was there. His management philosophy and professional approach were the reasons the Kiwis were enjoying any success. In those days, a more military style approach was needed just to keep the young crew under control and focused on the goal. When Michael stepped aside, the balance between discipline and disorder was upset. His management style was a combination of decisive action and consensus understanding. To my mind, it was just what was needed at that time in New Zealand yachting history. I thought he made all the right moves and certainly put together the strongest effort that could have been made at that time.

Likewise, I think Michael's decision to go with Chris Dickson was the best choice he had at that time. There was no one in New Zealand at that stage who could have put together a better programme than Chris and his father. But I bet that, in hindsight, the Dicksons regret the day Michael was moved out of the action. Here was the guy with the chequebook! As Michael once quoted to me:

"The campaign was run by the Golden Rule – he who has the gold, rules." It's critical for the guy who is the syndicate head to be involved with the day-to-day operations. He needs to know everything that is going on, and he needs to agree with everything that is going on.

While the "Michael issue" was being discussed, things got a little tense around the Kiwi camp and Chris and his tactician, Brad Butterworth, were having some communication problems and differences of opinion on the water. They were sent away from the team to a hotel in Perth to try to work it out. This move, coupled with the questioning of Michael Fay's value as a manager, were perfect examples of rookie problems. And when you add those to the inexperience of the team, the exodus of the old salts, the bickering among the designers and the bitter residue of the sailor-selection process, it's a wonder the team made it to the starting line, much less established the record they did.

The first race of the challenger finals was scheduled for January 13, 1987, a date that turned out unlucky for *Kiwi Magic*. Winds of 20 to 25 knots met the two teams at the starting line and Conner employed a pre-start tactic he would use throughout the finals and later in the Cup match. Rather than take on the more manoeuvrable *Kiwi Magic* in a head-to-head tacking and gybing contest to establish control, Conner steered *Stars & Stripes* away from the Kiwis and into the spectator fleet. He then played hide and seek and dodge boat until it was time to make a bee-line for the start. The tactic negated the quicker turning ability of the New Zealand yacht, prevented Chris Dickson from forcing Dennis into a foul and allowed *Stars & Stripes* to hit the starting line at full speed. It was a masterful strategy employed brilliantly.

The story of the 1987 challenger finals can be written in two words: boatspeed and experience. The Americans made boatspeed a high priority throughout the entire regatta, continuously changing, tweaking, tuning, experimenting. With this approach in mind, Dennis had selected a team of designers, co-ordinated under John Marshall, which was continuously working to improve the boat. Bruce Nelson, Clay Oliver, Britton Chance, Dave Pedrick and John Letcher were some of the key players in a team of designers that would define the model for the modern approach to an America's Cup design effort. They were a design team that left their egos at the door, rose above all individual agendas and were motivated by Dennis and John to develop the fastest boat in Fremantle and win the America's Cup.

There was another important factor behind the success of *Stars & Stripes*. Dennis had a boat full of sailors who not only had spent a lot of time on 12-metres, but had known and raced with their skipper for many years. I remember observers commenting that *Stars & Stripes* was "a quiet boat", meaning Dennis didn't spend much time issuing orders or instructions. These guys knew what to do and when to do it because they'd done it so many times before. This was another lesson I personally learned from this regatta and it was one of the reasons I spent a lot of time on the match-racing circuit with guys who joined me on Team New Zealand.

One of the sailors who had spent time with Dennis, who had actually sailed with him in Newport in 1983, was Laurent Esquier. He knew the American skipper well and he attempted to use that knowledge to prepare the Kiwi team. "Dennis will be at his best," he told a team meeting before the Louis Vuitton finals began. "*Stars & Stripes* has been modified and will be faster than at any time this year. Dennis has grown in confidence and he believes there is nothing that can stop him from winning."

Unfortunately for the Kiwis, his assessment soon proved to be disappointingly accurate.

I remember calling Michael Fay on the eve of the challenger finals after arriving in Perth to sail the 18-foot World Championships. He, too, suggested that the challenger finals were going to be a lot tougher than most people thought, and that it would be an interesting psychological battle between two great sportsmen. I recall he was astonished by the off-the-water behaviour of Dennis. The American had often been sighted very late at night in more than one Fremantle bar. His imbibing habits reached near legendary status, as did his remarkable powers of recovery. Friends have told me they would spot Dennis weaving through the streets at 3 and 4am, looking for all the world like the proverbial cat dragged in out of the rain. Yet there he was at 8am, fresh and chipper and ready to race. There are a thousand stories that accompany Dennis wherever he goes, but the one truth that I've never heard anyone familiar with sailing dispute is that he is one of the greatest helmsmen of our day. From my experiences on the race course, I would never argue with that and I know that Michael Fay has nothing but respect for Dennis as a competitor.

In the first race *Stars & Stripes* won the start by three seconds, extended the lead to 15 seconds at the first mark, and eventually won by 1:20. The second race was similar to the first, except this time *Stars & Stripes* went from an even start to a 38-second lead at the first mark. Boatspeed. The final delta was 1:36.

Race three went to the Kiwis as a result of failed snap shackle aboard *Stars & Stripes*. Although the Yanks had once again sped out to a lead on the first beat, this time by 21 seconds, when they hoisted their spinnaker the snap shackle opened and the chute descended. In the mad scramble to recover, one of the halyards was fouled and more time was needed to clear the problem. It was enough time for New Zealand to pull ahead and stay ahead, despite an America's Cup record of 55 tacks thrown at them by Dennis on the final 3 1/4-mile leg. The Kiwis won by 38 seconds.

Team New Zealand grinder Andrew Taylor later told me that those 55 tacks were the most strenuous he has ever had. The sailors knew that if they gave *Stars & Stripes* any breathing space at all, she would be able to use her superior speed to catch *KZ-7*, and so they had to match the Americans tack for tack. It was an effort they will all remain proud of for many years to come.

Dennis brought in fresh grinders for race four because the wind was again howling. *KZ-7's* crew remained unchanged. Taylor later admitted to me that he was physically fatigued after the previous race. Several opportunities presented themselves to the Kiwis but mistakes and bad luck prevented them from taking advantage. Gear failure and a crash gybe in race four ended that contest and resulted in a damaged masthead crane. Kiwi bowman Erle Williams probably did one of the most gutsy acts ever witnessed in the 1987 event (or any sailing event for that matter), when he free-climbed the top section of the mast in extreme conditions to cut the mainsail down. The courageous act was a combination of true commitment and the impulsiveness of naive youth. Even with the score 3–1 in favour of the Americans, Erle's ascent of the mast symbolised the team's heart to millions of viewers around the world.

Race five was similar in that the New Zealanders were close before a spinnaker change was messed up, and then a mark on the course was hit, ending any chance in the race and in the 1987 America's Cup. It was an inglorious ending to a glorious campaign.

Another factor, a significant factor I believe, should be considered when reviewing the fate of *Kiwi Magic*. The conditions in which the finals were raced tended more to the extreme than the normal for Fremantle. The high winds and large waves favoured the longer *Stars & Stripes*. The day after the last race between the Americans and the Kiwis, lighter winds and smoother seas returned. These would have favoured *Kiwi Magic*. It makes you wonder what would have happened if New Zealand could have pulled off just one more victory in the heavy stuff.

It has also been suggested that Conner used to allow a good deal of water to come into *Stars & Stripes* during the tow out to the race course. In strong winds this had the effect of sinking the boat slightly, which resulted in a longer waterline and added stability. You'd think that the more water you have in a boat the slower you would go, but in these conditions apparently the opposite was true. Conner, the experienced master, figured it out along with a lot of other changes as he went through the racing.

Despite the loss in the finals, the nation of New Zealand had adopted the *KZ-7* campaign. The "plastic" boat had proven a consistent winner. It was the first time New Zealand had ever been to the America's Cup and here they were, after losing only one race, up against the man who had become synonymous with the event. Kiwis were obsessed with getting news from Fremantle. People were convinced we were going to win and the Cup would come to New Zealand. They were buying coastline property in Auckland, investing in Fay, Richwhite whose Capital Market shares were soaring, and the papers were filled with Cup stories every day.

As far as most Kiwis were concerned, New Zealand had outsmarted the rest of the world by building the first fibreglass 12-metre yachts. And while the New Zealand designers and builders realised that we were coming into the game so late and so far behind the technology curve that we had to do something unique and radical if we were to make any kind of showing, there was a growing suspicion in the rest of the world that the "plastic fantastic" was built lighter in the ends and that explained why the boat performed so well. When Conner was coaxed by Tom Blackaller to say "Why would you want to build a fibreglass boat unless you wanted to cheat?" a firestorm of controversy erupted. Dennis immediately became the guy Kiwis love to hate, although we have a great respect for his sailing abilities.

Brad Butterworth, who raced with Dennis in the 1993/94 Whitbread Round-the-World Race, tells the story that when they were approaching Auckland for one of the stop-overs, he kept reminding Dennis of his "cheating" remark and telling him, "You know, DC, these people have never forgiven you. When you get there you're going to get eggs thrown at you, and maybe worse. They really hate you." Dennis became terrified and, as the boat approached Auckland Harbour, he was on the radio trying to arrange security and a quick exit out of Auckland before Butterworth told him he was joking. Of course, when he landed in Auckland, he was treated more like a hero than a villain.

And just like the Aussies in 1986 embraced him, I believe if he comes to Auckland in 1999 he'll be one of the most popular people in the country. Far from hating him, I think New Zealanders are intrigued by Dennis. When you look at him, he's an amazing guy. He's overweight. He drinks too much. Yet somehow he still performs. He still wins. We look at him and wonder how he does it.

Peter Montgomery tells a story about how I both annoyed and intrigued Michael Fay in 1987. After I had returned to New Zealand and resumed my studies, I still kept my hand in sailing by organising a team on the 18-foot skiff circuit. These exciting, competitive, difficult-to-sail boats are very popular in Australia.

On one of the nights during the final match with Conner, I was having mast trouble with the boat I was racing in the Perth 18-foot Worlds. I phoned Michael and asked him if we could use the New Zealand challenge's workshop that night. He couldn't believe I had rung him at home at 8 o'clock the night before the final about an 18-foot skiff that had nothing to do with the America's Cup. The following day he saw Montgomery and asked, "Jesus Christ, who is this guy who doesn't give a damn that we're racing in the America's Cup? All he wants to do is work on his skiff." But as he and Montgomery talked, it became apparent Michael was actually amused with the level of intensity that I adopted for my own racing. He told Montgomery, "Coutts makes Dickson look like he's distracted." That phone call may have gone a long way towards my being named to helm Team New Zealand in 1995.

When the team returned to New Zealand, you would have thought from their reception that they had won the America's Cup. New Zealanders are knowledgeable sports fans and they appreciate great effort, especially from underdogs. "America's Cup Fever", a strange ailment that seems to afflict those who have either participated in or closely followed sailing's most fabled event, spread through New Zealand. The symptoms of the malady are an intense desire to continuously participate in the America's Cup, no matter the sacrifice, no matter the difficulty. No known cure has been discovered.

So even before the parades were over and the streamers cleared away, Kiwis began wondering how the next challenge would take shape. Across the

Tasman, the man who had vanquished all challengers had done the same to the defenders, represented by *Kookaburra III*, helmed by Iain Murray. *Stars & Stripes* proved itself the best boat in Fremantle in 1986/87 with a 4–0 sweep of the Australians, winning by an average margin of 1:39.

For Dennis Conner, the comeback victory had to be sweet. He had been abandoned by the New York Yacht Club after his 1983 loss in Newport and now he was returning to his country, with the America's Cup in hand, as a hero. While winning the Cup under the auspices of the San Diego Yacht Club had given him and the California club the right to defend the trophy in the next contest, the failure to make a quick and expedient announcement to that effect began one of the most bitter and controversial periods in the entire history of the event. In the middle of it all was Michael Fay.

The next chapter in America's Cup, and New Zealand yachting, history is informally titled "The Big Boat Campaign". It probably had its origins in the fibreglass issue that grew into the hotly debated controversy of the 26th America's Cup. I say this because the Kiwi camp always felt the question of the legality of the New Zealand boats was raised and continuously pushed by Sail America, the syndicate representing the San Diego Yacht Club. The New Zealand legal counsel, Andrew Johns, became increasingly frustrated and irritated with the way Sail America handled itself. It became clear that New Zealand presented a real threat to the SDYC's hopes of displaying the America's Cup in their trophy case, and Johns, among many others, felt their off-the-water assault was unfair, unsportsmanlike and completely without merit. Johns and Fay believed the "legal" onslaught was motivated by the knowledge this issue would distract the Kiwi camp from training and preparing for the racing. So when Dennis won the Cup and took it to the San Diego Yacht Club, Johns saw their off-the-water actions in Fremantle as a precursor to how they would deal with the many questions and issues leading to the 27th America's Cup.

What was most strange about the exit from Fremantle by the Americans was they left with the Cup, but without any notice of the next event. In previous America's Cups, a so-called "pocket challenge" was immediately issued following the final race. This challenge was a pre-arranged agreement between the winner and the victor's hand-picked challenging yacht club. It was done this way to meet certain conditions of the Deed of Gift, the 1887 document that was supposed to be recognised as the rules of the game. The pocket challenge usually established the Challenger of Record, the type of boat the next Cup would be raced in, and a rough timetable for the next event. The duties of the Challenger of Record were to deal with the defending yacht club on behalf of all challengers and to represent their position on any and all issues that were proposed concerning the event.

But even after Dennis and his gang had returned to the States, were given a New York City parade, visited the White House and installed the Cup in the SDYC trophy case, no plans were announced about when or where or who would be involved in the next regatta. In the meantime, Andrew Johns went to the library. He began to study the Deed of Gift, amended twice since 1887, and his excitement began to grow.

And while Johns was studying, the SDYC remained officially silent. But rumours began to spread through the America's Cup world that an internal argument over who would manage the next event was taking place within the club. It was said that Sail America, an organised entity only loosely affiliated with the club, wanted to call the shots. The SDYC was saying no, we will run the event. And while the two fought for control, time was passing and the challenging nations were becoming more and more anxious to know details. Then it was said the next event wasn't going to be in San Diego, but in Los Angeles. Then we heard it was being moved to Hawaii, where Dennis had trained for the Fremantle event. Then word spread the whole thing was being shopped around and would go to the highest bidder. Clearly, the San Diego Yacht Club's America's Cup stewardship was off to an ominous start.

While all the rumours were swirling, those who were most closely involved in the challenger ranks believed that answers would be forthcoming at the 1987 12-metre World Championships in Sardinia. A meeting of the International Twelve Metre Association was scheduled and that seemed the likely venue for the SDYC to announce its plans.

Back in Auckland, Michael Fay was operating at full speed. He, like the rest of the world, anxiously awaited news of what his counterparts in San Diego intended. His involvement in yachting's highest-profile event over the past two years had left him with a severe case of America's Cup fever. Although disappointed in the 1987 Cup results, he had come close enough to believe that, with a few changes, his country could come home with the trophy following the next event. One of those changes was his decision to replace Chris Dickson as skipper. It was a decision that caused an uproar throughout New Zealand.

Dickson had received a tremendous amount of national and international exposure during and immediately after the Fremantle races. His age, his talent, his piercing blue eyes and the savvy way he conducted himself in front of the media had created an image of "the golden boy of New Zealand sailing". Any negative internal team issues were known to the public and the press. To them, Fay's decision was hard to understand.

Even more difficult to understand was Fay's silence on the issue. Although he was being questioned, even castigated, by the public and the press, he offered no explanation. I had always wondered why he chose this tactic and I recently asked him to explain.

"What I wanted to avoid," said Fay, "was a public post-mortem on Fremantle where the whole campaign would be taken apart piece by piece and examined. That tends to do more damage that good. The better way to do it, to be more constructive to those directly involved, is to do your debriefs as a team. You need to be honest with yourself, learn the lessons, build on the experience, and then act on what you've learned.

"My assessment was that I didn't believe that in Chris Dickson we had someone that naturally would go the team-building route. He is an undoubted talent and his record justified his skippering the first challenge. I thought at the time, and I still believe, he is one of the world's best yachtsmen. But I felt it was time to build the base, put a team together, and make this the goal for any New Zealand skipper who wanted to stick with it. I just didn't think Chris was that person.

"I knew my decision to open up the skipper position would be controversial. I also knew there was no point in making a public response to that controversy. It would have just fuelled the fire of the media debate."

So as Michael Fay was changing direction within the team, he was also preparing for the 12-metre World Championships, to be held in June. David Barnes was selected to helm *KZ-7* in the waters off Costa Smeralda. Rod Davis, who had begun working as an advisor to the Kiwis in Fremantle after his *American Eagle* campaign had been eliminated, replaced Brad Butterworth as tactician.

The story resumes in Sardinia as Fay and some of his close advisors were discussing the now oblique future of the America's Cup. It was clear there would be no statement on the anticipated San Diego defence. Despite a thousand questions from the assembled Cup officials, the SDYC was mute. They were stonewalling. It was evident that Sail America and the SDYC were still locked in a power struggle, five months after the *Stars & Stripes* victory in Fremantle. No one was sure who controlled the Cup, who was making decisions, if any decisions were being made.

Enter Andrew Johns, fresh from the archives of the New York Yacht Club, where he had studied the historical and legal documents pertaining to the running of the America's Cup. Johns counselled Fay that from his reading of the Deed of Gift he concluded that the America's Cup was intended to be a challenger-driven event. A challenger had every right to initiate a competition; in fact, was encouraged to do so. He advised Fay to draw up a formal, legal challenge based on the guidelines outlined in the Deed of Gift. Johns' excitement was infectious, and Fay made the immediate decision to draft such a document if the remaining Sardinia meetings provided no satisfaction. Fay then became a bit of a Cup scholar himself as he took Johns' admonishment to "read the Deed" to heart. He knew from history that there had been a number of different types of boats that had raced for the Cup, so it was obvious that no one class was mandated in the original Deed to be used. What he learned from the Deed was that anyone could challenge in the boat of their choice as long as the dimensions fitted the Deed's parameters and a minimum of 10 months' notice was given. Further, the trustee of the Cup, now the SDYC, was obligated to honour the challenge if it met the Deed's requirements and it was the first challenge submitted.

Fay's reading of the Deed made him conclude that the maximum length of a boat allowed to race for the Cup is 90 feet on the waterline. As he envisioned such a craft, he must have foreseen a glorious match-race battle between two like giants that would captivate spectators around the world. He then had dinner with designers Bruce Farr and Russell Bowler. Farr, of course, had been a large part of the "Plastic Fantastic" equation. The designers were told of the possibility Fay might issue a challenge for the Cup to be held in June of 1988 and they were asked to think about designing a 90-foot-waterline boat.

When the Worlds ended in mid-July, with *KZ-7* the victor, there still had been no word about the next America's Cup from SDYC or any of their representatives. Fay decided to act. He travelled first to Washington, DC on his way back to New Zealand, while at the same time Tom Schnackenberg flew to Annapolis, Maryland, to work with Farr and Bowler in completing the concept for the new boat. Fay needed the concept and required dimensions – waterline length, beam at load waterline, extreme beam and draught – as part of the notice of challenge. The designers had three days to complete their work.

From Washington, Fay then flew to Los Angeles and on July 17 he walked into the San Diego Yacht Club to have lunch with the commodore, Dr Fred Frye. A number of stories have circulated about that fateful lunch. Here's what Michael Fay recalls:

"Andrew Johns and I drove down from LA and I can remember thinking I must be getting used to this sailing philosophy because it was a fairly tense day, obviously, but I fell asleep in the car, much the same as some of the sailors go to sleep on the tow out to the start of a race. So, in that sense, we were quite relaxed really, although we anticipated a difficult experience explaining our plans to the commodore. But Fred Frye was pretty well known to the Kiwis and we'd been told he was a good guy, a reasonable fellow who would hear us out.

"While we were waiting for the commodore, we were looking at the trophy cabinet which had the America's Cup in it. I remembered back to the final dinner in Fremantle when the prizes were presented for the challengers' regatta. I was sitting with Dennis Conner and he'd become rather drunk. I was a bit drunk myself, I must confess. We got a couple of trophies and of course Dennis got a couple as well. When I woke up the next day, I found only one of the trophies. I was a bit embarrassed to tell the Royal New Zealand Yacht Squadron I'd lost one of their trophies. I didn't know where the hell it had gone.

"So I just shut up about it. But then I was standing in front of the San Diego Yacht Club's trophy case thinking, God, I recognise that trophy. Conner must have picked it up at the table and taken it home with him. So when I sat down with the commodore, I said I wanted to talk about the next America's Cup, but first, if he checked his records he'd find that's our trophy out there in his case and he just might want to send it back to us sometime.

"Then over lunch I quietly explained how much we had enjoyed the racing in Fremantle and we were looking forward to coming back. The commodore was very polite, very complimentary about our effort and he said he was looking forward to having us back. Then we chatted a bit and I said we'd like to come back a bit sooner than later. He asked what I meant, the regatta wouldn't be for three or four years. And I said, well, we have something a little different in mind, we'd like to come back next year. I'm not sure he took me too seriously at that point, but he asked if we were going to race *KZ-7*. I said no, we had something a little bigger in mind. He asked how big. I looked at Andrew, who could barely contain himself, and I told the commodore the boat would probably reach from here out to the car park. That got his attention.

"To Fred Frye's credit, he said that sounds very exciting. He took it very much in the spirit of the America's Cup and in the spirit of the challenge. Of course, his club didn't quite see it that way."

That evening Fay and Johns met back in Los Angeles with Alan Sefton, Peter Debreceny and Peter Montgomery. Alan has been a part of New Zealand's involvement in the America's Cup from day one and has been chiefly responsible for the press and public relations activities surrounding the various Kiwi challenges. He had been in Sardinia and had called Montgomery to tell him the broadcaster should get to Los Angeles as fast as he could because something big was up. That's all he could say. Just drop everything and get to the States.

Montgomery began filing reports back to New Zealand and Sefton began issuing press releases. The news of the challenge spread throughout the world like wildfire. To most Cup observers, it sounded like an exciting concept, but it generated a million questions. Chief of which among other potential challengers was, "Can we race, too?"

Twelve days later, both the Royal Perth (Australia) and Royal Burnham (England) yacht clubs announced they would join the big boat challenge as well. In the meantime, Fay, and the rest of the Cup world, waited for a response from the SDYC. None followed. On August 6, New Zealand formally requested an official response. The SDYC said there would be none. Then two days later the Californians officially rejected the New Zealand challenge. That forced Fay to petition the Supreme Court of New York, the legal custodian of the Deed of Gift, requesting the challenge be recognised. And then all hell broke loose.

What was supposed to be, according to the Deed of Gift, "a friendly competition between foreign nations" turned into a vitriolic contest of legal one-upmanship and personal attacks. As the rhetoric increased, Fay was accused of a "sneak attack reminiscent of Pearl Harbor" and of an "obsession to win the Cup, and thus spread his name throughout the world".

The SDYC went to war, waging a clever battle in the press. They kept referring to the challenge as a "sneak attack"; said they were "blindsided". And it worked. In the eyes of many, the Kiwis were made to look like the bad guys, out to steal the Cup in any way they could. Never mind that according to the very rules the SDYC was saying were broken by Fay, the Kiwis had every right to issue a challenge. Never mind that it was the SDYC's failure to act, failure to respond to the many potential challengers, that prompted Michael Fay to take the action he did.

I believe his intentions were simply to create an exciting event, but the results of his challenge turned into a public relations nightmare and caused considerable image problems for the event. As he once told me a few years later, what the press made of his challenge was similar to what happened to the

American politician Gary Hart, who at that time was considering a run for the White House. However, a photograph was circulated of the senator with a bikini-clad blonde, not his wife, sitting on his lap next to a yacht called *Monkey Business* from which the two had just disembarked. Despite denials of any monkey business, Hart's campaign for the presidency was immediately scuttled. For Michael Fay, the SDYC's portrayal of him as launching a sneak attack which created the image of him as the enemy was equivalent to the Hart case. Image and appearance became all important.

While the Supreme Court of New York was considering the matter, the SDYC announced that San Diego would be the site of the next defence. On November 20, 1987, the *San Diego Tribune* quoted a Sail America official as saying the defence would "jimmy the rules" if necessary to keep the Cup. Five days later, Judge Carmen Beauchamp Ciparick ruled that the challenge was legal and she disallowed SDYC's request to make 12-metre yachts standard. In December, the SDYC stated "no other challenge will be considered until this pending event has been decided. Fay argued for a multinational event, but SDYC resisted. This prompted Australia's Alan Bond to send SDYC and Sail America officials white feathers, symbolising cowardice.

At the end of 1987, the new commodore of the SDYC, Douglas Alford, stated, "The Deed of Gift clearly indicates that the challenger and defender each have the right to choose any yacht each wishes to use which complies with the dimensional restrictions set forth in the deed." Two weeks later Dennis Conner announced he would skipper *Stars & Stripes '88*, a 60-foot catamaran. Yet another uproar ensued.

At the end of January the Royal Burnham Yacht Club filed legal papers seeking to open the competition to other nations. Two weeks later the SDYC announced the site of the defence wouldn't be in San Diego after all, but up the coast at Long Beach. On February 24 Royal Burnham's case was heard in court and the SDYC then said it would accept a multinational challenge. Most nations agreed it was too late to build boats. In March the SDYC issued a statement that said the site of the defence would be San Diego.

By May, with everyone confused about when, where and in what the next America's Cup might be, Fay returned to court requesting that the SDYC be ordered to defend the Cup in a 90-foot-waterline boat, saying the Deed of Gift calls for a match race in two like and similar boats. In July Judge Ciparick ruled that New Zealand's suit was premature. She wrote: "The time has come for the sailors to be permitted to participate in the America's Cup. The parties are directed to proceed with the races and to reserve their protests, if any, until after the completion of the America's Cup races."

So race they did, although it was much more a "mismatch", as Fay termed it, than a match race. There is just no way a monohull boat, dragging a keel through the ocean, can keep up with a multi-hull boat, skimming over the water's surface. The races aren't even worth recounting as their outcome was never in doubt. Conner's cat won the first race by more than 18 minutes and the second race by more than 20 minutes. The races were staged simply to comply with the court order.

Motivation in the New Zealand camp must have been difficult. I can't imagine preparing for a race that everyone knew would not be a race at all. I'm reminded of an incident Team New Zealand business manager Ross Blackman told me happened during the lead-up to the debacle in San Diego. It began as a motivational device, but ended as something a bit different.

The story goes that Michael Fay gave Laurent Esquier the instruction at about 3pm one day to phone all the wives of key sailors and heads of departments. He was to tell them not to expect these team members home until quite late; no explanation was given.

The group was told only to meet at the team van. When the group of about a dozen people assembled, they began asking each other what they knew of this request. The questions were answered by shoulder shrugs all around.

"Perhaps we are off to the airport, about to be shipped home," was one speculation, offered only partly in jest.

Soon Michael arrived and was greeted by 12 voices asking, "Where are we going?"

Michael answered, "Let's have a beer first. It's no big deal."

Despite the leader's casual attitude, everyone was still suspicious and a little worried. After a short drive, the van arrived outside the Kansas City Bar-b-que, a watering hole that had become somewhat famous since its use in the movie *Top Gun*.

Inside, Michael ordered a jug of beer for everyone except Laurent, who was driving and would be responsible for looking after the group.

When that was finished he ordered another round or two until everyone except Laurent was feeling the effects yet still wondering what this was all about.

At eight o'clock, Michael announced that the group should get a "quick bite" and they were driven to a Spanish restaurant, where a table had been booked, overlooking the America's Cup harbour.

Michael asked the waiter, "What's your best red?" When the waiter replied, Michael said, "We'll have a bottle each for everyone." He then asked for advice on the best white, and similarly requested a bottle of that for each person as well.

At this stage, most of the guys began to realise this was Michael's way of getting them to forget the controversy swirling around them and help them feel closer to each other through some trying times.

As the wine went down, the voices went up. Soon a full-fledged party broke out in the best tradition of hard-working, hard-playing Kiwis. One of the revellers, feeling no pain, stood up and suggested this would be a good time for each of the diners to report on why he had decided to compete in this glorious competition known as the America's Cup. Each man got up and among heckling and verbal abuse gave reasons ranging from "for my country" to "for the money".

Through somewhat bleary eyes, one member of the team noticed that a table full of women was in close proximity. Feeling gallant, he offered an apology about the content of the discussion. Much to the amusement of all concerned, one young lady at that table stood up and replied in a very broad accent, "You don't have to worry about offending us mate, we're Australians."

Well into the night, Michael decided it would be a good idea if the group ventured over to the SDYC for a look at the Cup. After all, wouldn't that serve as an inspiration? Laurent, having been around Kiwis in similar circumstances long enough to know what might happen, and sensing the worst, suggested that maybe this would not be such a good idea.

Someone else suggested that "we should go to the San Diego Yacht Club and take the Cup because it is rightfully ours anyway".

Michael thought that was the best idea he had heard all night. Laurent, still stone sober, cringed at the thought. He began a short-lived campaign to dissuade the group of any such notion, but he was promptly told to shut up.

The group proceeded to drive to the San Diego Yacht Club where they used Rod Davis' pass to get through the front gate. As Laurent pulled the van up to the front door and the first of the Kiwis stepped out to storm the San Diego Yacht Club, a large group of very official-looking people dressed in tuxedos appeared on their way out of the club.

Apparently this brought a graphic sense of the reality to the act they were about to perform. The gang of Kiwi Kup Kulprits hesitated for a moment as the well-dressed San Diegans moved toward them. Recognising the New Zealanders, the Americans nodded and smiled their greetings. Even through the alcoholic fog that surrounded them, the little band of miscreants began to realise their plan had a certain downside to it. Might the club members miss the big hunk of Victorian silver?

Fay spoke for the group. "Ah guys, maybe we should reconsider this for a minute." Laurent immediately seized his opportunity, shoved the van into first gear, planted his foot on the accelerator and screeched out of the parking lot.

I've always wondered how America's Cup history might have been changed if not for a group of gentlemen in tuxedos! Then again, one could argue that had those Kiwi Robin Hoods succeeded in their quest, the 1988 event might have been saved from the far worse image it is now doomed to live with.

Probably the ugliest incident of all occurred in the final press conference. Dennis Conner, ever the public relations nightmare, began spewing venom as Kiwi designer Bruce Farr made an appearance. "Get off the stage," Conner yelled. "You don't belong here with winners. You're a damn loser." The words were captured on a tape recorder while a camera filmed from the back of the room. The two mediums were then put together and replayed over the next few days for all the world to view. An American friend later told me that he saw the clip on the national news and after it was shown broadcaster Connie Chung shook her head in disgust and said, "And they call that sport."

More legal wrangling followed the September races as the Mercury Bay Yacht Club, New Zealand's sponsoring club, sought disqualification of the catamaran. At the time, it seemed almost everyone had an opinion about how the Deed of Gift should be interpreted. As a Kiwi, I sided with Michael Fay, but I also understood how others could reach their opinions. While the Deed of Gift is considered the rules of the game, it doesn't consider all possibilities. As the America's Cup historian John Rousmaniere wrote at the time, "The Deed of Gift, like most trusts, wills and constitutions, does not include enough specific written rules to cover all eventualities. While the deed encourages the defender and challenger to reach mutual agreement on the ground rules, in case there is no agreement it makes specific provisions for only some issues. For example, the boats must sail a two-out-of-three race series around 39- and 40-mile courses with a seven-hour time limit. The deed says nothing specific about what types of boats can sail other than establishing minimum and maximum waterline lengths of 44 and 90 feet. While it explicitly requires the challenger to produce a yacht, it makes no such demand of the defender."

With the Cup back in court, Judge Ciparick reviewed the opinions of the New York Yacht Club and the Royal Perth Yacht Club, the two previous trustees of the America's Cup. On behalf of Royal Perth, Dr Stan Reid wrote before the races, "I am firmly of the opinion that the San Diego Yacht Club is in breach of its obligations as trustee of the America's Cup in purporting to select as its representative yacht a multihull. Such a vessel was never contemplated by the parties to the Deed. Certainly a multihull vessel can never be a legitimate defender of the Cup in the face of a bona fide monohull challenge."

After the races, Commodore Frank Snyder of the New York Yacht Club wrote, "For the SDYC to purport to defend with a catamaran what this court had determined was a valid challenge for the Cup by a monohull was, therefore, not a defense at all. There was no 'match,' as that term is used in the Deed of Gift."

As the case dragged on in court, powers-that-be in the Cup world resolved to prevent, at all costs, any similar situations from occurring in the future. They acted swiftly, a rare occurrence. By the end of November 1988, the syndicate savants had reached agreement on such issues as yacht design, course configuration, Challenger of Record, tentative schedule for the next races and who would settle future disputes. Perhaps of greatest importance was that the International America's Cup Class grew out of the design meetings that were held.

The new boats would be designed and built to a complex formula in which sail area, waterline length, displacement and weight were considerably adjusted compared to the 12-metre formula. The idea was to present marine architects and boatbuilders with a vast challenge to explore the speed frontier. The obvious result was a new look to the fading image of the America's Cup and the hope for closer and more exciting competition.

Although 12-metre yachts were for all intents and purposes the face of the modern America's Cup, replacing the majestic but anachronistic J-Boats and used for almost 30 years, by 1988 they were considered dinosaurs. Criticised for being too heavy and short on sail area, the twelves performed admirably in

Rob Tucker

One of the first times we lined up NZL-32 against NZL-38. We confirmed almost from the first day that 32 was the faster boat and we saved her until the challenger semi-finals.

Overleaf: During the early sea trials, NZL-32 sails in front of the Auckland skyline. In the year 2000 scenes like this will be repeated by many IACC boats. (Rob Tucker)

Dennis Conner congratulating Dean Phipps, Brad Butterworth, and Matthew Mason, all of whom were crew members of his yacht Winston *in the 1993/94 Whitbread Round-the-World race.*

Dirty Den & Paul Cayard, formidable opposition.

Australia's heavy weather, but it was feared they would give a slow motion perspective to the San Diego event, where the average wind speed is not even 10 knots (in Perth it is over 24 knots). By contrast, the IACC boats at 75 feet, with 70 percent more sail area and 30 percent less weight, were promoted as speed machines.

While it was assumed the next Cup would be held in San Diego, there was no confirmation from the court that that would be the case. As long as the law suit was still alive, there was a question of whether the 28th America's Cup would be held in San Diego or Auckland. Although designers for the potential challengers now had design parameters for the boat, it was difficult for them to get much past the concept stage because the wind and wave conditions of the two venues differ greatly, affecting the type of boat to be built.

Judge Ciparick finally made her ruling and for one brief moment in time the America's Cup belonged to New Zealand. Her ruling sided with Mercury Bay's lawsuit, but was later reversed by the New York Court of Appeals. The next Cup would be held in the waters off San Diego in 1992.

The long, acrimonious 27th America's Cup had finally come to a close. Its proceedings on and off the water did as much damage to the event's image as the Fremantle event did to raise it. People around the world have told me how they were glued to the television set watching the sailors pound through what appeared to be survival conditions in the Indian Ocean. The courage of the crews, the closeness of the races, Conner's dramatic comeback, and the Fremantle festivities were all caught by live television and on-board cameras to project the sport at its best. A new fan base had been established, only to be partially destroyed by the foolishness of the great mismatch.

And yet among all the ill-will and bitterness the Big Boat campaign generated, one good thing did come out of the entire mess. The trophy given to the Kiwis in Fremantle that Michael Fay spied in the SDYC trophy case on the day he issued the challenge was returned to the Royal New Zealand Yacht Squadron. It arrived many months later by surface mail, an indication of just how well the men in power at the California club at that time treated their mates from Down Under.

5

From Mismatch to Match Racing

L ike most of the New Zealand public, I was a spectator of the Big Boat campaign and the debacle that was called the 28th America's Cup. And since I wasn't personally involved, I was neither emotionally lifted nor deflated by the legal and sailing events that had occurred. Except that, like all Kiwis, I was concerned about our country's image after more and more false stories came out as Michael Fay and his advisors got deeper and deeper into the challenge.

There was, however, a moment when I wished I had been part of the campaign. It was the first time I saw the big boat sailing on Auckland's Waitemata Harbour. I was on a golf course overlooking the water and there was the white giant of a yacht, fantastic to watch cutting effortlessly through the waves. Once again I regretted my decision to leave Fremantle and return to university.

But I hadn't abandoned sailing altogether. I'd returned to racing in the Champion of Champions regatta in Auckland not too long after I'd flown out of Fremantle. And who should I meet up with but Chris Dickson, on his Fay-imposed sabbatical to find himself and unload some of the pressure leading up to the America's Cup.

After completing my Bachelor of Engineering degree in November 1986, I spent three months competing in the Australian Eighteen-foot class. It was a learning experience to say the least, especially for someone who came out of the single-handed Finn dinghy and, before that, the single-handed Laser. Stepping into a three-man trapeze boat in the form of a high performance

Eighteen footer was a baptism of fire.

Rob Brown, who was the world champion at the time, and I had a conversation just after I arrived in Sydney. Rob said that when he was told by the promoter that I would be sailing an Eighteen, he replied, "That can't be true. Those guys aren't that stupid." But stupid enough I was!

In truth, it was one of the most memorable and fascinating periods of my sailing career. In a lot of ways it was a breath of fresh air and like learning how to sail all over again.

The complexity of tuning those boats and the fact that they were so overpowered made Eighteen-foot sailing one of the most challenging disciplines I have attempted. The boats have been recorded at speeds in excess of 30 knots, which was a far cry from the six or seven knots that a Finn might achieve.

The rules at that time, simply put, dictated that the boat had to be 18 feet long and a monohull . . . end of story!

It was, therefore, possible to put as much sail area on the boat as you thought you could handle, which led us to have a number one rig 48 feet in height! This on a boat that was 18 feet in length. That gives you some idea of why the word "overpowered" has always been associated with this class.

I recall the first time we rigged those sails. We stood amazed and in fear at the sheer size of the sails. Photographers love to train their lenses on the wings of the Eighteens as the three crew stretch on trapezes as far outboard as they can in an often vain attempt to balance the forces of the huge sail.

Just before I entered the class, there was no limit on the wing width. As the sailors became more proficient at sailing these bucking broncos, and more courageous, so too did the wings become wider. Some of these guys were sailing with wings 35 feet in width, with masts up to 50 feet. That meant they were controlling the boat from $17\frac{1}{2}$ feet off the centre line! Even more ludicrous was the fact that some teams increased the height of the mast and the widths of the wings by several feet overnight to gain added advantage for the next race.

Problems started to develop as a result of this madness, not the least of which was the distance of a fall if (and in my case, when) the boat capsized. Several sailors received broken bones when falling off the wings onto the capsized rig at high speed. Thankfully, it was decided to restrict the width to just 22 feet just before I entered the class.

Just 22 feet? I can tell you first hand that this is still a very long way to fall.

Although not very successful with my initiation into Eighteens, and accepting that the bookies probably could only get people to take odds on us either finishing or not finishing the races, I did learn an immense amount about putting a crew together and sailing such a high-performance boat.

I took with me a rookie crew from New Zealand. None of us had any Eighteen-foot experience and we spent a lot of time trying to reinvent the wheel, operating more like a sailing school than trying to win races. It was a lesson that I would later apply to my match racing and America's Cup crew selections.

Towards the end of 1987, I spent a very intense three months in Europe training for the Olympics in a Soling, a three-man keelboat, which, at just under 27 feet and 2300 pounds, is the longest and heaviest of the Olympic classes. Having a cast iron keel to help keep the boat upright was a welcome relief after three months of Eighteen-footers and swimming in Sydney Harbour.

Again, although the people I chose as crew were excellent individual sailors, the balance of talent in the boat was not ideal for top-level competition. Our fifth in the Soling World Championships showed we were lacking both tactically and with our boatspeed at vital times, although we were the top New Zealand boat.

We then faced hard-fought Olympic selection trials in Auckland against a crew of Tom Dodson, Simon Daubney and Aran Hansen, the New Zealand representatives in 1984. The Dodson team took a more relaxed approach to their preparation and had as one of their de facto supporters the Leopard Tavern, the local yachting watering hole in Auckland at the time. In contrast the Coutts team were all serious, spending long hours preparing the boat, training on the water and working out in the gymnasium.

In hindsight, a balance between the philosophies of the two camps would have been the objective to strive for. My team probably didn't have enough fun and the Dodson team probably had too much.

We led the trials after four races until a strong southerly weather system appeared and set in for the next two days. Tom Dodson, who I would rate as one of the better heavy air sailors in the world, began to show his skills. Aran Hansen, making full use of his Leopard Tavern support by weighing in at over 20 stone, was a definite ballast advantage. They took over the lead and began to prove their superiority.

We had to beat them in the seventh and final race to tie the series up and force an additional sail-off race. The final race started in perfect light air conditions and we established a sizeable lead. On the second lap the race committee, responding to a wind shift, repositioned a mark. We noted the change and set off on what we thought was the correct course. Unfortunately, we had badly miscalculated and after correcting the error found Dodson, Hansen and Daubney hot on our heels. A tremendous match race occurred on the final leg with us crossing the finishing line first, a mere boatlength ahead. It appeared we had won but an incident 50 metres before the finish ultimately decided the result.

Dodson had approached on port tack and had to give way to us on starboard. He left his tack very late, probably too late, as we were forced to alter course slightly to avoid contact. Both yachts were now on starboard tack. We sailed on for about five seconds in a windward overlapped position. Then Dodson luffed hard, resulting in contact between the two boats. At the protest hearing we were disqualified. In truth, both yachts probably erred, yet that was irrelevant because we believed anything less than a win in that final race meant a trip home for us.

To make matters worse, the protest committee also found that Dodson was at fault in a previous incident and therefore we didn't actually need to beat them across the finish line. We didn't need to push it as hard as we did in the final 50 metres.

It was a very bitter pill to swallow. Although our campaign was only five months long, we had given total commitment to it. Our focus was on nothing but getting to the Olympics.

Because yachting allows only one competitor per country to compete at the Olympic Games, the dreams of many sailors can be spoiled by one bad race or a penalty call. After months, probably years, and sometimes even a lifetime of dedication, training and financial sacrifice, there remains only one chance to perform. It is tremendous pressure and a huge let-down if you are unsuccessful. In 1988 I once again began to wonder if sailing was in my future.

After the disappointment of the Olympic trials, I worked as an engineer, realising that from that day in 1984 when I rammed into the *Titianui*, my profile as a sailor was disappearing about as fast as that beautiful old committee boat would have sunk had it not been on a 24-hour pump-out watch.

Yet not all was doom and gloom. I felt I had accomplished something in obtaining my degree and finding employment. Best of all was the birth of my son, Grayson, in June 1988. Like most fathers I suppose, I count that day as one of the most joyful of my life. It has been a great pleasure to watch him grow through the years.

I may have succumbed a bit to some of the maturity I spoke about earlier, but I admit I was also becoming restless. There are few places in New Zealand where one can escape the ocean and, whenever I saw it, I thought about sailing. The sport is in my blood.

So in 1989 I decided to take another crack at match racing. As an international competition of the world's best sailors, match racing was the only game in town, so to speak. The America's Cup, now tarnished and competitively questionable, was still in court. The international match-racing circuit was now becoming the focus of organisers, sailors, the world's elite yacht clubs and the media.

Even more important than the attention it was receiving was the fact that match racing provided the world's best sailors the opportunity to continue developing their skills. Several prestigious match-racing events had established an enviable history, including the Gold Cup in Bermuda, first held in 1937, the Congressional Cup at Long Beach, California, dating back to 1964, and the Royal Lymington Cup in England, established in 1974.

As the events became better organised and attracted more of the top sailors, more and more television programmes were broadcast internationally. As well, the creation of a rankings system on the lines of that used in tennis has helped the sport grow in one decade from a handful of events and fewer than a hundred sailors to upwards of a 100 match-racing events and more than a thousand currently ranked sailors.

As match racing was growing, I realised that if I was going to get back into the sport and attempt to raise my profile so that I might be considered for a future America's Cup challenge, I should organise a team and try to get on the circuit. The first international event that accepted my entry was, ironically, the Citizen Cup. I vowed to keep clear of all bridges and committee boats.

As a prelude to the event, an unofficial team race was organised a couple of days before the match racing began. A US team of Tom Blackaller, Rod Davis and Gary Jobson was formed. Sailing for New Zealand were Chris Dickson, Brad Butterworth and me. The scars of 1987 and '88 had not yet healed. Chris, who had essentially been banished from New Zealand America's Cup consideration, was still voicing his displeasure with the status quo. He had won the inaugural World Championship of Match Race Sailing the year before and was currently ranked number one in the world.

"Where's David Barnes?" he would ask about the helmsman who replaced him in Michael Fay's syndicate and was absent from the regatta.

"Where's Rod Davis ranked?" he would ask about the American sailor who had turned Kiwi advisor and who was being talked about as the possible helmsman for any future Fay challenge.

While Chris' questions may have been self-serving, they were also being asked by many of the public who followed the sport. And although Chris may have been using this situation very cleverly to build a reputation as the misunderstood genius of sailing, an image and excuse he could offer potential Cup challengers in other countries, there can be little doubt he felt bitter about being shut out in his own country.

An incident on the day of the team race illustrates the point. Roy Dickson, the sailor's father and former Fay advisor, was walking near Rod Davis' boat, which was fitted with a US flag, and pronounced, "It must be nice to be able to switch your flag from the US to New Zealand and back again."

The Citizen Cup got me back into yacht racing on the world stage. I felt the excitement and the competitive juices began to flow once again. We ended up third in the regatta, which was something of an achievement.

Earlier in the year, we had raced in the New Zealand Match Racing Championships where Chris was the obvious choice to win. I was sailing with Robert Salthouse, who had been in the 12-metre Worlds, Murray Jones was my tactician, and Simon Ostick, David Brooke and Nick Willetts all had a great deal of experience. We put together a positive campaign and worked well together. We spent a good deal of time tuning and racing against Rod Davis, so we felt prepared going into the championships.

We sailed well and made it to the finals where, as anticipated, we met Chris. Although still long shots, we pulled it off. We beat the world champion and number one ranked match-race sailor. I had come to a stage in my sailing career in which I was mentally open to learning as much as possible about match racing and in which I was a good deal more comfortable with keel boats.

The victory earned us a sponsorship from Dominion Breweries and, after the Citizen Cup, we went to three other events on the circuit: the Australian Cup in Perth, the Kouros Cup in France and the Liberty Cup in New York Harbour. We made it to the finals in Perth, but Peter Gilmour received the cup. Peter is one of three skippers I most enjoy sailing against; Chris Dickson and Paul Cayard are the others. Over the years, these three guys have given me the most exciting competition and memorable match races.

In France we were again second, this time to Marc Pajot, and in New York, racing in the shadow of the Statue of Liberty, we tasted victory for the second time that year, beating Frenchman Bertrand Pacé. Our results in these five events were high enough to propel us into the top echelon of the match-racing rankings. And that ranking was high enough to earn an invitation to the World Championship in Lymington, England.

The World Match Racing Conference set up the World Championship of Match Race Sailing as potentially the most competitive event of the year. Ten skippers are invited, based on their world ranking. Initially, only the top 10 ranked skippers are invited and if any of those sailors are unable to race, the organisers go to number 11 and 12 and so on. At the time the invitations were made for the 1989 World Championship, we had completed our string of high finishes and were lucky enough to receive an entry after one of the top 10 declined.

The World Match Racing Conference, in its effort to raise the level of the game, contracted International Management Group (IMG) to sell the title sponsorship rights for the regatta. IMG is one of the biggest and most powerful sports marketing companies in the world, with clients ranging from top athletes in many sports to Wimbledon tennis to world tours by the Pope. Although sailing was new to the company, they soon worked out a three-year deal with Mazda motor company. Suddenly the sport had become serious; more than $US135,000 in prize money was at stake in this one regatta.

We finished sixth equal with Bertrand Pacé of France. It wasn't that we sailed particularly badly, it was just that five other guys sailed a lot better. I learned a good bit from the regatta, mostly that I still lacked experience and had a way to go before I could be grouped with the best in the world. But I also considered that our team had made a great achievement during the year. It wasn't too many months before that I had wondered if sailing was in my future at all, and now our team had made it into the World Championship. From a personal perspective, 1989 was the year that brought me back into racing and launched me on the international match-racing circuit. Over the next three years, I skippered in more match-racing events than any other sailor.

The best-of-three finals of the Lymington World Championship came down to Australia's Peter Gilmour and Chris Dickson. As defending champion, Chris was in peak form, but Peter took the first race and was well ahead in the second race when fortunes turned. With close to 25 knots of wind blowing, the Australian team rounded the top mark and began a gybe set. It looked like a risky manoeuvre, especially as they were well ahead in the race and even more risky when Peter's crew decided not to use the running backstays. The mast rebelled and the rig came crashing down. Chris Dickson rounded and cheekily set his spinnaker before gybing and sailing past his opponent. With the spar and mainsail in the water, Gilmour's hopes of a 2–0 sweep quickly faded.

In all the years I've known Chris, I've learned he is one of the most dogged competitors on the course. He never gives up, and if he detects an opening, even the smallest opening, he'll find renewed vigour and forge ahead. With new life at Lymington, he went into the deciding race determined to become a two-time champion. And full marks to him and his crew, as they took Peter over the starting line and then sailed brilliantly throughout the race to win. Dickson winning, Gilmour second and we were back in the pack. They were results that were typical of that era and results that I vowed to turn around.

I also noted that Dickson was supported by an excellent crew that included Simon Daubney, Joe Allen, Dallas Bennett and the heavyweight Aran Hansen, many of the guys who would end up in my team in later years. Hansen actually arrived at the regatta a little too heavy to make the weight limit and so was forced to go on a crash weight-loss programme. Daubney and Allen, realising a sauna was nowhere to be found and sensing a health risk if Hansen went jogging, devised another solution. They dressed him in multiple layers of sweaters and wet-weather equipment and sent him on a long drive in their rental car with the heaters turned up to maximum heat. He returned two hours later, much to the amusement of onlookers, with the inside of the car absolutely saturated. Yet when he was checked on the scales, he had only lost one kilogram. To this day, Daubney and Allen are suspicious that Hansen may have stopped at a fast-food establishment along the way.

As well as the match-racing regattas, I competed in the 1989 Admiral's Cup as tactician for Colin Beashel and the Australian team. Beashel is one of those soft-spoken but extremely talented sailors who ply their trade on international waters. I was greatly impressed by his ability to sail the boat fast and position it correctly around the marks. I still consider him one of the most underrated helmsmen of our era. We took top points in the One Ton class, in a very fast yacht designed by Bruce Farr. It seemed a fitting end to a year of renewal for me. I felt I was now in a position to be considered for a part, not a lead role, in the next America's Cup.

The 1990 Kouros Cup was held in one of the most beautiful and exciting sites on earth, St Tropez, France. Located on France's fabulous Côte D'Azur, this idyllic village is known to many people as the home of Brigitte Bardot; to sailors it's one of the most challenging venues in the world. While the Mediterranean Sea often appears inviting, conditions can change quickly from light to heavy air with windshifts close to 180 degrees.

With the match-racing success of 1989 bolstering my confidence, I asked Andrew Taylor, Warwick Fleury, Dean Phipps and Mike Drummond to accompany me to Europe. It was the first time the five of us sailed together and it's interesting to note that the same guys made up almost a third of the 1995 America's Cup sailing team on *Black Magic*. Back then, though, San Diego and the America's Cup were far from our minds. A little French cooking and a fast boat were more the subjects of the day.

Despite the fact that it was the first time we raced together, we made it into the finals. It won't be any surprise to tell you who was waiting for us. Yep, there was Dicko, still looking to increase his international profile. Chris had already accepted a job to helm the Nippon Challenge boats for the 1992 Cup and no doubt nothing would please him more than to knock off a boatload of Kiwis. But, in a surprise result, we beat him 2–0 and it was a solid 2–0 indeed. I felt a claw or two removed from the monkey on my back and it was also a sweet victory for Warwick Fleury, who had sailed with Dickson in many regattas until they could no longer agree on the level of compensation Warwick deserved.

Shortly after we crossed the finish line, six magnums of champagne materialised from the hospitable French spectators on the course. The drink of local crushed grapes, combined with the heat and exhilaration of victory, had a predictable result. All five of us were soon drunk as skunks. We didn't plan it, but I won't deny it. When we brought the boat in, we were asked to make our way to the informal prize-giving, a brief ceremony held mostly for the benefit of the press. The more formal award ceremony would be held later that evening to which several hundred guests of Kouros (a men's fragrance from Yves St Laurent), other sponsors, local dignitaries and yacht club officials were invited.

I'm told it took quite a while to assemble the winners on stage for the informal presentations and that our decorum was, let us say, not particularly becoming, although I do remember a good bit of laughter from the audience. Apparently our appearance, topped off by Andrew Taylor's spraying of the ceremonial bottle of champagne on the audience, which included the mayor of the town, was not something everyone found amusing. Although I seem to remember the mayor took it in good spirit, one of the corporate bigwigs from Kouros pulled me aside after the festivities had ended and suggested it might not be a good idea for us to attend the formal presentations that evening.

Somewhat offended (couldn't this guy take a joke?), but understanding, I pleaded my case. I'd get us all coffee and food, have us showered and dressed, and in 100 percent presentable fashion in time for the awards, I assured our host. He looked at me carefully, no doubt trying to work out some elaborate formula of alcohol and caffeine percentages. While he figured, I guaranteed. I had him convinced, I know I had him convinced; but just as he was about to relent, Andrew Taylor's father, who had shared both his son's elation and champagne, sort of stumbled over a chair, setting off a domino effect on a whole row of seats. That ended my discussion with the corporate suit, who walked away shaking his head.

I gathered together our little band of rascals and somehow we all got back to where we were staying. Rather than coffee and food, more champagne and a party were in order. In no time at all, Andrew had forced his way through some of the surrounding hedges and had appeared, all six feet four inches of him, outside one of the neighbour's windows. Certainly no harm was meant, but the neighbour, who had never laid eyes on this hulk, felt a quick call to the police was the prudent course of action.

In the meantime, Simon Daubney had joined our party and, realising the situation, began cooking up a pot full of spaghetti bolognese. He, too, believed food was the needed sobering agent. But while the spaghetti was cooking, the chef sampled some of the champagne and by the time the meal was ready, he was giddy enough to serve it in the Kouros Cup, which someone had, let us say, mistakenly brought back with him.

When the police arrived, they recognised, in true French fashion, a roaring but innocent party and they accepted our story of overdoing it just a bit after winning the cup. After all, we had the silverware to prove our tale was genuine.

During all the festivities, Simon Daubney asked me that evening if I was interested in having him sail in my team. It was one of the best questions anyone had ever asked me. I remember sensing that night, even through the champagne, that things were going to turn around over the next few years and it would be the beginning of a new era for me and my new team.

To my mind, and I think most sailors will agree, Bermuda ranks equal to St Tropez in any beauty contest, and as far as tradition and competition are concerned, the venerable Gold Cup for the King Edward VII Trophy tops the list of international match-race events. The origins of the Gold Cup date back to 1907 when it was given by King Edward VII for a featured race at the Tri-Centenary Regatta in Jamestown, Virginia, to commemorate the first English settlement in America. A famed American yachtsman named Sherman Hoyt won the cup and kept it for 30 years before offering it to the Royal Bermuda Yacht Club, which agreed to host a match race. Briggs Cunningham was the first skipper to win the cup, just as he was, with *Columbia* in 1958, the first skipper to win the America's Cup in a 12-metre yacht.

Since that time, some of the most famous names in the world of yachting have competed in the event. The first New Zealander to win the Gold Cup was Chris Dickson in 1987, and he did so again in 1989 by beating the Coutts team. But in 1990 we came into the event with solid performances behind us and full of confidence. Unfortunately that confidence didn't translate into great sailing in the early rounds, as we had trouble at the starting line and coming to grips with the International One Design yachts used in Bermuda.

In a memorable first round, Kevin Mahaney, who would later go on to skipper *Young America* in the 1995 America's Cup, had us firmly on the ropes. His team was 2–0 up in a best-of-five knock-out series and as we switched boats between races he remarked to Simon Daubney, "It's a long way to come from New Zealand just to be sent home early empty-handed."

I've always maintained that it doesn't pay to upset the opposition, unless you get them so upset that they simply can't concentrate. Most of the time smart comments only serve to fire up the opponent, exactly the effect Mahaney's comment had on us.

With renewed vigour, we drew the series level 2–2. We were determined to make it three in a row, but Mahaney got the better start in the deciding race and was sailing further ahead. We were all but out of the race when he turned around the mark for the last lap and set his spinnaker. I saw an opportunity and turned our boat onto a collision course with his. Before he realised what was happening, we were coming aboard his yacht. After a huge collision, we were locked together side by side.

He was clearly at fault, yet was so far ahead in the race that one penalty turn would not have made much difference. Simon Daubney and I, after breaking our yacht free from the mess, immediately lobbied the umpires to give Mahaney two penalties. We maintained that not only had he infringed the rules but he had impeded our progress when the boats were locked together. The judges were suitably convinced, Mahaney was made to complete two penalties and we narrowly won the deciding race.

Mahaney was, justifiably, very upset, and yet I couldn't resist, knowing that it was now safe, at least until we met in the next regatta, to remind him of his earlier comment. "Sorry Kevin," I said, "it seems you've come a long way only to be sent home early empty-handed."

In contrast to us, Peter Gilmour was having a terrific regatta, losing only one race the entire week. We met up with him in the finals.

In the first race of the best-of-five format, we had an intense battle in the pre-start and, as we approached the line, Peter was to windward and on the favoured side, perhaps a half boatlength in front. The gun went off and then a second gun, signalling one of us was over the line. I was relieved to see the race committee notifying Peter he'd have to return and cross the line once again. First race to the Kiwis.

The Aussies suffered even worse luck in the second pre-start. After the initial circling, both boats headed away from the line where we were able to manoeuvre into the controlling position. With less than a minute before the gun, we headed towards the committee boat. Peter's boat was to starboard of us and we continued to force them to the right, trying to "close the door" on them, giving them no room between us and the committee boat. If Peter determined he couldn't make it, he would have to tack behind us, losing time and distance. He knew that by tacking he'd give us an enormous advantage. I knew that too, so I opened the gap ever so slightly between us and the committee boat. When Peter took the bait, I closed the door again and he now had nowhere to go. His big, heavy International One Design slammed the corner of the race committee craft and was black-flagged, or disqualified. Second race to the Kiwis.

Although not amused, the race committee showed some humour by donning life jackets before beginning the pre-start sequence for race three. It was an even start and close all the way around, but we pulled ahead and won our first Gold Cup. It was the biggest win of the year.

By the end of 1990, I was number two on the world match-race rankings, behind Chris Dickson. Going into the World Championship, which was held in Auckland, the press was focusing on the two top New Zealand skippers, predicting yet another finals in which Dickson and Coutts would square off. I think both Chris and I pictured it the same way.

And that was our undoing. We tended to concentrate so much on each other that we took the rest of the field, the very best sailors on the globe, too lightly.

Neither of us even made it into the semi-finals. I ended up fifth and Chris was sixth. Not much of a showing for the top two skippers, sailing in their home waters.

Our trans-Tasman neighbour, Mr Gilmour, took the honours that year, beating Rod Davis. It was a significant effort by Rod, whose performance was sure to impress America's Cup syndicate leaders. But by ending the year so high in the rankings, I felt I might attract some Cup attention also.

By May of 1990 the America's Cup had made its way out of the American judicial system and the SDYC had announced that the next event would be held off Point Loma, the scene of the big boat/catamaran disaster, and all challengers were welcome, as long as their boat complied with the new International America's Cup Class formula. Some sanity had been restored to this venerable contest.

As challengers around the world announced themselves and began preparations, things were pretty quiet in New Zealand. No doubt still reeling from the 1988 battles, Michael Fay, now Sir Michael Fay in recognition of his contributions to the British Empire, wasn't saying much publicly about any plans he might have. But behind the scenes, he had quietly put together his third challenge. I received a call from him around the time of the match-racing world championship asking me to come and talk to David Barnes, who was spearheading the effort.

Fay was determined from the beginning to keep a very low personal profile in the 1992 campaign. I believe he had been stung by the idle chatter questioning his motives. Some people were saying he was involved in the Cup scene only to promote himself and not for the good of New Zealand. But I believe he would not have undertaken the 1992 campaign solely for the greater good of Michael Fay. I believe most of us who were involved in the challenge share the opinion that he sincerely believed winning the Cup was both unfinished business and very possible, and that by doing so it would do the country some good.

Regardless of the motivations prompting whomever to do whatever, there would be another Cup regatta in 1992 and New Zealand would be in it. The Farr design offices had been contracted, boats they designed were being built at the Marten Marine and Cookson boat yards and a sailing team was being assembled. The effort was full on, but the bells and whistles common to the past two campaigns were relatively mute.

In the meantime, the focus was still on the match-racing circuit. While a number of Kiwi sailors had been asked to consider joining the New Zealand America's Cup challenge, still more than a year in the future, no positions had been discussed and the job of helmsman was wide open. Skippers who did well in international competition would conceivably have a leg up.

Talk around the docks was that three sailors had the early lead in the steering sweepstakes: David Barnes, Rod Davis and Russell Coutts. Barnes had performed well in the big boat campaign and proven himself a team leader and an able skipper. Davis had become more and more involved with New Zealand yachting since the 1987 America's Cup and he'd done well in a number of match-racing events. Coutts had made his way back into the sailing scene with some good, although inconsistent, performances.

When the Congressional Cup in California called for entries, Chris Dickson's name appeared on the list. However, for the first time he was officially representing Japan on the match-racing circuit as well as the Nippon Challenge for the next America's Cup. His so-called "defection" was not unique, as American Paul Cayard also left home to skipper for Italy. And, of course, American Rod Davis was in the thick of things in New Zealand.

While the press and some of the competitors tried to make a big issue out of the "hired gun" trend in the 1992 America's Cup, many people were beginning to understand the moves as part and parcel of a sport that was becoming totally professional. Many sailors, myself included, have sailed in events such as the Admiral's Cup for other nations. Yet the America's Cup is by far the biggest and most prestigious sailing event and thus attracts the most attention. And because it is still very much a contest between nations, it receives the most scrutiny of all sailing regattas.

There is no doubt that the rumoured six- and seven-figure salaries and bonuses offered to some of the top sailors as an inducement to defect from their country of origin has been a leading reason for the increasing trend of mixed nationalities in America's Cup teams.

The 1991 Congressional Cup ended up in another Dickson-Coutts final. I'd beaten the Davis/Barnes team earlier in the regatta, but I'd also recognised that they were working very well together and developing into a strong tactical team.

I'll remember the finals of this regatta for many years to come. Chris pulled off a brilliant manoeuvre at the start of the second and third races that I'd previously discarded as too risky in most boats. We'd won the first race and needed only one more victory to capture the crimson jacket, the Congressional Cup's symbolic championship attire. We were racing Catalina 36s, which perform as fairly big boats in most situations except when the sails are backed and the boat begins to sail backwards.

Chris had no doubt noted that the keel was situated well forward on the hull with the rudder attached well aft, which, unlike most boats, made the Catalinas very fast and easy to sail backwards. The rules at the time stated that the yacht in front had rights over the yacht behind, yet the rule made no distinction as to what direction the yachts were moving!

Chris set a trap and sprung it with perfect timing. He suckered us into the controlling position in the pre-start, which was directly astern of him. In many cases, it is from this position that the trailing boat can choose where to start in relation to the opponent and thus dictate. Yet as I happily set up in this position, somewhat confused by the gift Chris was apparently giving me, all was not as it appeared.

As we approached the line, Chris began to sail backwards and, before I could react, he had won a foul against us. He went on to win the final race and was fitted for the colourful blazer.

It was after the Congressional Cup that my wife and I decided to separate. She had been tremendously supportive of my efforts to become a successful yachtsman, but the strain of continuous competition and travel had taken its toll. She is a tremendous person, yet we unfortunately decided to get married when we were both too young to weigh up what our individual objectives in life were.

I felt the best way for me to get over this huge change in my life was to focus on my career as a professional yachtsman. That took me to the next event on the match-racing schedule for 1991, the fifth annual ACY Cup in Rovinj, Croatia. Despite the on-going war, the regatta attracted 10 skippers from eight countries to compete on the wind-swept waters of the Adriatic Sea. The ACY Cup was one of the first match-race events to offer prize money and this year the purse was $US50,000. We put together a strong performance, winning the round robin with a perfect 9–0 record and then beating England's Eddie Warden-Owen in the finals.

From the Adriatic we travelled to St Tropez, where the Kouros Cup was in contention. My first act upon returning to France was to see if any remnants of Simon's spaghetti bolognese could be seen in the cup! It was clean and shiny, but our night of revelry from a year earlier was not forgotten. Added into the Notice of Race was a new clause giving notice to sailors that any behaviour during the competition which caused the regatta or its sponsors any embarrassment could result in expulsion. The sentiment, known informally among my peers as "the Coutts Clause", was adopted by a number of other events on the circuit.

The final of the $US100,000 1991 Kouros Cup was once again a Dickson versus Coutts match-up. Still a bit chagrined from the pre-start fiasco in California, our team was determined to perform at top level. We split the first two races, setting up an exciting and lead-changing showdown in the determining contest. This time we had the controlling position in the pre-start but we avoided any possibility of Chris backing down and causing us to foul. When the start gun went off, we had used the controlling position astern to force Chris over the starting line and we were on our way to the first mark. We rounded 30 seconds ahead, but on the downwind run Chris caught a windshift which gave him a narrow lead at the next mark. Then racing luck fell our way as we tacked and, with Chris trying to cover, his jib sheet fouled, slowing him enough for us to regain the lead and win the Kouros Cup for the second year in a row. I don't remember whether champagne was offered or if we refused, but in any case we got out of town unscathed.

Up to that point it had been a good year for us. We'd made the finals of three major international match-racing regattas and had won two of them. Not only did that record put some money in our pockets, I thought it would also add some persuasion points to the decision makers in New Zealand when the time came to select the helmsman for the 1992 challenge for the America's Cup. But Davis and Barnes had done well also, and the competition became more and more intense.

I remember answering Michael Fay back in 1985 when he asked me how I thought we should conduct the campaign. I told him to form two teams and let the best team, with the best helmsman, prove themselves in competition. I guess I felt the same about the 1992 challenge, but I now realise that method, instead of promoting team unity, simply promotes individual agendas. I was out to beat Rod and David and they were out to beat me. There was no information sharing, no working together, no real co-operation.

Both Rod and I came into Bermuda's Gold Cup that year anticipating a shoot-out between us. I think we both figured whoever won the Gold Cup and then the World Championship, to be raced in Bermuda the following week, would be selected to helm the New Zealand boat in the America's Cup. As predicted, we both made it through the largest field on the circuit of 24 teams to meet in the semi-finals. We got to 2–2 and, as we lined up for the deciding race, I suspect anyone reading our faces would have known we both believed the winner would soon be steering the New Zealand boat in San Diego. Davis took the race and then lost to Eddie Warden-Owen in the finals. But being runner-up rather than champion probably meant little to Rod at the time. His big victory had come at my expense.

In the next day or two, most of the sailors who had participated in Bermuda had returned to the America's Cup syndicates they were involved in or attempting to be with. While we were away, David Barnes and most of the rest of the New Zealand Challenge had been testing a new secret weapon – a tandem keel that in many ways was as radical as the winged keel that Ben Lexcen had designed for the Australians in 1983. There were conflicting reports as to the success of the tests, yet there was little doubt that the management, the sailors and, perhaps most of all, the designers were all hoping this keel would provide the substantial speed advantage needed to enable New Zealand to win.

For the next seven months, the focus of the yachting world would be on San Diego and the one event every sailor and yacht designer in the world dreams about at one time or another.

6

Of Bowsprits and a Boat in a Box

With the match racing in Bermuda concluded, my focus returned to the New Zealand challenge. The match-racing circuit had provided many of the sailors who would race in the 1992 America's Cup the opportunity to improve tactical and strategic skills. On the circuit, the emphasis is on sailing ability as the boats are identical in make and equipment. In the America's Cup, although the format is match racing, the emphasis is on innovative design, construction and equipment which the team as a whole must learn how to best develop.

For more than 140 years what has characterised the competition has been the quest for a breakthrough in new technologies. The original race in 1851 between the American schooner *America* and 15 British yachts was the result of an invitation to the New York Yacht Club to demonstrate the scientific achievements of its country's boat-building industry. Since then, the America's Cup has been more of a design contest than a sailing competition. And through the years design issues have caused as much of the controversy the event is so well known for as any other issue.

The 1992 America's Cup joined its predecessors of 1986/87 and 1988 in the design controversy category on the first day of the International America's Cup Class World Championship. It was on May 4, 1991, that the new IACC boats made their debut. Nine yachts, never before sailed in competition, lined up off Point Loma in San Diego for the fleet-racing portion of the regatta. At the end of the week the top four boats would advance to a match-racing format.

The coming-out party of these new Cup contenders was anything but auspicious. Atypical San Diego conditions of 15 to 20 knots of wind stirred up sloppy seas, resulting in an estimated million dollars of damage. *Nippon-6* was dismasted after it appeared that the huge loads applied from the boom vang buckled the spar as the vang was not released when rounding the windward mark. *Nippon* also suffered a man overboard on the tight reaching leg of the course when a sail was washed off the deck, carrying the crew member with it. Chris Dickson, at the helm of *Nippon*, must have been wondering about the inexperience of his new Japanese crew. *Spain '92* lost her steering system and America[3]'s *Jayhawk* suffered hydraulic and genoa-track problems. Dennis Conner finished the last half of the race sailing under headsail only after having stability problems with his new mast. We nursed the New Zealand boat around the course to finish third, with the boat bending, creaking and groaning all the way under the huge sailing loads.

The carnage across the course prompted Bill Koch, the American multi-millionaire who was relatively new to the sport of sailing and brand new to the America's Cup, to angrily declare at a press conference, "The guys who designed these boats are idiots." Actually he meant the guys who were responsible for the rule that led to the design, but Bill had a lot of trouble with his words at the 1992 press conferences. Although no one was injured, Koch thought the fragile boats were "incredibly dangerous".

His opinion wasn't shared by many, but it did begin the Cup season with yet another dispute. Chris Dickson took immediate issue with Koch.

"They're a challenge to the world's top sailors. I think they're a fantastic boat to sail and exactly what the America's Cup is all about. Only the best sailors should be out there. These boats are like Formula One race cars. An amateur shouldn't drive one."

Obviously the target of Dickson's comment, Koch replied, "I am an anachronism out there. I'm not a hired gun."

The Cup year wasn't even a full day old and already the venom was spewing.

New Zealand's boat in the IACC Worlds, like most of the syndicates, was a prototype which would never see America's Cup action. Rod Davis was behind the wheel and I was positioned as the tactician. Because we had already built three boats and had been set up in San Diego for more than four months, we were expected to do well. And we did, but we didn't win. The Italian's newest boat, *Il Moro di Venezia-15*, beat us in the finals by a little more than a minute.

Six months later, after returning from Bermuda in late October, I didn't feel we'd made much progress towards putting together a solid effort to win the Cup. We were one of the first syndicates to arrive in San Diego, we had already built three boats and a fourth was expected to arrive in another six weeks, yet we still hadn't selected a sailing team nor a helmsman nor even an afterguard. And it didn't seem the lessons of the IACC Worlds had been assimilated by our designers.

Although our light-displacement boat had won the fleet-racing part of the Worlds, we were beaten in the match-racing portion by *Il Moro di Venezia*. The Italians, like all other syndicates, had built at least one heavier boat. The IACC rule allows a displacement range between 16,000 and 26,000kg, yet all three New Zealand test boats were built in the middle of the displacement range.

The Italians had clearly outperformed us in all but the medium-strength wind conditions, yet I felt that in those early stages our sails and our sailors were better tuned in comparison to the rest of the world. This begged the question of why our performance was weak in the high- and low-wind conditions.

Many of us were questioning the displacement issue when more new boats were launched such as *America³* in August 1991. This boat, like others debuting at the time, was in the heavy-displacement category. Was the rest of the world really that stupid to not consider a light-displacement boat like ours? Were our Kiwi designers simply that much better than everyone else that they had got it right while everyone else had it wrong?

We consoled ourselves with the fact that our designers, Bruce Farr and Associates, had led the way in innovation in other classes of yachts . . . at least, that's what the promotional material said! It was not unusual to read, particularly in the New Zealand sailing publications, that Bruce Farr and Associates were the best designers in the world, even though they had not yet won the premier design competition, the America's Cup.

The secrecy surrounding the design details of the fourth yacht was at an all time high. Most, if not all, of the sailors in the New Zealand challenge were unaware of what the final product would look like. We had no access to any technical data as a veil of secrecy was extended over the entire syndicate. The first time we got any hint of what *NZL-20* was like was after it arrived in San Diego and was unpacked from its box.

Even David Barnes, who was the co-ordinator between the Farr office and the sailing team, was surprised that the boat again weighed in at the same displacement as the other three boats. *NZL-20* had been built in New Zealand and shipped to the US where the boat would be assembled late, too late for the opposition to react and copy our "breakthrough design".

The decision to go light-displacement was puzzling indeed, yet several factors may have contributed to the decision. The first was that all the previous full-size testing was in light-displacement boats and therefore the designers may have been reluctant to change their thinking late. It appears that even the early technical studies focused on the displacement ranges close to the final design, so perhaps no clear advantage was evidenced from those test results. The other factor may have been the overriding considerations for the engineering and usability of the tandem keel that would eventually be fixed to *NZL-20*.

The tandem-keel concept was a truly radical approach which, if successful, no doubt would have firmly cemented the designers into the history books. And after 1988, when Dennis Conner had pronounced, "We're racing a cat, and they're racing a dog," if the tandem had been successful, it would have provided sweet revenge for the designers. The media would have focused on the success of the designers, taking away all the questions raised by the defenders about the relative performance of the 1988 big boat against a similar monohull yacht, had the Americans chosen to build one.

Yet the options for the type of boat to be considered for 1992 would close down pretty quickly once the tandem concept was chosen. Displacement, hull shape and sail proportions were, in all likelihood, based on accommodating the keel.

And so, when *NZL-20* was taken out of the box, there was a lot of talk that this was the most advanced boat in San Diego. So many new technologies were used in her design and construction, it was said, that she was the highest of the high-tech boats that would sail for the Cup. She was glued and riveted, similar to construction methods used in the aircraft industry, rather than using the traditional boat-building methods of bonding and taping. The internal structure was different. Most significantly, a tandem keel with two rotating fins would be placed on the yacht's undersides. Finally, a bowsprit was fixed to the front, giving the New Zealand boat the appearance of the fantastically radical breakthrough boat that it was promised to be. I found it interesting that, in the end, it was the bowsprit controversies and protests that many people singled out as the undoing of the 1992 challenge.

But long before the bowsprit became a contentious issue, the boat itself opened up some rather heated discussions within the Kiwi syndicate. On the day we were ready to transfer *NZL-20* from a cradle to the water, when a crane began to lift her the boat almost immediately began to crack and bend. She was placed back in the cradle for another two days while the boatbuilders reinforced her. When the boat finally began sailing, the side decks began to buckle as the running backstays were loaded up.

I remember one of the sailors saying, "Look at that bulge. What the hell are we supposed to do with something like that?"

The design advice given, with an element of humour, was, "Sit on it. That will straighten it out."

Once again the boat went back to the workshop where additional webs and struts were added to help stiffen her, all of which meant more weight.

The mast "development" programme was similar. Six masts were built, at a cost of roughly $400,000 each, and in reality it was hard to judge whether they were pretty much the same or if they represented a progression in design and construction. It was often very difficult to understand the underlying philosophy of this designer-driven programme. Yet, through it all, the confidence of the syndicate managers remained. The general feeling was, well here's the new boat, it's a world-beater, all the sailors have to do is take it out, shake it down a bit, and then go win the America's Cup.

This attitude followed precisely what the New Zealand challenge PR machine was cranking out to the rest of the world and there's no doubt we began to believe our own bullshit.

The tandem keel has been described as an upside-down balance beam arrangement with twin moveable fins for steering. In simplest terms, by separating the keel fins, the keel's design reduces the size of the wave trough generated by a single-fin keel and hence a tandem reduces the drag associated with the wave trough. Wave drag created by the hull and appendages becomes a bigger component of the overall drag as the windspeed, and therefore the boatspeed, increases. In Fremantle, for example, when the 12-metre yachts sailed in strong winds they created a huge wave trough. Yet in the lighter winds off San Diego the wave effects of the more easily driven IACC boats with deeper keels was of less importance. The tandem keel probably resulted in more surface area and greater defections of the huge bulb of lead sitting some four metres below the surface. In truth, the concept seemed like an exciting proposition, but in reality the tandem keel was extremely complicated to use. As such, we probably never realised its full potential, even in the conditions for which it was best suited.

On a big boat the helmsman does not have a great deal of feel in steering; with the tandem keel there was no feeling. And we had to be constantly aware of the optimum angles that the foils were set at because, if the angles were incorrect, the combination resulted in increased drag and the boat was slowed. As the wind increased or decreased, even a fraction of a knot, so too did the balance of the boat change, sometimes radically. With each change in balance, the mast rake and hence the sail sheeting angles had to be adjusted to rebalance the boat. It was little wonder, then, that at times the performance of *NZL-20* seemed quite good yet at other times it was quite ordinary.

We were not the only syndicate to use some version of the unusual keel configuration. Dennis Conner experimented with the radical underwater appendage in round one of the defender trials and Iain Murray's *Spirit of Australia* also carried articulating twin keels. But neither team was as successful in its use of the tandem keel as was New Zealand. Both teams struggled to achieve the proper balance of the foils. This is where Bruce Farr and Associates excelled in their design. The basic keel configuration that they conceived worked well in steady conditions, no doubt the result of thorough tank testing and persistent hard work, the trademarks of Farr and his company.

Members of the eventual winner of the 1992 America's Cup, *America³*, claimed to have tested the concept in a wind tunnel, but thought better of it. My own view is that they probably didn't explore the concept in much detail.

"We rejected the idea," said one of their top scientists, Jerry Milgram. "We thought it had possibilities, but it's very difficult to engineer. The two fins together can't be any bigger than one normal fin if you're going to avoid extra wetted surface. And the fins must have a thin core. With 30,000 or more pounds of lead hanging from them, it's hard to prevent the smaller fins from bending sideways under load."

I've always believed the engineering was not our undoing. In fact, I think the engineering of the tandem keels was one of the best areas of that programme. What did us in was that our full-size testing of the concept was not complete. We did not develop the single-fin concept enough to test it as a benchmark against the tandem keel. Even if the tandem keel had been right for San Diego, we did not have the time to properly develop the technology and learn how to apply it on the race course.

In the meantime, while the design and construction issues were being played out, mostly in secrecy, the sailing team became more and more anxious. All of us were competing for a position on the boat and, instead of working as a team, we were battling each other as individuals.

One place that provided members of the challenge some refuge from the daily internal political battles was a bar in Coronado called Bula's Pub, owned by Steve Lindsay who became a good friend of the Kiwis. In one of the opening press conferences, Michael Fay stated that the team's previous experiences in San Diego would help in reducing costs and understanding the logistics involved in campaigning far from home. Then he said, "And we all know the way to Bula's Pub; mind you, I'm not sure that's necessarily an advantage."

Steve Lindsay became an honorary Kiwi after the great hospitality he showed us, and stories of incidents in the bar became legendary. One of my favourites occurred in 1988 during the Big Boat campaign. Michael had called the team together and told them the San Diego Yacht Club would host a party in honour of the New Zealanders and he expected everyone to wear the team uniform. "It's important that you look after your uniform," he lectured. "Don't lose it, give it away, or trade it to anyone for any reason."

The party at the yacht club was pleasant, if tame, so as it was winding down, Michael called Steve and said he was bringing the team of 70 crew back to the relative safety of Bula's. The result, predictably, was a great New Zealand blow out.

As the party progressed, a young lady who had followed the Kiwis to the bar from the yacht club, obviously sensing an increase in action, began to make her presence known in a fairly demonstrable way. It seems she had taken a fancy to the team shirt and, as the night progressed and the drinks flowed, she became determined to take one home. Actually, it just wasn't any shirt she wanted, it was Michael's and she wanted it right off his back.

Her strategy was rather unique. She took a seat at Michael's table alongside his wife Sarah and his business partner David Richwhite. After attempting several unsuccessful ploys to get the shirt, she simply removed her blouse and offered to trade it for Michael's garment. In the confusion of the scene, heightened by considerable noise, the hour, and a good deal of frenetic activity, it took Michael a little while to realise the lady was not wearing a bra. Sensing it was probably prudent to cover her up before a photograph made its way to the newspapers, Michael relinquished his shirt and the lady left, smiling the smile of the victor. As she left, several of the team members repeated in unison their leader's words about the team uniform: "Don't lose it, give it away, or trade it to anyone for any reason."

About halfway through the 1992 campaign, Peter Blake was brought in. A veteran of three Whitbread-Round-the-World races and the wire-to-wire winner of one of them, Peter had established a high profile as a skilled sailor, an even higher one as a manager. Although Fay, Barnes and Clinton were nominally in charge of the campaign, when Blake was hired there was little doubt among most of us that Bruce Farr was really controlling the programme.

In the early days of the 1992 campaign, none of us on the team knew what position we would have. That was the case up until November, right before the new boat arrived. The Cup was scheduled to begin in January. Rod Davis and I were called to a secret meeting where it was announced that Rod would be helmsman and I was selected as the tactician. Surprisingly, this didn't leave anywhere on the boat for David Barnes, who had been with the campaign from day one and had put his heart and soul into the effort. I was in an awkward position and felt badly because I hadn't performed very well – I wasn't happy with how the team was coming together and, more importantly, I didn't feel like I controlled my own destiny.

Politics were already playing a huge role in the campaign with Barnes and John Clinton attempting to have Peter Blake replaced and Michael Fay, somewhat distant from the action, being led in all directions. Davis, having come out of the American campaign with Blackaller, Cayard and his own ill-fated Eagle programme, was well experienced at the political games that are a big part of the America's Cup. He already had a major influence on the shape of the programme. I began to feel that, if the programme went awry, I was being set up as the sacrificial lamb. I felt like I was taking up a place on the team, but I had no part in any decision making.

When I was selected as tactician, I asked Peter Blake if I could think about it overnight. At first he said that was fine, but an hour later I got a phone call from team coach Eddie Warden-Owen who said I had to commit right then or I wasn't on the team. The change of mind irritated me and I said, "Okay, don't put me on the team." It was a stupid way to react, but I also think that someone in the senior management of the syndicate should have stepped in and tried to work things out. But they didn't and I became the back-up helmsman, which in many ways was ultimately the best position for me.

One of the biggest strengths of the '95 team was that we didn't have knee-jerk reactions to major issues. Blake had been through it before; so had I. That selection incident stayed with both of us for a long time and we both learned from it. Everyone has highs and lows and when you're involved in such a pressurised and competitive environment you sometimes say and do things on the spur of the moment. The difference between '92 and '95 is that we learned to handle the outbursts and the off-the-cuff decisions that individuals made which seemed detrimental to the team. Instead of saying, "Okay, if that's the way you want it," we'd sit down and analyse the best way to handle the problem until the final decision was the right choice for the team.

That incident between Blake and me is an example of what went wrong in the '92 campaign. There wasn't a strong enough and active enough management initiative. On the other hand, I was thinking and acting too much as

Russell Coutts the individual rather than Russell Coutts the team player. As I reflect on my role, I believe I didn't really have it in my heart to sail the trial boat in the best interests of the team. I'm not sure anyone on the back-up team approached the whole task with the best attitude. And no one in the syndicate tried to sort out the problem.

The irony of all this is that we really thought we had the fastest boat and the best team and we were going to win the Cup easily. In the early races, the "A team" had the boat going well and we believed we were better organised and the boat was better sailed than any other in San Diego.

I remember coming out of the 1991 IACC World Championships thinking our boats were better organised, better sailed, better campaigned and we had a better sail programme, but we were still beaten. Perhaps we should have considered a heavier displacement boat. But all the model testing, all the VPP analysis, all the on-the-water testing had been done with lighter-displacement boats. When you think about what individuals wanted to achieve out of winning the Cup, instead of what is best for the team, maybe it wasn't in the designers' interest to come out with a boat that was similar to everyone else's and have the sailing team win it. Maybe they wanted to come out with a magical boat, like another plastic fantastic, and people would say "that's the reason we won the America's Cup". Whether that was true or not, the overall impression I was left with was that the team approach took a back seat to the personal agendas in 1992. But it can also be argued that if things didn't happen the way they did in 1992, and we didn't concentrate on learning from our mistakes, we wouldn't have won in 1995.

I look back on the 1992 skipper selection and at that stage there's no way I was experienced enough to do the job. I believe Rod Davis was the better choice at that time. He was initially more experienced at the game and a skilled sailor in big boats. His biggest problem was that he wasn't born a Kiwi, which I think is hugely detrimental to a New Zealand campaign, especially if you're trying to get the public behind you. But that problem may have also been his biggest asset as there may have been personal considerations that helped sway some of the decision-makers towards a non-Kiwi. The thinking may have been that the New Zealand public and media aren't going to focus on the sailors if there is an American driving the boat. Instead, they'd focus on the boat and the designers.

Whatever the underlying reasoning was, the first few months of the 1992 America's Cup challenger trials seemed to prove that thinking correct. Farr and his design team had produced a very competitive boat. Davis, with Barnes as his tactician, and a boatload of very talented sailors were performing well. Eight boats were vying for the right to race against the American defender in the Cup, which was scheduled to begin on May 9. Of those eight boats, four would advance to the challenger semi-finals after three round robins held from late January to mid-March.

Round robin one ended with *New Zealand* and *Nippon* each with six wins. Italy's *Il Moro di Venezia* and France's *Ville de Paris* were close behind with five victories each. *Spirit of Australia*, *Challenge Australia*, Spain's *Espana 92* and Sweden's *Tre Kronor* proved to be not competitive in this round or the two that followed.

Our only loss in the first round was to *Il Moro*, which had beaten us to win the IACC Worlds some seven months earlier. We knew the Italians had put together a very strong programme, headed by the multi-millionaire industrialist Raul Gardini and skippered by American-born Paul Cayard. Gardini and Cayard had teamed together to form successful maxi-boat campaigns for about five years and they were formidable opponents on any race course. Even in these early days, predictions of a New Zealand-Italian challenger final were written in the international press and heard along the waterfront. While there was similar speculation within the New Zealand compound, we knew it was very early and that Chris Dickson's Nippon campaign and Marc Pajot's French campaign presented stiff competition as well.

Dickson's boat seemed particularly fast and I would have to say, with the hindsight of our 1995 research programme, that his yacht was probably the most correct of the challengers in terms of hull design concept. Yet Nippon, as with New Zealand, had chosen a radical keel concept, a canard design with a bow and stern rudder. This meant that their performance was often erratic and highly dependent on them forecasting the correct wind speed at the beginning of the day to allow the correct rudders to be fitted to suit the conditions.

Dickson probably faced an even more complicated task than Davis and the team on *NZL-20*, and yet he had less depth and skill to draw upon in his camp to help him find the best solutions.

The New Zealand team sailed a perfect second round, while *Il Moro* lost only to us and *Nippon* was outsailed by the Italians and the Kiwis. *Ville de Paris* was beaten by the three leaders. In the third round robin, it was *Nippon*'s turn to go undefeated. Dickson beat New Zealand for the first time as did Pajot. Cayard fell to us and to *Nippon*.

With the close of the three round robins, the challenger semi-finals were set. Because of the points weight of the three rounds (1, 4 and 8), *Nippon* was high points winner after the round robins, but actually both the Japanese and New Zealand teams were tied with 18 wins each. The Italians had 16 victories and the French 14. Joining the two teams from Australia on their way home were the Spanish and Swedish syndicates.

There was little doubt that Brad Butterworth, myself and most of the others on the back-up boat were becoming more and more distanced from the *NZL-20* campaign. For most of the important decisions, we were no longer consulted and our role became simply to tune up the race crew before the races and provide competition for them between the round robins. We enjoyed our races and practice against the team on *NZL-20* and often performed reasonably well against them, but we were also quick to seize the opportunity to enjoy ourselves off the water. Our objective was often to pack the back-up boat up as quickly as possible at the completion of the day's duties and get to the golf course to begin the real competition.

Somehow, we believed our activities away from the compound were not attracting any attention. At least, until Michael Fay's helicopter flew over the first fairway of the Coronado golf course and caught Butterworth and me red-handed, smack in the middle of heated battle!

When later asked about the incident, we justified Fay's discovery by saying that we were working on our time and distance for the pre-starts. Fay looked somewhat puzzled at this until we further explained that Butterworth called the distance to the line in terms of the distance that the various golf clubs hit the white ball. Thus a driver, five iron and sand wedge was the terminology we used to gauge distance. And who could argue? We were actually doing reasonably well against the "A team" in the pre-start practice sessions!

After that close call, and drawing upon the unquestionable wisdom of Butterworth's advice, we took Fay's acceptance of the situation as the green light for future distance development. We chose to further refine our skills by taking on the boat an eight iron, a golf mat and some range balls. We were working, you understand, on "distance refinement" during the hour-long tow out to the course area.

The behaviour was understandably met with dismay by most on the *NZL-20* team. They considered we were not taking our role seriously enough. Yet as the humour on the back-up boat developed, the performance was getting better. While the guys on *NZL-20*, admittedly under considerable pressure, didn't really appear to be enjoying themselves, the team on the back-up boat were having a ball – and learning heaps about sailing (as well as correct club selection) in the process.

It was one of the key lessons that Butterworth and I took into the 1995 campaign: above all else, we had to have fun and enjoy the moment.

Surprisingly, it was about this time, just before the semi-finals, that Davis approached me and suggested that he was considering replacing David Barnes as tactician. He asked if I wanted the job.

It was obvious to me that what he really wanted was to remove me as the back-up helmsman but I was very surprised that he was apparently prepared to sacrifice David Barnes in the process. Barnes had been his tactician for some time on the match-racing circuit and it was Barnes who had really given Davis the opportunities in the early days with the New Zealand challenge. I wondered what would ultimately happen to me under a Davis regime and I politely said that I was quite happy providing the competition on the back-up boat.

In the semi-finals, *New Zealand* and *Il Moro* proved the best performing boats. Of the nine races, *NZL-20* lost only to *Ville de Paris* once and *Il Moro* once. The loss to the Italians was memorable because it was extremely close all around the course and *NZL-20* actually beat *Il Moro* over the line by one second but was disqualified for hitting the finish mark. The guys on board claimed that, although they were very close to the mark, they had not actually hit it. But the umpires claimed that they not only saw the mark move, they heard the sound of the yacht scratching the synthetic mark. Some ears they had; hearing this over the sound of their outboard motor!

The Italians lost four races in the semis, but the real surprise was the collapse of *Nippon*. After their undefeated round robin three, they lost six of their first seven races in the semi-finals. For Chris Dickson, who had had his problems with Michael Fay and had left his homeland to join the Japanese effort almost five years earlier, it must have been a particularly bitter defeat to have his campaign officially ended by a 31-second loss to New Zealand.

Chris was quoted after that race as saying, "I'm depressed. It's not so much that we're losing, but that we had the ability to win." Explaining exactly why the wheels came off is better left to those inside the Nippon challenge, but I prefer to remember their effort by a race they had against *Il Moro*. It was the sixth race day of the semis; the winds were gusting and the seas sloppy. In the pre-start manoeuvres, *Nippon's* carbon-fibre boom splintered and began shedding glasslike needles across the deck.

Amazingly, the Japanese did not request a delay, which was permitted under the rules until the actual starting signal was displayed. They could have replaced their broken boom with a spare and started a new race. Yet they chose to remove the broken components and continue with the pre-start. They had come all that way, had developed a very fast boat, but were overlooking the obvious solution to a major problem at the eleventh hour.

I couldn't help but consider that, in a lot of ways, Dickson appeared on his own in the Nippon group. In a true team environment, that situation would never happen. Somebody would have backed up and advised on the rules issue, while Dickson no doubt was focused on the repair, the pre-start and how they were going to retain the slightest chance to win the race. He obviously had his hands full with the Nippon group, so much so that he apparently didn't get a chance to fully read and consider the rules of the regatta. To me, the mistake didn't reflect badly on Dickson but on the syndicate as a whole.

Nippon finished the race sailing the whole course without a boom, and never more than two minutes behind *Il Moro*. It was a dramatic effort that won the sailors the respect of most who witnessed the incident, and high praise from the media. Yet for those who knew the rules, it represented a huge opportunity missed.

Nippon lost another key race when one of its rudders failed after they had established a commanding lead over the French. Although the Japanese had achieved their goal of making the semi-finals, I could understand Dickson's frustration in losing a great opportunity to win a place in the final of the Louis Vuitton Cup. Those opportunities don't come along very often!

As in most sports, statistics only tell part of the story. To see a record of 25–5 for the Kiwis versus 21–9 for the Italians, you would think we should have been pretty confident we could take out *Il Moro* in the challenger finals and advance to the America's Cup match without too much difficulty. And we were pretty confident, but behind the scenes things were not going as smoothly as our public face might have shown. Political battles within the group were being waged. A number of the sailors felt *Il Moro* had progressively improved in speed and tactics while *NZL-20* was starting to show weaknesses in the upper and lower end of the wind spectrum. The sails were receiving a fair amount of the blame from those not on the boat, but in truth the New Zealand sail programme was probably more advanced than most of the other groups.

Davis was having a tough time getting off the starting line and there was no doubt that the boat had a serious weakness in tacking and with low-speed manoeuvres in the pre-start. The tandem keel was beginning to look less and less like the major breakthrough we had all come to believe it was.

All in all, conflicts within the compound were beginning to create cracks in our armour. In the nine days between the semi-finals and the finals for the Louis Vuitton Cup, the Italians made considerable changes to their boat and trained their crew hard. Much later, Paul Cayard told me they had experimented with a different set of wings on the boat and immediately realised an increase in boatspeed of two-tenths of a knot. That may not sound like much, but for boats that average about $8\frac{1}{2}$ knots, it is a considerable increase. As well, we already had one one-second finish with *Il Moro*. What might have happened if they'd had that two-tenths of a knot increase then?

The other part of the story is that as they picked up this increase going upwind, the new wings did not cause any loss of speed going downwind, an unusual occurrence. It was theorised that although the wings added surface area and therefore increased viscous drag, as the yacht bumped up and down over the waves, the wings actually propelled the yacht in much the same way as flippers work for a diver. But even more than the immediate speed increase, the knowledge that they had improved their performance that much gave their team a great boost in confidence. They began to feel they were peaking at just the right time and they reminded each other of what had happened to the Kiwis in Fremantle when Dennis Conner's team peaked at just the right time.

There was another significant improvement to *Il Moro*. She was outfitted with new downwind sails that kept her even, if not helped her outperform *New Zealand* on the runs.

It was rumoured that the Italians had tested spinnakers and gennakers from other syndicates and had had non-nationals design some new downwind sails that were faster. Of course, if this were true, it would be highly illegal under the Cup rules, although very difficult to prove. The New Zealand camp became very agitated over the rumours as we felt we had been squeaky clean with all the Cup rules. There could be no doubting that some of the other syndicates, particularly the Europeans, would have much preferred the Cup to go to Italy rather than New Zealand. The Italians appeared to be getting considerable help on some fronts.

On the other hand, New Zealand wasn't getting much support from the other challengers and in many ways we were fighting issues such as the bowsprit on our own. Many outside the camp were saying that the arrogance of the Kiwis was finally catching up with them. We had set up camp away from everyone else in Coronado. We had made frequent claims that our boat, our sails, our sailors and everything about our camp was far superior to all other contestants. Journalists and the general media complained about the lack of accessibility to the sailors and the very secret, restrictive and stand-off policies the New Zealand challenge had adopted.

The Italians worked hard to look after the media. Cayard was "just a sailor", accessible, articulate and very good at convincing the reporters that the Italian perspective was the most believable. All in all, New Zealand didn't have many friends as we were about to enter the battles that would develop both on and off the water.

While the Italians continued to develop their boat, their crew and their confidence, we began to struggle. Rod felt he needed starting practice and on the day before the challenger finals he and I lined up against each other for six or seven starts. With Michael Fay and many of the sponsors watching, the back-up team won every start, additionally embarrassing Rod and the team on *NZL-20* by gaining penalties on them and pushing them over the line early in three of the starts. It couldn't have helped his confidence at all and, if I'd been more concerned about the team than proving I could outgun the guy who won the helmsman position over me, I might have approached those starts differently.

To make matters worse, when we returned to the dock, fitness instructor Jim Blair asked how the day had gone. Jim had requested that we go easy on Rod and the boys and let them win a few, being the day before the finals. I replied "pretty good", and before I could explain the real situation, he headed over to Davis presuming that Rod had had a good day.

Jim said something to Rod like, "Great day Rod. Sail like that and you'll do great tomorrow." Rod was not amused!

Although all of this created increased pressure on the entire team, it wasn't particularly noticeable in the first race of the finals. Rod had a brilliant start and the team sailed well while Cayard and his crew were out of sync throughout the entire race. *Il Moro* crossed the starting line 18 seconds after the gun and never got close to the Kiwis. After the race Cayard said they had misread the conditions and had the wrong sail inventory on board.

The second race was one of the most exciting America's Cup races ever. This was heart-pounding stuff. The two boats were never more than two or three boatlengths apart over the 20.3-mile course. Cayard sailed the right side of the course towards the first mark but Davis found a little more breeze on the left and rounded the mark 13 seconds in the lead.

Then *Il Moro* began to catch up, showing her superior downwind speed. By the second mark the Kiwis' lead was just five seconds, but *NZL-20* was only able to increase its lead by three seconds on the second weather leg. Davis continued in the lead through the Z-legs, continually feeling the presence of Italy's bow whipping across his stern like a scimitar coming ever closer.

On leg seven, Davis attempted a manoeuvre known as a "slam dunk". It occurs when two boats approach each other on opposite tacks and the yacht on port has to dip behind the yacht on starboard. If the starboard tacker tacks at precisely the right moment, the port tacker becomes trapped beneath in the lead boat's dirty wind. What's worse, the boat behind is now trapped on the same tack as the boat in front and when it finally creates enough room to tack, the lead boat can tack also, in phase with the other yacht.

Davis went for the slam dunk but turned slightly too late. Cayard judged it perfectly, with the two boats missing by about a foot. He did the counter-move perfectly, putting the bow down early to gain more speed, then, just as Davis was crossing, Cayard dialled the 25-ton yacht up towards a collision course thereby forcing Davis to sail a little further before he could tack. At the very last moment, Cayard pulled the bow away to avoid a massive collision and sailed straight through Davis, who was still trying to build speed after the tack. It was brilliant sailing by Cayard.

The light New Zealand sled got rolling off the wind, and closed at the finish line in a replay of their semi-final photo-finish. This time, *New Zealand* was not eliminated for hitting the mark. But she lost anyway. Italy, to weather, snuck her bow across first and won by just one second.

By the afternoon of April 25 it looked like the Italians would soon be making reservations for an early return to Europe. The Kiwis won races three, four and five as Rod sailed superbly and the Italians made a number of blunders. *Il Moro* let a 33-second lead in race three evaporate by failing to cover Davis as he went right. Soon, the wind followed the Kiwi boat and *Il Moro* fell behind, eventually losing by 34 seconds.

New Zealand won the fourth race by a whooping 2:26 and then, on the 25th, we surged to a 4–1 advantage with a 2:38 victory. The Italians held a 4:20 lead going into the last leg. As the breeze died, Davis and crew set a downwind sail that was noticeably faster than the light-air gennaker the Italians had chosen. On that one leg, New Zealand gained an incredible six minutes and 58 seconds on her opponent.

I found it remarkable that the Italians had been in San Diego longer than anyone else, had an almost unlimited budget, yet had such serious weaknesses in their sail inventory. With the hindsight of our 1995 programme, I have little doubt that the Italian boat should have performed better in terms of speed versus *NZL-20* than it did. Cayard and the Italians, at the very end of their programme, were starting to show some of *Il Moro's* advantages in certain conditions over *NZL-20*.

Even though *NZL-20* was now 4–1 up, the Italians had been leading in three of the five races and the New Zealanders had sailed well and been somewhat fortunate to catch up some large time deficits and turn around the results in those races.

Another remarkable thing happened after race five. Paul Cayard, realising the Kiwis needed only one more win to advance to the Cup match, chose this afternoon to raise the protest flag; claiming an infringement of Rule 64.4. Thus began the great bowsprit debate.

The small white spar appeared on Bruce Farr's fourth design, and was a controversial item from the outset. I remember discussing the possibility of a technical protest over the bowsprit in October 1991. Since I was considered one of the sailors who had a good understanding of the rules, I was called into a meeting with Davis, Barnes, attorney Andrew Johns and John Doerr, an international umpire who advised us through the 1992 campaign. We discussed possible reactions to the spar and then, in a good idea, we set up a mock protest.

In the protest I took the position that use of the bowsprit presented a problem. I felt that during a gybing manoeuvre, when the real spinnaker pole was temporarily disconnected, the bowsprit could be viewed as a spinnaker pole. Since it was not connected to the mast, it could be construed as illegal.

I was told, "There's no way you'd ever win a protest based on that argument." It was decided the bowsprit was no big deal and let's go ahead.

However, it did become a big deal. Beginning in January 1992, the Louis Vuitton Cup Jury, the International Jury, the America's Cup Organising Committee, the Challenger of Record Committee and the New Zealand and Italian syndicates exchanged enough paper on the subject to fill a set of encyclopedias. There were numerous hearings from which rule clarifications, decisions, amended decisions and revised definitions were issued. Even the most knowledgeable sailors found themselves pondering a sea of technicalities.

On March 5, between rounds two and three of the challenger trials, the International Jury made a ruling that served as the basis for the Cayard protest of almost seven weeks later. Requested by the Challenger of Record Committee and the America's Cup Organising Committee to review the issue, the International Jury knew their opinion was non-binding on the Louis Vuitton Cup Jury. This in itself was controversial. In essence, the LVC Jury was saying "think anything you want, you'll get your turn soon enough, but right now we're in control".

Regardless of who had the power at the moment, the America's Cup Jury, led by Goran Petersson, gave the opinion that to attach the gennaker sheet to the bowsprit without using the spinnaker pole was a violation of Rule 64, which reads, in part, "No sail shall be sheeted over or through an outrigger . . ." At the time the ruling had no impact because the LVC Jury refused to be bound by their counterpart's decision. "Here we are contesting the most prestigious sailing regatta in the world," said an angry Peter Blake, "but the referees can't agree on the rules. Where does that leave the competitors?"

Where it left them was in the jury room on the evening of April 25. Cayard, armed with video tapes, diagrams and a rule book, spoke long into the night. He contended that our method of rigging the spinnaker to the bowsprit by leading an adjustable rope called a strop to a ring under the spinnaker was illegal. It was much the same argument I had used in our mock protest some six months earlier, but it was also an argument our rule advisors believed had been reviewed many times and cleared. Yet the use of the bowsprit had in fact never been properly resolved.

Michael Fay said when the protest was lodged, "We come here with an independent jury whose opinion should be respected. I think it's quite inappropriate for any competitor to cast aspersions on their integrity and reputation." From the Italian side, syndicate head Raul Gardini countered with, "New Zealand has been racing in the Louis Vuitton regatta in an unsportsmanlike manner." To which Cayard added, "Mr Gardini considers the Louis Vuitton Cup over and *Il Moro di Venezia* the winner."

In the end, the LVC Jury, citing several technicalities, ruled ". . . For approximately eight seconds, after gybing, the tack of the gennaker was being controlled by a line from the tack of the gennaker through a block near the end of a bowsprit." While they affirmed Cayard's protest, they did not give him the race. Instead, *New Zealand's* win that day was "annulled" – the first annulment of a yacht race in anyone's memory. The Kiwi lead was cut from 4–1 to 3–1 in what would mark the beginning of the end for Sir Michael Fay's third challenge.

For some time following the protest and even after the regatta itself, analysis of the bowsprit issue in many camps tended more towards the psychological than the technical. Many observers believed Cayard had the faster boat, but *NZL-20* was sailed better. Cayard's gambit, so the thinking went, was a ploy more to upset our crew than to have the use of the bowsprit outlawed. In the end, he did both. Many saw the manoeuvre as a clever head-game designed to unsettle Davis and the crew. It is true that Cayard knew Davis well from having sailed with him on *Defender* with Tom Blackaller.

It is also very true that Rod appeared to suffer from the heat of the enduring arguments, the protests and the self-imposed pressure of perhaps being one of those singled out as responsible for losing the America's Cup. Cayard was reportedly infuriated over the use of the bowsprit and was fuelled by a burning desire to see it corrected. He fought the issue hard, apparently not being concerned about having to roll over his good friend of previous years. Some of the New Zealand management questioned if Davis had the same conviction and determination to take on Cayard.

We had gone from recording the most wins in the challenger trials and semi-finals to a 4–1 advantage in the finals. But from this position, on the brink of victory, we fell off the cliff.

What happened? I believe it was a combination of things. One was the bowsprit. The successful protest did unsettle the Kiwis. The way the team on *NZL-20* used the bowsprit to trim and gybe reaching sails was unique. "We had to practise a whole new technique in the middle of the finals," Rod Davis said after Cayard's protest was upheld. These are critical manoeuvres and we basically had to go back to the beginning and learn all over again.

Most of the boats were loading their poles with 8000 pounds of aft pressure when reaching with an asymmetrical sail in medium breeze. With the bowsprit, we were down to around 800 pounds. Without the use of the bowsprit, there was an enormous effect on rig, gear and sailors.

In hindsight, the bowsprit may have been a good idea as it facilitates sail handling, and it's probably safer. But taking it into the world's most litigious regatta was chancy at best. Aside from last-minute boat-handling changes, the psychological effect perpetrated by Cayard was, as Rod Davis said, "Intimidating.

Having the win taken away ticked everybody off. It was a harsh penalty."

Peter Blake was outraged by the protest ruling. Generally fairly mild-mannered, Blakie lost his cool at a press conference, telling the world's media we had been "shafted". Michael Fay's preference for a low-profile, "quiet" campaign was shattered as the former Whitbread superstar became more and more visibly angry. Literally shaking with rage, Blake suggested a conspiracy at work.

Behind the fences of the Kiwi compound, none of us were feeling too charitable towards either our opponents or the jury. After the experiences of the last two Cups, it seemed as if our competitors began to believe if they couldn't beat us on the water, they'd get us in the courtroom or the jury room.

Boosted by their protest coup, the Italians began sailing inspired races. *Il Moro* came surging back in races five and six to tie the series at three wins each. While we weren't exactly in panic mode, there was considerable talk about what we should do to reclaim our winning form. I think most of us now believed *Il Moro* was a tough match for *NZL-20*. Cayard and the Italians were really sailing well, dominating the starts and always getting the first shift correct. Races five and six were all over in the first few minutes as the Italians on the first cross had established big leads. Cayard was now sailing *Il Moro* to its potential and perhaps even beyond. They were getting in front of the Kiwis and then protecting their lead by tight covering, forcing *NZL-20* to tack often and to sail in a lower mode of sailing. Cayard was exposing the weaknesses of the tandem keel and the design of the "breakthrough" New Zealand boat.

Talk began to circulate that *NZL-20* was not being sailed as well as it was in earlier rounds. It was said that Cayard had Davis completely psyched out and that Rod's starts were the biggest problem.

Immediately after the race that tied the series, I received a phone call from Peter Blake who was on the water and had observed the race. I had been booked to fly out that night to return to New Zealand for a fundraising dinner for my Barcelona Olympics bid. I had timed the dinner thinking it would be straight after *NZL-20* won the Louis Vuitton Cup, which I reasoned would have everyone in a happy and generous mood, perfect for raising some much-needed dollars.

Blake asked me if I would cancel my trip to New Zealand and start the boat in tomorrow's race. I told him I would only if Davis, Barnes and the rest of the team agreed and I had the total support of the crew. Blake said he'd talk it over with the team on the way back to the dock and he'd let me know.

I felt that having me start the boat possibly had some merit. In practice, there was little doubt that Rod was having a tough time with his positioning and timing. Having me start the boat and then hand the wheel over to Rod might have been beneficial.

When the team arrived at the dock, I was informed there had been a management decision to make a more significant change than just add me as the starting helmsman. The decision now was to replace Rod and David with me and Brad Butterworth. I was dumbfounded. In the space of an hour or so, a subtle change had turned into a major transition. My immediate reaction was that it was a crazy decision. I remember asking, "Are you sure you guys want to do this?" I said I thought having me start was the better way to go. No, came the answer, we think we need a wholesale change. In hindsight, I wish I had stuck to my guns.

David Barnes and some of the other guys on *NZL-20* were also keen for a change. Barnes stepped off the boat and was the first to suggest that we should make a change for the seventh race and that I should replace Rod as the starting helmsman. I believe he was genuine in his wish to give the New Zealand challenge the best possible chance, yet I also feel that, as with some others, he was thinking that he alone did not want to be blamed for the campaign failing.

As I was trying to decide whether to jump into this situation, Brad Butterworth came by. He and I had come to know each other quite well through the campaign; in fact, I'd have to say strengthening that relationship was the best thing for me about the whole 1992 challenge. It was also an important ingredient in the success of the 1995 challenge. We went over the pros and cons and convinced ourselves that we might just be able to pull it off. We knew there was a huge downside should we lose and that in many ways it would provide the designers, Rod Davis, David Barnes and many others with a perfect excuse. I knew it was an incredible longshot, but I was also conscious that it was an incredible opportunity.

What's more, what the hell if we were not successful. It was probably New Zealand's last effort in our lifetime anyway. In many ways, that was the attitude that was needed if we were to have any chance at all.

As Butterworth and I stepped onto *NZL-20* on the morning of race seven, pitman Dennis Kendall remarked that we would all know if the change had been successful after the first two minutes of racing. As we towed out past Steve Lindsay's new bar, the Bay Beach Cafe, Midge Marsden and Herbs were performing at full volume in an attempt to get the New Zealand team cranked up.

And at the beginning of race seven it seemed as though the gamble had paid off. We won the start and crossed ahead of *Il Moro*. Butterworth chose the right side and we received a healthy right-hand shift that put us firmly in control. At the time the feeling on board was electric. I can recall thinking there is no way I would rather be anywhere else than right here, right now.

Cayard then gained on a left shift yet we were still in front as we approached the windward mark. Then Cayard pulled off a great dip as I failed to perform the slam dunk. When *Il Moro* missed us by about six inches, I remember thinking Cayard's judgment is either very good or he is extremely lucky. In reality, it was probably a combination of the two. Cayard gained the lead which he never let up, beating us by 20 seconds.

I was both disappointed and encouraged. I felt we could beat the Italians and that they had simply sailed a better overall race, but it was very close. *NZL-20* was higher but slower than *Il Moro* upwind in the medium conditions with the overall result being pretty even. Downwind, *Il Moro* surprised me as she was faster.

For the next race we made some more crew changes, brought David

Barnes back on board to assist with sail selection as well as using his overall knowledge of *NZL-20*.

We were beaten easily by the Italians. The wind was stronger and the speed difference reminded me of what I had seen in the World Championships in 1991. *Il Moro* was faster. They got a slightly better start and used their speed to get to the first big right-hand shift. Barnes advised we needed a more powerful headsail then, after we changed, the wind picked up, *NZL-20* became overpowered, and we went from bad to worse.

By the first mark they had a massive lead and went on to clinch the Louis Vuitton Cup with a 1:33 victory. The Coutts/Butterworth change had proven unsuccessful.

Four months of racing had come to an end. Our overall record was 28–10 (with an additional win in the "annulment") and the Italians had posted a 26–12 score. But, as I said, statistics don't always tell the full story.

7

Schnack Attack

As the Italians prepared to go into the Cup match against Bill Koch and his America[3] team, the Kiwis broke camp and drifted off to resume their lives. For as many as three years, men and women who had come into the New Zealand challenge as sailors, designers, engineers, mechanics, cooks, lawyers, accountants, from all types of varied vocations, had worked together towards one goal, one ideal. We all believed we could bring the America's Cup back to our country. For the third time in a row, we left the regatta empty-handed.

In San Diego, *America*[3] put on a dominant display of superior boatspeed and took out Cayard and crew in five races, losing only the second race and that by a mere three seconds. While Koch and the media didn't take much of a liking to each other, resulting in the multi-millionaire Kansan's achievement being written off in some press circles as a matter of out-spending everyone, most of the Kiwi team grew to respect the American's scientific approach to the game. And none of us believed the argument that Koch "bought" the Cup. If it was as easy as that, Raul Gardini's more than $US100 million would have taken the silver ewer back to Venice or the $US85 million the Japanese spent would have the Cup in Tokyo. Koch and his team simply produced the fastest boat and sailed it better than everyone else.

We were acutely aware that Michael Fay had given New Zealand every chance to win. In terms of our budget we hadn't wanted for anything, yet we had not made the best use of our resources or time and, in comparison to the *America*[3] programme, we were left far behind. Lack of money was not the reason for New Zealand's failure.

But there was no question that money was one of the critical factors in the 1992 America's Cup. It made it easier for the likes of America[3] and the Italians to cover greater areas of research, yet there was little doubt that there was considerable wastage in their spending versus performance improvement.

Some estimates have more than $80 million being spent by the two defending syndicates and a whopping $418 million by the eight challengers. Compared with just nine years earlier, when an estimated $7.8 million went through two defenders' wallets and seven challengers spent $25.5 million, it's easy to see why there was such an outcry that the cost of mounting a Cup campaign had almost eliminated the chances of competing for everyone except the very richest nations. For a country like New Zealand, spending that kind of money just to win the America's Cup was considered obscene. The country had been going through some tough economic times after the 1987 sharemarket crash and most of us wondered if we had seen our last America's Cup.

Our loss in 1992 had a devastating effect on me. I was totally deflated, both mentally and physically. I went from believing we had the best team and we would win to being thrown into the middle of an impossible situation and coming out of it thoroughly depressed. While Rod and David never voiced it publicly, or privately as far as I know, they had the perfect excuse: "If they'd kept us on the boat, we might have pulled it off." Bruce Farr wasn't about to be blamed. The suggestion was that the boat was fast, but the sailors were not able to understand the technical complexities involved in sailing it to its full potential. The unsuccessful afterguard change at the end provided the perfect excuse and it didn't even need to be stated. That was the obvious reason.

Publicly, there weren't any real recriminations voiced at me. New Zealand people tend to look at sports pretty realistically. They don't make too much out of victory or get too unbalanced by defeat. But I think it can be said that Kiwis generally were fairly bitter about the 1992 America's Cup. Not because we lost, but how we lost. Even for the most avid yacht-racing fan, the technicalities of the bowsprit issue were difficult to understand, much less care about. To the man or woman in the street, the whole thing must have appeared Machiavellian at best and downright corrupt at worst.

For Sir Michael Fay, the dream of capturing the America's Cup must have become a nightmare. If he didn't leave San Diego feeling pretty paranoid, believing the world was out to stop his efforts at every turn, he must be a great deal more mentally tough than most people. I know that when the sailors left the States, you couldn't have found a taker who'd bet New Zealand would return to this yachting competition for many years to come. I think we all felt we'd just about had it and that it would be next to impossible to put together another campaign on the back of the 1992 results. The question most asked was, "Who'd want to be a sponsor now?"

While I'll admit to an emotion bordering on disgust and filled with disappointment concerning the 1992 America's Cup, my enthusiasm for sailing, for the pure sport, had not diminished. Simon Daubney, Graham Fleury and I had planned a Soling campaign in the same boat in which I'd made an unsuccessful run at the 1988 Olympics.

And because part of the Olympic format in the Soling class is match racing, I returned to the Omega Grand Prix. Our first regatta following the Cup was in St Tropez, where we'd done so well in the past two years. But apparently not all of the enthusiasm I just spoke about had returned as we finished a lowly seventh.

Our Olympic campaign didn't fare much better. Several factors came into play, chief of which is I just didn't sail very well. Because we had so much experience in match racing and we were the highest-ranked match racers in the Soling class, it was to our opponents' advantage to try to eliminate us in the fleet racing portion of the regatta. Only the top six teams advance from that format into the match racing. So we found ourselves at various key times during the regatta being camped on by competitors trying to keep us in the back of the pack. That's not meant as an excuse as the simple reason we didn't do well was that we just weren't fast enough in the Soling. Besides, it is actually a pretty sound strategy for teams who are stronger in fleet racing than match racing to try to push the better match racers to the back.

The gold medal in Solings went to Jesper Bank of Denmark and the silver medal was won by American Kevin Mahaney. I'd met up with both sailors on the circuit and in just a few weeks I'd be seeing Kevin at the World Championships of Match Race Sailing, held in August at Long Beach, California.

During our Olympic build-up we had trained with the South African team and got to know them reasonably well. From my observations, South Africans and Kiwis have a fair amount in common. They both love the game of rugby, enjoy having the odd beer with their mates and understand the mentality of giving your close friends a hard time, just for the sport of it. After the final race I was relaxing, having a few beers and chatting with some of my South African friends. A young woman was standing among the same group and my South African "mate", out of the blue, asked what my opinion of the Spanish Royal Prince was.

I had actually never met him but chose to use the situation as a joke and proceeded to loudly describe him in less than complimentary terms. "Oh the Prince. He's a bloody ———!"

The entire bar went silent in a matter of seconds except for the raucous laughter of my South African mate who was obviously enjoying the fact that he had set me up beautifully. He escorted the young woman over to me and said, "Russell, please let me introduce you to the Princess of Spain."

Over the next few minutes I was back-pedalling as fast as I could, realising that the situation was a lot more serious than either I or my South African friend had anticipated. The Princess did not take kindly to my assessment of royal blood, nor did those in her considerable entourage. We were clearly outnumbered and we made a quick exit. I kept a low profile in Barcelona until I was able to get the hell out of there.

Although the bad taste of the America's Cup experience had not left my system completely, nor had St Tropez and the Olympics done much to bolster my confidence, I looked forward to the Long Beach competition. Aside from Mahaney, fresh from his Olympic success, the field included Peter Gilmour, Chris Dickson, Ed Baird and, somewhat fresh from the America's Cup, Mr Cayard. It promised to be interesting.

And interesting it was. Chris, showing no visible adverse effects from what he termed his Nippon disappointment, completed the round robin part of the regatta with the most wins. Mahaney, Gilmour and myself were the other semi-finalists. In the double round robin, we had beaten Chris in both our match-ups. Knowing Peter is always a tough customer, Chris chose Mahaney as his opponent, leaving me and Peter to do battle. My crew of Warwick Fleury, Dean Phipps, Mathew Mason, Peter Evans and Lars Linger handled the boat exceptionally well and we advanced into the finals with a 2–0 defeat of Gilmour.

Although we expected to race Chris, Kevin came back after losing the first race to win the next two and enter the finals. Mahaney had a very strong team that included the American tactician John Kostecki. Kevin had studied and practised match racing for the previous four years and he was a force to be reckoned with.

Our races were not without controversy. In the first race, Kevin led us on the first leg and was just in front as we approached the windward mark. During the rounding, Kevin cut it close, but we were able to place our bow between his boat and the mark. That's all we needed to call for buoy room; when he didn't give it, we raised a protest flag. The on-the-water umpires agreed and the Mahaney team was forced into a penalty turn. The rest of the race was skintight throughout as Kevin caught up with us but was unable to pass. We won by one second.

The protest didn't sit well with our opponent. At the press conference later that day, he answered a reporter's question by saying, "Coutts didn't hit us, and he didn't hit the mark. Just how much room does he need? I can't say I agreed with the call."

The second race was even more heart-breaking for our opponents. Again, it was very close and, again, it turned on a penalty call. This time they were penalised at the last mark after leading the whole way. They tried to cross us on port and realised too late they weren't able to, and this time there was a collision. We had won the World Championship.

Winning that series for the first time was a special moment for our team and in many respects it helped to rejuvenate my career. Rod Davis later articulated what I think a lot of my fellow sailors were thinking at the time. "You know, Russell," said Rod, "after failing in the America's Cup and then the Olympics, I thought your sailing career was over."

I had never really thought of leaving the sport, especially not after the setbacks. Instead, I decided to change my approach to match racing, not my career. I asked Peter Evans to sail with me as a designated tactician, calling the tactics after the start. Under my old system, the crew had fed me information and I'd made the tactical calls.

In the next three months we entered the ACY Cup in Croatia, the Omega Gold Cup in Bermuda, the Nippon Cup in Japan and the Steinlager-Logan Cup in Auckland. We came second to Chris in Croatia and won each of the next three events. Despite a world-wide economy in a downturn, each of the regattas offered prize-money and in the space of 12 weeks we'd won more than $US100,000.

Perhaps the most personally satisfying victory was our win over Paul Cayard in Bermuda. The Gold Cup is probably the most competitive event on the circuit – it is one of the favourite venues of the sailors and traditionally attracts fields of 24 teams. We got by Holland's Roy Heiner in the semis and Cayard beat Dickson. The press made a big deal about a Coutts-Cayard match, playing up the America's Cup angle of just five months earlier.

Cayard was sailing particularly well, his strong team including former Olympic medallists John Kostecki and Steve Erickson. The umpire for the match was John Doerr, the former rules advisor for the New Zealand challenge. In our second match, Cayard received a penalty, prompting Erickson to yell across the water, "Hey Coutts, is Doerr still working for the Kiwis?" I answered by turning to John and yelling, "Great call, ref, you sure know your stuff."

With the series level at 2–2, in the deciding race we managed to force Cayard over the starting line early, thus turning the final race into an easy win. While the circumstances were completely different, our come-from-behind win took away some of the sting of the Cup experience.

The Nippon Cup brought me to the attention of some of the Japanese America's Cup leaders, and vice versa. I had a short discussion with Mr Yamasaki, chairman of the syndicate, and I had conversations with a few of the other managers. The talk was pleasant, non-substantive, but I had a feeling the meetings might lead to something more serious in the future.

And they did. Soon after the event, I was contacted by the Nippon challenge and asked if I'd consider a position with the team for the 1995 America's Cup. It was a very interesting and challenging proposal. I wanted to give it a great deal of thought. The residency requirements of the Cup at that time called for sailors to have established residency in the country for which they were to sail by May 6, 1993, exactly two years before the America's Cup match was to begin. That gave me about six months to decide whether to move to Japan or some other country. It also gave me, or so I thought, some time to decide if I truly wanted to go through another America's Cup campaign.

That schedule was slightly disrupted when Alan Sefton asked me to meet with him just after the Steinlager-Logan Cup. He said he wanted me to know he was planning to put together another Cup campaign. I heard him out, but I was very sceptical. I had already spoken with Michael Fay, who made it pretty clear he would be sitting out the 1995 event. I wondered how Alan thought he could put together another run without Michael's involvement. I also wondered where he thought he'd find the sponsorship.

Sefo told me he was teaming up with Peter Blake, which I thought was a positive. Then he mentioned they had established a preliminary budget of $25 million. I put that statement in the category of "if cows could fly . . ." He did let on that they hadn't raised a cent yet, but he was hopeful that some of the leads they were working on would come through. I was asked to give it some thought.

It was hard for me to believe anyone could pull this off. The atmosphere in New Zealand was not exactly conducive to putting together $25 million. We were still reeling from the sharemarket crash. The previous three Cup campaigns seemed to illustrate more what we couldn't do than what we could do. The PR for both the big boat campaign and the 1992 team wasn't terrific. It looked like Fay was out of the game. The '92 team was in disarray.

With the possible exception of the two guys who were trying to get it going, there wasn't too much this new challenge had going for it at that point. Sefo had been closely involved with every New Zealand challenge since the first. Blake had obtained hero status in the country because of his long-distance races and was no doubt as much of a drawcard to sponsors as anyone. Between the two of them, they certainly had the connections. But I wondered if the strength of these two personalities was enough on which to base a complex and expensive America's Cup syndicate.

The next meeting I had was with both Sefo and Blake. It was a little strange because we met in the Fay, Richwhite Building in Auckland. Had Fay really divorced himself from the Cup? Was he involved, but only removed from the action?

Blake confirmed what Sefo had told me. I saw that he was serious about this effort and that, like Sefo, he thought it was a real possibility to find the sponsorship, put together a strong campaign and win the Cup. I'd heard all this before, although something ignited inside me for the briefest of moments, something that told me this really could happen. But, in truth, that spark died within minutes of the meeting ending. Blake had told me, however, that if I was interested, they'd have an offer in front of me in the next few days. Still sceptical, I told myself I'd believe it when I saw it.

While I think Peter and I had developed a mutual respect over the previous few years, I can't say we were best of friends. During the 1992 campaign we had established a good working relationship, but I'm not sure either one of us put forth too much of an effort to go beyond that. It's also fair to say we didn't always see eye to eye on some of the core issues that confronted the '92 team.

So I was a little surprised that he and Sefo had approached me so early in the game. And while I might have had some doubts about the money side, I didn't think twice about Peter's abilities to lead a sailing team. I'd heard too many positive reports about his Whitbread races from guys who had sailed with him and, of course, I'd seen him in action through the previous campaign. I resolved to give the idea of joining this effort some serious consideration while I spent time at my parents' beach house north of Auckland.

As I was doing just that, I received my next surprise. Ross Blackman arrived one day acting as an emissary for Alan and Peter. He delivered the offer Sefo and Blakie had spoken about. Well, semi-offer would be a better way of describing what Ross had brought. In the simplest terms, the offer was we don't have any money now but we're going ahead with this and we think we'll have funding by May of 1993. Since there wasn't any money to pay anyone, those committing to the effort now were asked to accept a deferred salary until May. Since I was still considering the Nippon offer with the same deadline, I thought this was reasonable, but my immediate thought was the Nippon challenge is solid and nothing I've heard yet tells me the Sefton/Blake dream is anything more than that – a dream.

Then Ross casually mentioned the clincher. "You know, Russell, we've given this a lot of thought and we want you to be the skipper and helmsman. We're going to do this a little differently than the Kiwi challenges have done in the past. No helmsman try-outs. No selecting the sailing team at the last minute. We think settling all of that going in will prevent problems down the road. Peter believes you're the best guy we could have behind the wheel and he wants it to be your boat and your team. He and Sefo and I will handle the finances, the PR, the administration and the legal. You'll be in charge of putting the design team and sailing team together. Included in those responsibilities are the weather and rules guys, the coaches, the sailmakers and the boat and equipment manufacturers."

He stopped and looked at me. I was stunned. I hadn't expected this. He seemed amused by my expression.

"I guess Peter figures if you're going to drive, you ought to know what you're driving. And I mean every inch of it!"

Truthfully, I have no clear recollection of any immediate response I gave to Ross. I probably tried to collect myself and say something intelligent, but trying and doing are two different things. I'm sure I mumbled something to the effect that I'd think it over, but already the adrenaline was pumping and in my mind I was no doubt in the middle of the final leg of the final race of the 1995 America's Cup. And in the lead, I should hope!

After Ross left, the instant euphoria was quickly balanced by reality. I realised nothing had really changed since I'd first heard of this possible run for the Cup. There still weren't any sponsors, there wasn't any money. The indifferent, if not negative, attitude of the New Zealand press or public hadn't changed. The sharemarket crash still loomed over us all. Michael Fay wasn't rushing to the forefront. All in all, putting together another challenge was still one hell of a longshot.

On the other hand, the way Peter and Alan were approaching this was intriguing. By designating a skipper and helmsman this early in the game they were immediately negating the individual competition that had led to anxiety, jealousy, resentment and low morale in the past. Instead of playing off sailor against sailor, the skipper could base his selections on how the individual fitted in with the team, how he would affect the chemistry of the unit. I'd just been through a very successful period on the match-racing circuit and I knew one of the major factors behind the success was that each guy on the boat worked well with both me and every other crewman. Why couldn't the same concept be applied to an America's Cup boat?

The more I thought about this approach, the more excited I became. I realised Sefton and Blake had obviously given this a great deal of thought and it appeared they were open to learning as much as they could from the previous three challenges. They had determined to use what worked in those campaigns and discard what didn't. It was a new, fresh way of looking at things, but it carried with it a respect for what the past New Zealand efforts had accomplished. That appealed to me.

In comparing this offer to that of Nippon, I felt I'd have more freedom here to help put together the team than I would in Japan. I also knew there was unfinished business at home and if there was to be a New Zealand challenge, I'd want to be a part of trying one more time to bring that silver trophy to Auckland. Something deep inside told me this might be the time.

As Christmas approached, I figured I had about four months before I'd know for sure whether the Kiwi deal was a go or whether I should acquire a taste for sushi. In the meantime, I realised I had an opportunity to gain as much information as I could about what makes a boat go fast. I felt it necessary to increase my understanding of yachting's physics. I told the fledgling New Zealand challenge I was on board with the understanding that if by "nationality day" of May 6, 1993, there was nothing solid, I could look in other directions.

So I set off to receive a post-graduate education in America's Cup history, yacht design, velocity prediction programmes, computational fluid dynamics, wind tunnels and tank testing and all sorts of arcane subjects near and dear to the hearts of yacht designers the world over. Dean Meyers would be proud.

By this time, the Kiwi effort had grown by leaps and bounds – we now numbered six. Peter Blake had worked and sailed with Mike Quilter in the past and had a thorough trust of his skills and intelligence. The two had sailed a Whitbread together and knew how each other reacted to a wide variety of situations. Blake asked Mike to oversee what was happening and advise him on the critical early actions and decisions while he himself was away for more than four months, competing in the Jules Verne Round-the-World Race. Alan and Ross were running around like the proverbial one-armed paperhangers and I'd asked Simon Daubney to hang around a bit. Scott Chapman, formerly of Fay, Richwhite, became involved as well.

I began my information quest by working the phones. I'd made a list of every America's Cup designer and technician I thought had made a significant contribution during the past three or four America's Cups and I began to ring them. I was immediately surprised and impressed by how co-operative and forthcoming these experts were. Contrary to the secrecy and security that surrounds Cup campaigns, particularly the design offices, away from the battlefield these guys were amazingly open. Almost without exception, my questions were answered without hesitancy and with care and concern that I understood the points being made. Intended or not, I considered this the highest form of sportsmanship. Maybe the Cup wasn't the contentious, hostile minefield it sometimes seemed to be after all.

Of course, I wasn't so naive to think I could obtain this wisdom for the price of a phone call or a jug of beer. As in everything in life, you have to give a little to get a little. I'll tell you something about the New Zealand designs if you tell me something about why you did this or what you thought about that. My advantage was that they were talking to one guy and, before it was all over, I had talked to dozens. In the process, I was able to fill in many pieces of the puzzle on what the best brains in the business thought made boats go fast.

And while it was never flat out said or asked, I knew the implication of my questions was that the Kiwis were putting together another syndicate and we were reviewing all options on designers and technicians. And since the talk of the yacht design world as we approached the nationality date was "who're you going to work for?" no doubt those I talked to figured their services might be needed.

After the preliminary phone calls, I made arrangements to meet with more than two dozen of the world's top design, engineering and technical minds. But before I set off on what resulted in pretty much a world tour, I read as much as I could about the history of the Cup. It's ironic that Dennis Conner, that old "Dirty Den" from the fibreglass controversy and the big boat/catamaran fiasco, should provide me with some of the ideas on which we based our design team. I had always been greatly impressed by the way he had put together his 1987 effort in Fremantle. When it looked like our plastic fantastics would run away with all honours, Dennis and his Stars & Stripes team kept improving and making the right design choices at the end of the programme to give them the best possible chance.

I sat down and read the book *Comeback*, which takes the reader inside the campaign and reveals a great deal about how and why certain things were done. I was particularly interested in the chapter titled "A Bunch of Picassos". It made a case for using a team of designers instead of one person or a single design firm. It also provided good advice on dealing with the artistic temperaments of "a bunch of Picassos".

The chapter starts with Dennis and his long-time mentor Malin Burnham visiting a super-high-tech company called Science Applications International Corporation. There the two sailors were shown, in scientific terms, how and why the wing keel of *Australia II* had made the difference in the 1983 America's Cup. As Dennis writes: "The analysis revealed that, compared with a conventional keel, the wing keel provided the boat with added stability and maneuverability, as well as increased lifting qualities. While the scientists had everything neatly defined in terms of formulas and percentages and quotients, sailor Dennis translated it all to mean that the little white boat from Australia turned on a dime, headed higher into the wind, and footed lower off the wind."

The point is that while all the other syndicates believed there wasn't much new to get out of the 12-metre formula, the class of boats used in the Cup for 45 years, the Australians had experimented with the wing keel and had changed the rules of the design game forever. As the two Stars & Stripes men left SAIC, they discussed the new era of yacht design in which computer modelling and tank testing were becoming key tools. Malin told Dennis that when the Americans decided to accept the challenge of putting a man on the moon, their space agency didn't go out and hire just one contractor or one engineer. "They harnessed the best and the brightest from all across America."

The concept of building a team, using the skills and expertise of a wide spectrum of talented individuals working towards one goal, was not unique to the Stars & Stripes team of 1987. Michael Fay had tried the approach by using Farr, Holland and Davidson. Where the Americans succeeded was in designating one guy as the design co-ordinator. Dennis started out as the head of design but, to his credit, he realised he was in over his head. He brought in John Marshall who was both an Ivy League graduate and an America's Cup veteran of four campaigns. As Dennis says, "He is the guy who talks the same language as the eggheads and the jocks."

In discussing the use of many different talents with our small group of Kiwi '95 pioneers, the new approach received unanimous support. We knew from the beginning that the choice of a design co-ordinator was perhaps the most critical decision we would make in the entire process of forging the campaign. In an ideal world the person would have strong management skills, be technically adept at a whole range of complex design and engineering issues, be able to communicate with "eggheads and jocks" on an equal basis, be able to diplomatically accept and eschew the many ideas offered by the diverse team without undo praise or scorn aimed at anyone, and be able to clearly define and develop a programme of testing methodology conforming to the restraints of time and budget. It wouldn't be a bad idea if the person could cook dinner and wash windows as well.

Clearly, the ideal world and reality are in conflict, but the one name that kept coming up as the candidate who most closely fitted those demanding requirements was Tom Schnackenberg. His credentials were, as they say in the corporate world, impeccable.

Schnack's America's Cup experience dates back to 1977 when he worked with the Australians in their sail programme. He's been involved in every Cup since then. I guess if he was asked what he does, Tom would say "sailmaker". That's a little like describing Ernest Rutherford as a "research scientist". Schnack is something of an innovator. Here's a partial list of his accomplishments: developed North Sails' first 3-D sail design computer software in 1977; developed the first leech-cut genoas in 1980; developed "TAC", a match-racing computer program, in 1983; developed the first tri-radial genoas in 1983; developed the first modern 12-metre gennakers in 1986.

John Bertrand, the first non-American skipper to win the America's Cup, credits Tom with developing the sails that powered *Australia II* to victory in 1983.

As the Aussie's sail co-ordinator, he specialised in building the mainsails for the winged wonder, but Bertrand believes it was Schnack's innovative spinnaker designs that won them the Cup. Before Tom concentrated on the downwind sails, *Australia II* was routinely getting thrashed on the runs by *Challenge 12*, a yacht they chartered from the Victoria syndicate, when the two boats sparred against each other in pre-Cup training. After the sailmaker's focused effort, *Australia II* became a dominant downwind performer.

Tom is also a dedicated sailor. He loves the action. I guess it's a special thrill to see something you've created come alive on the water. He's raced in Admiral's Cups, Kenwood Cups and the 12-metre Worlds and he coached in the 1992 Olympics. There are few people in the world that equal Schnack's practical and theoretical experience.

Schnack and Mike Quilter, who also worked in the sail programme for Australia II, are the only New Zealanders who in 1993 could say they had won an America's Cup. I knew the strong ties he had to the Australian Cup people and I knew they desperately wanted him. John Bertrand was coming out of yacht racing retirement to put together a syndicate for the 1995 Cup. One of the first people he called in hope of recruiting to his effort was Schnack. The two had forged a strong bond 10 years earlier and I knew we were up against a lot of personal and emotional history.

We had determined that it was important to hire the design co-ordinator early in the game so that he would have the major say in selecting the team he would manage. I spoke to Schnack about our infant campaign and our ideas for a design team. He seemed interested, but said he was considering the Aussie campaign. I asked if the position they offered had the same weight and responsibility we wanted him to assume. I knew Bertrand was going down the same team path, but I also had heard he was bringing in designers by the truck load. I was pretty sure the Aussies had Tom pegged as one of many while we thought of him as the one.

What we were offering Schnack at the moment was little more than a wing and a prayer. With most people, the lack of secure money to fund the campaign would have been a deterrent, but with Schnack the most important thing we had to convince him of was that he would have fun in the programme and have the freedom to operate in a non-restrictive environment. Besides, we had confidence that Peter Blake would find the cash; we'd just have to wait a bit.

Peter had taken off on a trimaran in quest of setting a world record in the Jules Verne race. Actually, it's not quite as nuts as it sounds. Although we didn't know it at the time, there was a method to Peter's madness. The trimaran was named *Enza*, after the New Zealand apple-marketing authority. Peter, in quest of America's Cup sponsorship, had approached Enza proposing they become involved in the 1995 campaign. They had an interest, but wanted more immediate exposure. Ideas flowed back and forth in several conversations until a deal was struck which went something like this: Peter, go win the Jules Verne trophy, set a world record, prove to us you're a winner, and we'll back your America's Cup team.

Of course, all Schnack knew was we had seven guys running around with this big dream and the leader of the band was off to conquer the world. Across the Tasman, John Bertrand had the same dream, but he also had money, an organisation which was building daily and, generally, a sure thing. It must have been an agonising decision, but in Tom's usual stoic way, he simply called me one day and said he was in. That may have been the most important telephone call in the 1995 campaign.

In the end, I believe Tom simply felt he could make more of a difference with us than with oneAustralia. I also suspect that the challenge of putting this all together excited him intellectually. One thing was for sure, there wouldn't be much chance of boredom.

From that day until the end of the last race more than 30 months later, Tom and I communicated with each other in person or by e-mail, fax, telephone, or regular mail almost daily. Our first talks focused on establishing a basic approach to selecting members of the design team. We were in agreement on the team approach, so what was left was to fill in the blanks. When we began to consider the tasks needed and the expertise required to make a fast boat, it was initially overwhelming. As Malin Burnham had said to Dennis Conner after they left the SAIC mini-seminar on the benefits of the wing keel, "If we're going to catch up to and surpass the Australians – and surpass them in this technology game – we're going to have to land our own man on the moon." What he meant was what Tom and I were beginning to see very clearly now; to win the next Cup meant going beyond conventional thinking, going beyond even state-of-the-art, going beyond what we thought was going beyond. The America's Cup had begun as a design contest in 1851 and its modern-day editions had developed into technological warfare. A wing keel in 1983; fibreglass in 1987; a new class of yacht and a total reliance on science and technology in 1992.

If we were to win in 1995, it appeared we'd have to out-tech the techies. But wait, something was missing here. Bill Koch had won the Cup and he'd spent $US64 million. The Italians had gone into the Cup match and they'd spent more than $US100 million. Peter and Alan had established the 1995 Kiwi budget at $25 million. And that was 25 million New Zealand dollars, not the US dollars in the figures above. Didn't high-tech cost big bucks?

Maybe not, Tom and I concluded. In those early days, Schnack went down the same information-gathering path I was on. He, too, studied past America's Cups, spoke with designers and technicians, shook the trees for as much wisdom and advice as he could gather. We realised that if we couldn't buy all the human resources we needed, we might be able to borrow just enough to fill the holes. Schnack was receiving the same openness and co-operation from the guys he was talking to as I was. Our methodology was similar as well. After I spoke to someone, I would immediately sit down and write notes on what we'd talked about, what I'd learned. Schnack and I spoke daily, deciding who should call whom, what we needed to ask, what we could tell them in return.

What was more important than finding out what designs that designers

18-foot skiff sailing, hanging out on a wing with a prayer.

The Team New Zealand crew, minus Peter Blake, heading ashore after the final practice session before the beginning of the Louis Vuitton Cup. There was a great deal of excitement and anticipation aboard that day.

A familiar sight to the crew of oneAustralia *during the 1995 America's Cup was the stern of* **Black Magic.** *Here the Australians 'go fishing' with their spinnaker after the second mark in the sixth race of the challenger finals. That effectively ended the race.*

NZ Herald

A rare sight for us, as one Australia sails in the lead during Race 4 of the challenger finals.
This was the only race we lost 'on the water' during the entire 1995 campaign.
Overleaf: Team New Zealand pictured at our compound in San Diego. Compared to most
America's Cup teams, our numbers were small. (Rob Tucker)

STANDING – LEFT TO RIGHT

1 Richard Dodson – Crew, Measurement. 2 Craig Monk – Crew, Fitness, Sails. 3 Simon Daubney – Crew. 4 Mike Quilter – Instrumentation, Crew, Cul... Adviser. 5 David Pizzini – Security. 6 Peter Blake – Syndicate Head. 7 Geoff Smith – Security. 8 Craig Oxenham – Boat Builder. 9 Jon Williams – Boat B... 10 Roy Mason – Shore Boss, French Language Consultant. 11 Peter Wilson – Boat Builder. 12 Ross Blackman – Business Manager. 13 Neil Wilkinso... Design Engineer. 14 Laurie Smith – Boat Builder. 15 Sue Ashby – Sailmaker. 16 Steve Wilson – Spar Builder, Chief Look Out. 17 Neville Thorpe – B... Builder. 18 Tim Gurr – Head Boat Builder, Diplomacy. 19 Doug Peterson – Head Designer. 20 Michelle Hebditch – Receptionist, Top Assistant. 21 Kristen Sneyd – Personal Assistant. 22 Jonathon Peters – Accountant. 23 Laurie Davidson – Head Designer. 24 Burns Fallow – Sail Designer. 25 D... Egan – CFD & CAD Designer. 26 Bob Rice – Weather, Country Music Consultant. 27 Godfrey Cray – Electrical Technician, Maker of fine scones.

ABSENT/OTHER TECHNICAL CONTRIBUTORS

Paul Gugeon – Sailmaker. Aran Hansen – Morals & Morale & Ballast. Mickey Ickert – Sail Designer. Philip Jameson – Chase Boat Driver. Richard K... Designer Acrodynamist. Kerry McIntosh – Crew-Support Vessel. Chay McIntosh – Boat Builder. Barry McKay – Boat Builder. Chris Mitchell – Mast De... Engineer. Ian Mitchell – Draftsman. Paul Murray – Sailmaker. Geoff Parsonage – Skipper/Owner support vessel. Don Robertson – Administration. Alan Sefton – Welshman. Wayne Smith – Structural Composite Engineer. Mike Spanhake – Sails & Crew. Steve Cruickshank – Security. Carl Pederson – S...

urkis – Security. Sir Tom Clark – Director. Roger France – Director. Richard Green – Chairman. Jim Hoare – Director. John Lusk – Director. Prof Jackson ersity of Auckland. Richard Flay – University of Auckland. Andrew Claughton – University of Southhampton. Ian Campbell – University of Southhampton.

SITTING – LEFT TO RIGHT

Shoebridge – Crew, Sails, Weather Boats, Height Consultant. 2 Murray Jones – Crew, Spars, Sheep Farmer. 3 Morgan Trubovich – Shore & Backup Crew, or. 4 Clinton Newberry – Draftsman, Boy. 5 Sean Reeves – Rules, Night Watchman, Foreign Affairs. 6 Joe Allan – Crew, Mechanics, Touch Football Referee, a^3 Consultant. 7 Jamie Gale – Crew, Weather, Whale Watching. 8 Nick Heron – Crew, Rigging, Underbody Maintenance. 9 Ed Baird – Tune up Helmsman, d Specialist. 10 Brad Butterworth – Crew, Head of B.I.A. 11 Russell Coutts – Crew. Warwick Fleury – Crew, Battens, Sails. 13 Mike Drummond – Designer, ural Engineer, Weather. 14 Robbie Naismith – Crew, Sails, Lie Detection. 15 Jeremy Scantlebury – Crew, Boat Captain, Show Jumping. 16 Mathew Mason – Crew, Boat Captain. 17 Dean Phipps – Crew, Sails. 18 Ross Halcrow, Crew, Sails, Hair Preserver. 19 Andrew Taylor – Crew, Listening Devices.

KNEELING – LEFT TO RIGHT

Maury Leyland – Computer Analyst. 2 Chris Ward – Crew, Maintenance. 3 Tony Rae – Crew, Sails, Fitness. 4 Tom Schnackenberg – Design Co-ordinator, Astronomer. 5 David Alan-Williams – Designer, Soap Supplies.

John Bertrand, Rod Davis and the oneAustralia team wave congratulations to us after the final race of the Louis Vuitton Cup. We had won the right to advance to the America's Cup match against the American defender.

Peter Blake, second from left, headed the syndicate. Having him on board was a big advantage to our entire programme and differed from previous New Zealand campaigns in which the syndicate head stayed ashore.

New Zealanders living in California were a big part of our support system. We couldn't miss this group's affiliation as they watched the races off Point Loma.

Black Magic *on the 'Reveal Your Keel' day before the Louis Vuitton Cup finals. I was happy after comparing our appendages to those of the other boats still contending for the America's Cup.*

The first downwind leg of Race 1 of the America's Cup match gave an indication that our opponent might be fast sailing to downwind.

The red socks phenomenon just got bigger and bigger. It seemed that all of New Zealand was waiting for our arrival when we returned on our specially chartered flight.

had come up with in the past was what their thinking was on certain issues. How did they attack a certain problem? Why did you go in this direction rather than that? I understand you didn't like so-and-so's idea on the initial keel shape. Why not? As more and more information came in and we began fitting more and more of the design puzzle pieces together, we began to see it was almost as important to understand what ideas these guys didn't like as it was to discover what ideas they did like, did experiment with, and did use.

We became more and more amazed at what people would tell us if we just asked. Now no one was exactly breaking out blueprints or handing over formulas, but the intellectual process of getting from step A to step B was freely discussed. And what was becoming clearer with almost every discussion was that the fastest boats in previous America's Cups had resulted from the interaction between designers and skilled technicians who weren't necessarily yachtsmen and sailors who weren't necessarily well-versed in the technical aspects of design. When both sides worked together on a particular problem or concept, both were forced to articulate their understanding and their vision of how to accomplish whatever needed to be done. Most importantly, the group thought long and hard about what was really important and had to justify those decisions to each other before embarking on projects that would lead to little benefit. A lot of time and money was saved just by spending a lot more time thinking about the problem and the processes.

It was gratifying to have the leaders of the yacht design industry confirm our decision to form a design team which would work under the management of a design co-ordinator. That decision had not been easy because our choice of design co-ordinator meant cutting ties with Bruce Farr and Associates, the design firm that had been such an integral part of all of the New Zealand America's Cup challenges and who had had an enormous influence on each of them.

Almost immediately after I committed to this campaign, I opened a dialogue with Bruce. I wanted to know the extent of his interest in another Kiwi Cup effort, what he might bring to the table, what assets from past campaigns he owned, what he thought he could do for us. I'd have to describe his attitude as lukewarm tending to the cool side. At first, I don't think he took me too seriously. Then, as we continued discussions and I pressed him on certain issues, I sensed he became somewhat defensive and almost resentful that I was asking for certain explanations.

In the end, there were three major issues that, in my mind, turned us away from the Farr shop and in the direction of organising a team. As I talked to so many of the design gurus from the 1992 Cup, I received a solid consensus that they didn't feel *NZL-20* was all that special a boat. They reiterated the same concerns I spoke about earlier: the light displacement, the bow shape, the excessive flare in the top sides and the tandem keel concept. Yet, quite obviously, the boat did have some very good features that counter-balanced the negatives, otherwise it would never have won anything. However, when I questioned Bruce about these points, he replied that there was nothing much wrong with the boat in terms of outright speed, except that they had underestimated some of the tactical advantages of racing a heavier boat with more sail. In fact, he suggested we could take *NZL-20* back to the 1995 Cup and, with a few modifications, we ought to do pretty well! That seemed to me to be the highest form of fantasy.

Farr also said his firm wished to keep their options open this early in the game and they would not commit to any syndicate until just before the nationality date. This implied he was talking with other countries, which I thought was natural and had no problem with, but his thinking didn't coincide well with our timing. Then there was a television appearance by Bruce during which he said he had placed a priority on the commercial aspects of offers he expected to receive and that he would have to seriously consider those, which we took to mean Bruce would choose to go with a foreign syndicate. Within our small band of Cup hopefuls, we agreed that if Bruce was seeking the most lucrative deal, then the money he was seeking wouldn't be found in our coffers.

With the May 6 nationality deadline approaching, if we didn't have Bruce signed and we hadn't moved to secure alternatives, then we might have ended up losing all our options.

We also believed unanimously that Bruce Farr would have difficulties working within our team environment. This was brought home in spades when Peter received a letter from the Farr office after I'd gone to Annapolis and met with the designer. I had outlined our thinking and our objectives and I'd explained how we saw the management and administration of the campaign. The letter was in the form of a "report card" which gave letter grades giving a critical analysis of the management aspects of our programme. The letter gave us a D, and then suggested that, considering recent communications, the grade might be downgraded further.

We were astonished. I could understand why he might have a bone or two to pick with me because I'd questioned some of the design aspects and explained what the consensus view was. But what I couldn't understand is how or why he would upset Peter.

Peter was the one who enlisted Farr to design *Ceramco*, the first competitive Farr Whitbread boat. Peter also went to Farr for the *Steinlager Two* challenge. There was no doubt that Farr had provided great boats on both occasions, but there is also no doubt that Peter provided great, well-sailed record-breaking programmes which one would have thought were of great benefit to Bruce Farr and Associates, particularly in their infancy.

Actually, I was rather amused by the "report card". I sort of filed it under "consider the source". But Blake, who most close associates would probably describe as pretty even-tempered, was outraged. He didn't say much other than "How many America's Cups have they won?" but the obvious slight burned inside him for more than two years. In the official team video produced after the 1995 Cup, Peter could contain himself no longer. Looking into the camera, he said, "I don't particularly like being told that my management approach was going to get a D, or no, maybe an E for concept. I didn't think we were going to get along too well at that point."

Bruce Farr's work will stand as a testament to his creativity and to his many achievements in yacht design. He is a fantastically talented designer and some of the fastest boats ever built have come from his ideas. Together with Russell Bowler, he has formed one of the most successful and committed design partnerships working today. In many ways, they have helped to reshape the modern approach to naval architecture. They had also been involved in all New Zealand challenges and could very well have been part of a winning team in 1987, aided by some more America's Cup experience and a little bit of good old-fashioned luck.

Why that letter was written will forever remain a mystery to me. After we won the Cup the team travelled to Washington for a reception and, to their credit, Bruce and Russell were there to congratulate us. I couldn't help but ponder what it would have meant to them had they not taken themselves out of contention. It seemed to me that a huge design talent had been wasted.

On the other hand, it is conceivable to view the report card as a major contribution to the success of Team New Zealand. Had it not been written, we might not have focused so strongly on our own design team. Perhaps the chemistry between Tom Schnackenberg, forever questioning and poking his nose around, and Bruce and Russell, having to justify their decisions to someone else, would not have worked.

And, as I've said, I think most, if not all, of us on Team New Zealand could have been exchanged for others of similar talent and the results of the 1995 America's Cup would have been the same. That statement does not apply to Schnack.

8

It's A Go

As Schnack and I went through our list of expert designers, technicians and managers, we received a great deal of information not only on many aspects of design but also on how the top guys in those fields were perceived by their peers. The world of America's Cup designers is a pretty tight, insular group. Everyone knows everyone else. Many have worked with each other on one project or another through the years. Like any group of people, certain biases, egos and personality quirks are to be expected. In order to fully understand what we were being told, Tom and I had to filter out some of the personal and professional prejudices and concentrate on what lay under the surface. Schnack's radar is particularly adept at this.

As our information quest intensified, we placed increasing emphasis on the America³ personnel. It was logical to attempt to gain as much information as we could from the people who had won the most recent America's Cup. Since there had been a great deal of analysis on the yacht *America³* as well as considerable talk along the docks, we felt we had a pretty good idea of the final product. What we were after is how the team had arrived at the final design. What thinking went into the crucial decisions? What ideas made the most sense and why were others discarded? What led to the use of that particular rudder and keel and mast?

One of the most important lessons we learned from the America³ group was a mild warning for tolerance. It seems there were a number of heated arguments between the many individuals who made up the A^3 design team. Sometimes egos got in the way, we were told, sometimes personalities clashed, and sometimes there was an honest difference of opinion. The design process is as much about challenging intellectual concepts as it is about putting lines on paper; if a team was to go beyond the status quo, it had to confront certain standards. Within that environment, the atmosphere becomes ripe for friction.

There may have been disagreements, even some fist pounding and perhaps a few unfortunate words exchanged, but what kept the America^3 group together was the work itself, the goal they were all striving to reach. In the end, what mattered most was the final product. And that's really how it worked out. Cup observers recognised the brilliance of the yacht and credited the team for its conception and its execution. No one person was said to have "designed" the yacht. The names Jerry Milgram, Heiner Meldner, Doug Peterson, John Reichel, Jim Pugh, Buddy Duncan, Penn Edmonds, Phil Kaiko and Jim Taylor were just a few mentioned either as members of the team or for specific contributions, but with more than 100 people working on the design, technical and construction teams, it's obvious this was a highly collaborative effort. Though he probably never received due public recognition, design co-ordinator Vincent Moeyersoms earned the respect and admiration of each of the hard-boiled design types we spoke to.

We liked what we saw in the America^3 group. Although we understood we would have neither the financial nor human resources they used to win the Cup, it's fair to say our challenge and theirs were similar in several areas, particularly in emphasising team over individual and in how to manage the team.

One of the "Cubens" who visited us and for whom we gained considerable respect was Dr Jerry Milgram. Described in America^3's official version of the 1992 campaign (*To The Third Power*, by Paul Larsen) as ". . . a heady innovator and something of a mad scientist", Jerry is a professor of Ocean Engineering at the highly regarded Massachusetts Institute of Technology. As also described in the same book, "Jerry Milgram was amongst the first to apply high-end scientific technology to yacht design with success. He created a stir in the 1960s when he used photographic measurements to create models of 12-meter sails that he tested in the wind tunnel."

Milgram had been a key member of the research and design staff that undertook a five-year programme to design the maxi-boat *Matador*^{2}. During that period, extensive testing and experimenting was done, more so than on any recreational yacht ever built. Some of the methodology, data and scientific tools developed during that programme were used in designing and building the 1992 America's Cup winner. One of the many tools that were created or refined was the Velocity Prediction Program (VPP), actually initiated in the 1930s but rarely used by Cup designers until after the late 1970s. The VPP was begun at Massachusetts by a man named Justin E. Kerwin, who was a professor in the same Ocean Engineering department where Milgram now teaches. Milgram had been working with VPPs long before most others caught on to their benefits and probably had as much experience with the algorithms and equations that produce a VPP than any other academic or technician. That was one of the chief reasons we wanted to talk to Jerry. It was also one of the reasons we wanted to see if he would consider working for our campaign.

At the time we spoke to Milgram, and indeed, all of the A3 men, syndicate head Bill Koch had not made any commitment to defending in 1995. In fact, just the opposite. Koch was often quoted as saying he was leaning towards sitting out the next America's Cup. He felt there was nothing more to prove.

The first meeting I had with the professor was in late January 1993. While I remember disagreeing with some of his thinking, I was very impressed by his intellectual energy and his obvious knowledge. Much of our discussion was theoretical, with an emphasis on testing and data-checking procedures. He had an incredible skill of simplifying his reasoning when describing complex issues, proving that he has a very thorough technical understanding of a lot of areas. I felt it was like referencing an encyclopedia without opening the pages.

Dr Milgram felt their tank testing was particularly beneficial, but only after establishing the proper procedures. Basically, models of yachts are towed down a tank and the forces are measured and compared. Some key decisions for this procedure include the size of the models in the tank as well as the various checking methods adopted. Yacht research has progressed immensely, but it's accuracy is still being continuously refined.

Such things as water temperature can affect the results of tests so they developed procedures that reduced the chances of condition differences. When scaling and comparing different variables, the methods used to strip and separate the various components of drag often determine the final results obtained. He believed the supervision of the model construction was one of the more important aspects of their quality- control programme, which started as a weakness in the early days but developed into a real strength. And the more Jerry talked about quality control and the checking mechanisms adopted in other parts of their program, the more evident it became the America[3] syndicate paid a great deal more attention to this than most syndicates. This was an area in which we resolved to place a much higher priority in our 1995 challenge.

Another area they felt was critical to the overall programme was the checking of the data and the results their tests produced. A number of different VPPs were used to estimate the full size implications of their test results. One was apparently written by Milgram and the other by an independent technician. The VPPs were run simultaneously and Jerry felt they were invaluable as a cross check. If the VPPs didn't agree, the scientists questioned the results and perhaps ran more tests.

It was interesting to learn that one of the more dramatic changes made in their design resulted from observations. While a lot was learned from tank data, much was also learned from observing the models or studying videos of the boats sailing. A lot of the shapes resulted from simply watching models go through the water and thinking about the dynamics and forces of the water flow.

Jerry also said that when they saw our boat they were initially worried. But as they continued to analyse the performance of the boat as best they could, they became convinced they had made the right choice. They were, however, impressed with our upwind sails. While he didn't tell me anything further, I learned they put a lot of effort into measuring the sail depths of the other competitors' boats and it was from that data they concluded we'd made the most of our upwind sails.

America[3] had had their masts and some other spars built by a high-tech aerospace firm in Utah called Hercules. Some people in the A[3] programme believed their use of special high-grade composite materials made a huge difference in the stiffness of their spars. Milgram indicated it was no secret to them that we had gone the light-displacement route and that he realised our masts were built to accommodate the lighter weight. But he also believed those same masts could be modified to handle more displacement and he recommended we look into that. He obviously had already concluded we would abandon the light-displacement theory!

As I departed, Jerry said he was very interested in exploring ways he could work with us. He confirmed that he'd been approached by a number of groups, but he told me the New Zealand possibility excited him the most. We continued interesting the professor but, in the end, Bill Koch decided to launch his novel women's team and Jerry returned to work for his longtime friend.

While our meetings with Milgram were very productive, a meeting I had about a week later may have been the most influential one I had. It was with Bill Koch who summarised so much of what so many of the designers had told me. I was impressed by his candour and sincerity. He seemed to be genuinely concerned about the future of the America's Cup and how he might have some input, as the defending champion, into the entire process. He and I also share a similar desire to advance the sport of sailing in any way we can.

Koch once again emphasised the team approach. He felt it was necessary to establish a creative environment in which everyone working towards the goal of producing the fastest boat in the world could offer any idea he or she felt worthwhile, no matter how crazy it might sound or what kind of response it might elicit. Koch's philosophy is that science should be used as the final arbiter on the wisdom of such ideas.

He believes that traditional yacht designers become too wedded to their ideas and that they have a hard time letting go of ineffective or illogical concepts. He says science is totally objective whereas individuals are not.

Koch's ideas about teamwork were well publicised throughout his 1992 effort. When he first got into yacht racing in the maxi-boat division, he bought a boat and filled it with some of the best-known sailors in the world. It was a disaster. He said they argued among themselves, they tried to prove they were right and the guy next to them was wrong, and they never worked together as a team. When he decided to enter the America's Cup, he resolved that building a team was one of his highest priorities. In fact, as he said the day he announced his

Cup intentions, the name of his syndicate, "America cubed", stood for talent, teamwork and technology. They were three watchwords we paid a good deal of attention to in Auckland, and I believe Bill Koch is owed a special thank you for his early advice and sportsman-like attitude towards a potential competitor.

During the first few months of 1993, our small band of America's Cup evangelists had many discussions about what we were hearing from abroad. During those months we talked with Bruce Kirby, Doug Peterson, Brit Chance, John Reichel, Jim Pugh, Grant Spanake, Bruce Nelson, Clay Oliver, Robert Hopkins, Per Anderson and many others, including several leading thinkers at New Zealand universities. It became increasingly apparent that the more input from as diverse a group as we could assemble should produce a variety of ideas and opinions. If we could monitor these ideas, test them correctly, encourage a difference of opinions, establish the creative atmosphere Koch had spoken about, we might achieve the breakthrough boat everyone in the game was seeking.

Bruce Kirby, probably best known as the designer of the Laser, a popular small yacht, made a number of points which resonated with us. One was that he thought Doug Peterson of America[3] had more to do with that team's victory than was generally acknowledged. Interesting that Milgram and others agreed that conceptually, Peterson was very good. He also said that during the early trial races, the great sailor Buddy Melges, who was one of Koch's helmsmen, called Kirby to ask about an acceleration problem the boat was having coming out of tacks. Kirby the designer began to discuss the problem in terms of the keel. Melges the sailmaker (he's also a highly regarded boatbuilder) began to discuss the problem in terms of the sails being used. Kirby's point was that solutions to problems are often arrived at by bringing different viewpoints together. Maybe no one on their own will reach the total solution if he comes from his discipline alone, but a group might solve the problem if several or many disciplines are involved. The cross-pollination of ideas is vital.

This was a recurring theme. We heard it repeatedly from Koch and his men, but the ironic thing was that these same people told us about all the arguments and friction they had. We heard that at times ideas were suggested and were belittled, causing embarrassment and humiliation. When Schnack and I discussed this, we determined that we somehow had to establish a culture which encouraged creativity while the rejection of suggested ideas was not to be taken as demeaning to the author of the idea. It was key to get everyone working together and not to be afraid of asking questions and learning about the science of yachting. Just how we were to do that may have been the biggest mystery of the campaign.

We resolved that everyone we brought into the group had to accept that their particular expertise would be open to questions from everyone else. It was established that the sailors were the clients of the syndicate. They were to request the performance requirements for the boat and they would approve the boat concept before construction. This way we were all in it together. There was no compartmentalisation, where the design team would go off and design, deliver a boat, and say "OK sailors, go and win the Cup." We wanted the sailors to understand the concepts behind how and why the boat was built. It was also critical that the designers understood the needs and desires of the sailors.

As we began to seriously interview individuals for the design team, a number of questions growing out of the 1992 America's Cup remained to be answered. Among them were: Why did we end up with the light displacement option? Was it accurate to have used smaller models than some of the other syndicates had used? What was the current state of wing and appendage technology? Why did most other syndicates opt for meter bows when our full-size testing indicated destroyer bows were good? What were the best test methods to employ . . . tank, tunnel, half-size boats, full size? What were the advantages and disadvantages of these tools? What was our degree of confidence in the tools?

In order to proceed, we believed we needed to come to a full understanding of the immediate past. We needed to learn from our mistakes in 1992, take advantage of what we had learned over the last two or three months, and try to immediately pull equal to America[3] in order to surpass them over the next 24 months. That yacht had set the standard we needed to go beyond.

We unsuccessfully tried to get access to the design test data from 1992. We did have knowledge of all the full-size data but it would have been nice to also view the tank and wind tunnel test results. That programme had, of course, been funded by Michael Fay with the help of some New Zealand sponsors and we felt, with Michael's support, we had as much right to that data as anyone else. Michael Fay didn't hesitate to give his full approval to release the data, but when we approached Bruce Farr and Associates, they advised they would not release the data until they were convinced we had someone technically competent enough to understand and interpret the results. After more delays, we gathered a greater insight as to what the '92 data might provide and decided not to bother pursuing its release.

As the months rolled by and other syndicates throughout the world began to sign up designers, we knew we had to make some firm offers. But we still faced the major problem of no money. It was hard to convince designer X to come on board in the hope we'd have sponsorship in the next month or two when other teams were writing cheques. Peter was due back from the Jules Verne race at the end of April, which didn't leave much time before the nationality deadline. How he was going to raise the money to even enter our challenge, much less support a fully fledged campaign, left us all shrugging our shoulders.

Although Peter was at sea for several months, he was not entirely out of touch. Modern technology kept him in communication with us and, perhaps even more important, allowed him to keep potential sponsors updated on our plans and developments. I believe that while Peter was setting world speed records, he was solidifying in his own mind his personal commitment to winning the America's Cup. Not that it really needed solidifying. While he tried to keep it quiet, several months after the fact the story got out about how we initially entered our official challenge.

Alan called Peter one day and told him the deadline had arrived to submit a challenge. Sefo observed we had no money. Blake told him he'd take care of it. The money was raised and the challenge was entered. Peter did indeed take care of it – by putting up $75,000 of his own money! It was that type of selfless act that was fundamental to our team and to our success. It was also indicative of Peter's leadership.

Knowing Peter had made such a large personal commitment in those early days made it easier for Tom and me to justify the use of our personal funds for travel and expenses related to Team New Zealand business. But I remember at one point Schnack asking me if I thought our names would appear on the boat as sponsors!

We faced another money crisis just after Peter had returned from the Jules Verne. As the nationality date approached, we knew we had to raise enough money to begin putting our plans in motion. A number of the people we had talked to had received encouragement, if not downright offers, from other syndicates. If we were to sign non-New Zealanders to help us in the design area, we'd have to do so now and, to do so, we needed at least some seed money.

A date was set as the day on which we would either abandon our challenge or go forward. The determining factor was money. Peter had met a number of potential sponsors and submitted proposals. His preliminary talks had generated the most interest from five groups: Steinlager, TVNZ, Toyota, Enza and Lotto. They, in turn, had met with each other and discussed a type of partnership which was sort of, "If one of us goes in, we'll all go in." These are five of the most dynamic corporations in New Zealand and we knew if they rejected our challenge we wouldn't have much of a chance to raise the money elsewhere.

Put-up-or-shut-up Friday came. We expected a call from the potential sponsor group before the end of the day. At 5pm, no call; 5.30, no call; at 6pm it looked like our dreams would dissolve before we ever had a chance to chase them. By 6.30 there were some long faces around the table on which the phone sat. The room was totally silent. No one dared to speculate on what might have happened or to suggest where we might go from here. When the phone rang, Peter answered. As all eyes focused on him, he said nothing. He listened and hung up, the expression on his poker face unchanged and not a thing indicated. Then he looked up, broke into a grin as wide as the Tasman, and said simply, "It's a go."

It is a testament to Peter's powers of persuasion that he was able to find sponsorship in the economic atmosphere of the time. Some five months after Alan and Peter had first told me they were putting together a challenge which would have a $25 million budget, it looked like their fantasy would become reality. While we were still a long way from $25 million, it was clear Peter's commitment and vision had been articulated clearly enough to convince this powerful and financially cautious group. I think we were all impressed by the fact that if these hard-nosed businessmen found enough promise in our game plan, then there was a good chance we were on the right track.

With the seed money promised, we took immediate steps to secure the design team. Peter hired Doug Peterson and Laurie Davidson as our main designers and went out and convinced both of them that we were for real and couldn't do this without them.

Davidson, of course, was not new to New Zealand America's Cup efforts. He'd been either in the middle or on the perimeter of design work since the 1986/87 challenge. We thought of him as a brilliant yet underrated conceptualiser, the type of creative mind that can draw the lines of a world champion contender on the back of a napkin over lunch – a natural.

Peterson and Davidson were given the responsibility of creating the hull lines and the overall design concept. The two men represented a good mix. Peterson brought much of the future thinking of the America^3 group and was considered a brilliant designer. Davidson similarly brought years of experience and practicality. He was not tainted by the mentality of coming from a winning team last time and thinking that everything they did was better.

Mike Drummond, Wayne Smith, Neil Wilkinson, David Egan, Richard Karn, Steve Wilson and Chris Mitchell were also brought in to work on technical aspects of the design. Mike and Wayne were given the shape of the boat by the hull designers and their responsibility was to devise the materials and structures which would make the boat strong enough and stiff enough for the anticipated conditions. David and Richard were our appendage wizards who concentrated on the hydrodynamics of such things as the keel, its stem and its wings as well as the aerodynamics of the rig. Neil was responsible for the appendage structures and mechanics. The different sets of spars were the responsibility of Steve.

While most of the focus had been on the design side of the campaign, we did begin to sketch out what we felt our needs would be for other aspects of the challenge. We made lists of the tasks required and the skills needed to fill the different jobs, both on board and on shore. As names to fit the jobs began to come up, we considered sailing talent, family constraints, compatibility, cost factors and so forth. I had already roughed out a list of the sixteen positions on board and who I thought was the best man for each position. Over the months the names changed as I "mixed and matched" the line-up, much as any sports team manager does. We had at least three guys equally qualified as sailors for each position on the boat, but some were more suitable for the role because of their other skills as boatbuilder or sailmaker or spar maker. Since I had known and sailed with so many of the candidates for many years, it was extraordinarily difficult for me to inform some of them that there was no place on the team, not even as back-ups, for them. Unlike previous challenges, there was now an abundance of talent.

It occurred to me how far New Zealand yachting and Kiwi yachties had come in a decade. I remembered back to those first days in Fremantle when none of us had had any real big boat experience. As I wrote my lists of sailing team candidates, I noted how many had been involved in the Olympics, on one or more Whitbread races, and on the match-racing circuit. These guys were now on an equal level with the most experienced sailors in the world. This time we wouldn't have to send a Laurent Esquier up the mast to free a halyard. This time we'd all know how to perform a float drop on a 75-foot racing yacht.

Difficulties of the 1992 campaign we tried to avoid this time around were complaints and arguments over money. By telling each sailor up front exactly what his role would be, what we expected from him, what that job would pay, and what the general pay structure for different jobs was, we hoped to diffuse possible problems down the road.

We soon began to see the management of the design team and the sailing team as a balancing act of fitting all the different components together to optimise the performance of both the boat and the crew. Consider the boat for a moment. It begins with a hull whose relative speed is the result of hundreds of different considerations, a few of which are length, depth, beam, weight and shape. Onto the hull will be placed a keel. A few considerations here are size, shape, how and where it is attached to the boat, the material it made of and so on. Onto the keel go wings and with them are a myriad of considerations as well. Then there is the rudder. And the trim tab, which is generally a vertical, movable flap on the aft portion of the keel which provides more lift than a symmetrical fin. How big should these appendages be? Narrow or thick? How best to operate them? And, perhaps most important, how do all the considerations of the underwater appendages affect each other and the overall concept of the boat? The process is thus one of continuous iteration.

Now let's go topsides. Mast, boom, rigging, steering wheel, winches, halyards, instrumentation, hydraulic system, cockpit layout, deck layout, and so on. Where should we put them? What should they be made of? Then there are the "engines" of the boat, the sails. Size, shape, weight, strength, material.

So a balancing act is performed just to get the boat right. Then it has to be sailed to its optimum, so the balancing act continues with the sailors. If the design team has done its job right, all the components will work both independently and together to produce a fast boat. Make that "potentially" fast boat, as I believe a boat can only reach its optimum speed if it is tuned correctly. Tuning is a series of adjustments to all the components mentioned above so that they do work together.

That's where the sailors come in on our balancing act. They are the ones who will fashion their own systems for the hundreds of tasks they need to perform during a race. In an America's Cup research programme, hundreds, if not thousands, of hours are spent testing how this keel reacts with that rudder when those sails are used. It is the sailors who must experiment with the modes of the boat and request from the designers the changes they desire to better race the boat. They experiment with different sheeting angles, mast rakes, rudders and wing and trim tab angles. They test sail shapes and sizes and then report the findings back to the designers.

Throughout the entire process, the sailors are expected to ask questions that might increase the boat's performance. What if we rake the mast two degrees more? What will happen if we change the sheeting and depth of the sails? What if the winches were forward three inches, the steering wheels aft two inches, the mainsheet trimmer behind the wheels, the boom blocks this way, the chain plates that way? How about turkey on rye instead of wholemeal? Well, it did get a little crazy.

But the interaction between sailors, designers and builders was extremely important and it was considered a huge advantage for the whole group to have an understanding of all the concepts. Many of the subtle design improvements were from non-designers.

As the fund raising and design teams began to come together, Peter Blake, Tom Schnackenberg, Ross Blackman and I received an interesting letter in April from Dr Pete Mazany, who teaches in the School of Business and Economics at the University of Auckland. Pete has a strong and varied background in management, specialising in developing competitive strategies, team-oriented cultures and the necessary supporting control systems. He studied at the University of Auckland and received his PhD from Yale University in the United States.

Pete wrote: "I work particularly well with organisations that are entrepreneurial, output-oriented and privately owned . . . You may ask what has this got to do with the NZ challenge. My approach has involved a long-term relationship with these organisations that includes managing the process of developing a strategy that the whole team can understand and commit to. This has involved organising strategy and team-building workshops of 3–4 days where strategic focus, communication, team building and fun are key objectives . . ."

Schnack had previously spoken to Pete and was impressed by his ideas of how he might help our team. As we discussed his proposal, we were in unanimous agreement that our management approach needed to be fresh and that it should incorporate many of the concepts we were using to build the design and sailing teams. Pete's ideas as expressed to Schnack and in his letter seemed in line with the approach we wanted to establish.

Further discussions led to a "Planning Workshop" on 18–20 May, followed by another on 30 June. Attending either one or both of the workshops were Blake, Schnackenberg, Quilter, Daubney, Davidson, Blackman, Sefton, Peterson, Karn, Mike Spanhake, Tim Gurr, David Alan-Williams, Steve Wilson, Chris Mitchell, Peter Jackson and me. Pete presented us with an outline of what we would discuss, what the objectives of the workshops were, what expectations we should have for the sessions, and a session-by-session overview. It was a new approach and concept for many of us and although we vowed we'd stop short of sitting around the room naked staring at each other, in the end we all agreed these initial meetings were keys to establishing our goals and our working relationships.

In Workshop I we were to "Decide and agree on a winning programme – what we will do, how we will do it, how much we will spend, how we will measure progress." In Workshop II we were to "Update key aspects of the programme, agree on next steps, and update the strategy document."

The workshops produced the fundamental architecture of how we were to manage the team. In the initial meeting, our first session was entitled "What is our vision?" We discussed the major principles we thought should be the cornerstone of the programme and how we could encapsulate our views in a summary statement. After some discussion, Pete took suggestions and tinkered with different thoughts until he wrote what seemed to be the words of all of us in the room. They were the words we tried to live by for the next two years: "To build a challenge in which we could be proud; a challenge of which all New Zealanders could be proud." It sounds simple, but it was sincere. It also served as a motivational goal.

There was more to the full statement. Each individual present was asked to read the entire statement and sign it, signifying his agreement. It read:

We want a small, informed and fully motivated team that:

- works in an environment which encourages every member to make a meaningful contribution;
- has a high degree of personal integrity and group honesty;
- recognises personal goals but not hidden agendas;
- continuously monitors and improves its performance;
- is fun to be in.

The last point may seem a bit frivolous, but in many ways it was of more importance than each of the others. Having fun, enjoying ourselves and each other may have been the one characteristic that most distinguished the 1995 challenge from each of its three predecessors.

Once the overall vision had been established, we discussed what assets we had and those that might be made available to the team. Michael Fay may not have been personally involved in this challenge, but that didn't mean he was out of the game altogether. He controlled the boats and equipment used in the 1992 campaign and he could have sold the assets, traded them, given them away or put everything in his backyard. Instead, we found it all in our backyard. Sir Michael was never publicly linked to Team New Zealand, but it was because of him that we got a huge head start. The four boats built for 1992 were made available for our use.

This presented us with a number of options. Should we use *NZL-20* as our base boat the way it was configured or should we make some changes to her based on what we had learned from our talks with the designers? Should we use her with a tandem keel or conventional keel? As a cost saving measure, should we build a new hull and appendages while using the existing deck?

Then we discussed the question how many new boats do we want to build and when? Our options were numerous: build one new boat; build two new boats in late 1993 and mid-1994; build two new yachts launched approximately one month apart which would be variations of the same theme. Simon and Mike Quilter proposed a unique option – sail *NZL-20* and give the trimmer and navigator one million dollars each. That option received only two votes!

We initially decided on building two boats, one in late 1993 and the other in mid-'94, but as our design and testing programmes yielded positive results, we decided to delay the first boat, spend more time testing, and then build two boats with no break in between. This would give us the luxury of testing two similar boats in our full-size test programme.

Other discussions centred around the 1995 IACC World Championship. Do we want to enter? If so, which yacht or both? That led to questions about how much time should we spend in San Diego. Servicing our sponsors needs was a consideration on this issue, as was the question of how valid the testing in Auckland was compared with doing the same on the actual site of the Cup racing.

The composition of Team New Zealand was next on the agenda. How many people did we need, who should they be and when should they start? A preliminary list of some 48 individuals was drawn up which included management, sailors, design team and design consultants, shore crew and extra sailors who would be needed for straight line and race testing in Auckland and others who we'd fly in to San Diego. Compared with other teams, particularly the 1992 America[3] syndicate which grew to more than 300 people at one point, we were thin to say the least. But we needed to work within a relatively tight budget and we believed efficiency of effort was an important management concept to follow. That's one of the reasons we looked at the additional skills the sailors brought to the team. If Dean Phipps could handle the bow while we were sailing and help build sails when we weren't, we wouldn't need to hire another sailmaker.

At the end of the three-day workshop we were a bit numb and slightly dazed, but I think each of us felt we had accomplished a great deal. At the very least, we were made aware of what it would take to create the type of successful programme we wanted to achieve. With his flow charts, overhead projections, management models and case studies, Pete Mazany had given us the framework from which we could move on to develop our management principles, philosophies and methods of communication.

After the 1995 America's Cup was over, Pete published a valuable little book called *Team Think*, which is advertised as "A 'vision-driven' model for managing extraordinary teams, projects and organisations." It is an account of the team-based management system and consensus decision-making style Team New Zealand employed.

Tom Schnackenberg wrote the foreword and, with Pete's permission, I have excerpted some of Schnack's words which tell a good deal about how we put Team New Zealand together:

> The task of designing, building and racing a winning America's Cup yacht is very easily defined but it is very hard to achieve. Simply put, we have a finite amount of money, a finite amount of time, and we have to design, construct and campaign two or fewer boats and in the process do it better than the other guys.
>
> We have observed, and anyone who studies the America's Cup campaigns over the years notices, that by and large syndicates waste a good portion of their budgets. This is obviously so in the case of syndicates which build a slow boat, but even syndicates which win are not immune

from this. In 1992, America[3] seemed to waste a fair amount of their budget "chasing rainbows," and these were the guys who won and who claimed they had done things right!

We talked amongst ourselves and thought that if we could avoid wasting a third of our budget, cut this down to 1/4th, 1/5th, 1/10th, or even 1/20th, then we might actually make some serious progress! We also talked with a number of friends in Auckland posing that question and out of these discussions came the suggestion that we might try to become more methodical in our planning.

The results of these efforts speak for themselves. I can say that not only did we win the Cup but, as we look back, we didn't waste even 1/20th of our budget. It was tight all the way through. We did not chase any "rainbows." All of our testing programmes were carefully thought out, thoroughly planned and executed and all came through on budget and as expected.

So that basically is what our challenge was about. Most of it is teamwork and the team culture. Team members were selected on the basis of ability and compatibility. However, seldom do these two things go together and there were plenty of instances in which individuals would feel that they could do fine without any help from their friends. It was part of the task and the goal of the "Team Think" to put aside all these differences and to produce a combined effort which was a focusing of the individual efforts to something greater than the sum of each. This demanded that people march, not necessarily in step, but at least in roughly the same direction!

The important decisions needed to have input from all the individuals. We were not like the army, where decisions are made on high and promulgated down through the ranks with no questions asked. We followed an "empowered" model, where plans were formulated by the people actually carrying out the tasks and passed along for approval by those "voting the money."

Consider our "two boat programme" for example: very early in the campaign we roughed out a budget which included enough money to build and campaign two yachts. The logical thing to do was to build a trial horse first and to use this for practising all our systems, designing, building, etc. Then we would sail this on the water, checking things out, testing against the old *NZL-20*. Finally, using all that we learned from this, we would build a race boat.

This is pretty much what the Japanese, oneAustralia and the French did and this was in fact our initial plan. What we actually did, however, was to think, talk, decide, re-think, argue and slowly revise the scheme many times and in the process we changed our plans completely. At some of these meetings every available person in the Team was present! The result was two boats built almost simultaneously and which were equal partners in the testing and racing programme.

Tom's words summarise our management approach perfectly. The continuous process of team involvement which resulted in the two boats being built almost simultaneously instead of months apart is probably the best example of our team-based decision-making style. In the first round of tank testing, which began in June 1993, several of the tank models gave us a few indications about certain design factors, but nothing that really jumped out at us. The next series of models were an improvement as there were good features about some of the models and good features on other models, but we didn't feel we had all of the components together just yet.

At that point, our intentions were still to build a first boat, trial it against *NZL-20*, learn as much as we could, then design and build a second boat. Actually, other options had been discussed as well. One of these was to build the first boat, then build another boat and register it with a different yacht club and use that as yet another trial boat. After all the testing had been completed on the two new boats, a third boat would be built and that would be raced in the Cup. We later discovered one Australia had a very similar plan, but there was one big difference between the two. The Aussies actually built three boats, while we looked into the new two-boat rule and decided against proceeding with our plan. That decision was based on what we believed to be the spirit and intent of the rule, which is simply that each syndicate was allowed to build two new yachts. We realised there may be clever arguments to get around the two-boat rule, but one of the tenets of this challenge was to steer clear of any risk of major controversy or protest.

The Aussies' building of three boats was challenged and we felt a lot of their focus was taken off their racing programme and put on defending the protest. We believed one Australia did violate the rule, but they were not penalised in the strict sense; although I've always felt their chances of winning the Cup were diminished by having to concentrate on defending themselves in front of the international jury.

As more tank studies were completed, we felt we were getting closer and closer to our ultimate design. Differences of opinion were common among the team over the results that we were receiving. As more and more data came in, some members believed we had gone as far as we could and we had enough information to produce the fastest boat possible within the time limits we had. Others wanted to keep testing, try new models, push the time limits to breaking point in hope of discovering even more pieces of information that might make the boat even one-tenth of a knot faster.

Although we had already ordered carbon fibre and other materials for the first boat, we had postponed the construction for a month. When the most recent test analysis was received, we found we had a very exciting result. We had made the breakthrough we sought and decided to further delay the building programme in order to find out more about the precise reasons for this huge improvement.

The tank testing had been done at the University of Southampton in England supervised by Andy Claughton, Ian Campbell, Schnack and Richard Karn. When Tom travelled back to Auckland to present the results, he would often couch them in the most conservative terms, although we could see he was barely able to contain his excitement. From what we were able to piece together about *America³*, we built a tank model that we thought was an improvement on the 1992 Cup winner. We compared our models to that base boat, and when we achieved our breakthrough, we calculated that the boat we were about to build would beat the base boat by several minutes around the course.

While the first boat, which became *NZL-32*, was being built, I was concentrating on improving my sailing skills by match racing in Europe with some of the guys I'd asked to join the team. When we returned, I visited the shed where the new hull was lying. My first thought was, "My God, this thing is narrow. Really narrow." Right outside the shed was *NZL-20*. I walked outside, looked over the 1992 racer, then went back in to mentally compare the '95 edition. "Really, really narrow," went through my mind. It was so extreme, I actually wondered if we had got it right.

I recalled the story of how a young American designer, Britton Chance, had developed a very different looking boat for media giant Ted Turner back when the New York Yacht Club was defending the Cup off Newport, Rhode Island. Apparently the tank results had shown considerable promise for a boat with a fairly blunt bow and radical stern. When Turner finally came to test the yacht's performance versus an old trial horse it was very apparent the model programme had given the wrong advice. After being frustrated by the yacht's speed, Turner, in typical straight-to-the-point fashion, reportedly said to Chance, "Hell Brit, even turds are pointed at the ends!"

Interestingly, Chance was able to come back and win the America's Cup as part of the Stars & Stripes Team in 1987. But, if our boat was wrong, I wasn't sure that I would ever be able to come back!

It was around July 1994 when I brought most of the sailing team out to see the new boat for the first time. I explained to those who had joined since the testing days how and why we had arrived at this particular design. "When you see the boat," I told them, "you'll probably be a little shocked."

About a dozen guys marched into the shed. As we entered, they were talking and laughing and joking with me that I was making some big deal out of this whole thing. How could we be shocked by the look of a boat? Was it in the shape of a horse, or maybe it was square? But suddenly the shed turned totally silent as each sailor took in his first view of the boat we thought would win the America's Cup. The silence was finally broken by a single profanity, followed by nodding of heads as all agreed with the sentiment expressed. Shocked? No, closer to a stunned disbelief.

Then they took the same route I had taken, outside to study *NZL-20* and back again to view *32*. Once again, the one word profanity seemed to sum it all up. Someone muttered, "They either got it horribly wrong or it's terrifically right."

The answer to that would have to wait for the next 10 months.

9

A Rocket Ship She Was

While the design team was being assembled and the boats were in the process of being built, I was involved in a number of other tasks. One of my responsibilities in the 1995 campaign was to select the sailors who would work the boat while I drove. As with the design team, a lot of thought and discussion went into the balance of talent needed and the compatibility of the group as a whole. My long-time teammates Simon Daubney and Warwick Fleury helped to provide the candidate lists and to analyse the expected workload for each area.

It was important that Simon had the sail trimmers and grinders on board that he could best work with, just as it was important for Tom Schnackenberg to have the sailmaking talent on board that would be open-minded and stimulate good ideas.

Warwick Fleury didn't have quite the same choice. "Warwick," I said, "your mainsail grinder and traveller operator is Peter Blake."

"Err . . . sounds like a great idea to me," was Warwick's only reaction.

We also had to be able to split the crew and run a test programme with two boats on a daily basis and keep up with the workload.

Everyone selected stayed with the team throughout the campaign, with the exception of one guy we lost to illness. There's an old saying among sailors that helmsmen win races and crews lose them. Nothing could be further from the truth. When you really think about it, steering a boat, especially a boat as fast as ours, is one of the easier jobs when you have a crew as experienced and skilful as

I had. From bow to stern, Team New Zealand was filled with talent, and everyone performed a variety of tasks.

Crews are vital to the success of any boat sailed by more than one person. They rarely get the credit they deserve. I'm reminded of a story that Paul Cayard tells about the late Tom Blackaller. The famed helmsman once joked to Cayard, his jib trimmer at the time, that if the job of trimming the sail was important, he would be doing it. Of course, in reality Blackaller surrounded himself with the best guys because he knew the importance of the crew.

As I've mentioned, one of the biggest differences between Team New Zealand and the previous challenges was we decided to select our racing sailors in the beginning of the campaign rather than towards the end. By eliminating the competitive aspects associated with who would perform what duties, we felt we could begin moulding the team culture that had been developed earlier.

I asked Dean Phipps to be our bowman. He was also our back-up sailmaker, having been with North Sails for many years. Dino had been with the Victory 83 syndicate in the 1983 America's Cup, with Alan Bond's Australian team in 1987 in Fremantle, and with the New Zealand challenge in 1992. He is also a Whitbread veteran as well as being a valuable member of several international match-racing teams, including mine from 1990 to '92.

Joe Allen came aboard as our mid-bowman and he usually worked with me in calling the start, signalling how close we were to the line and where the opponent was, and whether I could swing the bow of our 75-foot yacht past the stern of the other boat. His years of sailing experience stretched back to junior days and with the first Fay challenge for the Cup. He handled the starts because he is very definite and direct when communicating the facts. He's a carpenter by trade and also did a lot of the trouble-shooting on board as well as helping to build the sail loft and workshop in San Diego.

I've heard Joe complain only twice in all the time I've known him. Once was the day before round robin one when he pointed out we had been putting so much emphasis on testing that we hadn't performed a single gybe set or a float drop the entire time we'd been on the boats. The other time was when he was sent off our touch rugby field after treating the competition like it was a State of Origin rugby league match.

Two of the youngest members of our support team, fresh from Harold Bennett's Royal New Zealand Yacht Squadron youth squad, were Clinton Newbury and Morgan Trubovich. They were assigned to Joe to help set up the compound and sail loft. Joe also took it upon himself to instil in them a little discipline and education. It was undoubtedly the hardest two weeks of their lives. For simplicity, Joe re-named them Molly and Dolly. When they were painting the dock, Molly turned and looked at *Black Magic* approaching at the end of a full day's testing. "Don't even look at those guys," barked Joe. "They are yachtsmen . . . you are painters." I couldn't help but feel sympathetic.

I thought the mast position was perfect for Matthew Mason. A boatbuilder by trade, he became one of the boat captains and acquired an excellent knowledge of the hydraulics on board the yacht. Any extra boatbuilding that was needed, Matthew would stay behind to assure the programme ran to schedule. He'd been with our match-racing team when we won the world championship in 1992 and had been the boat captain on Dennis Conner's *Winston* in the 1993 Whitbread.

One of our grinders was Craig Monk, who was new to this class of competition. An Olympic medallist in the Finn Class, he approached me saying he wanted to be a grinder and that's all he wanted to be, although what made him attractive to the programme was his capability of performing a number of roles. "Monkey" is a deep thinker (especially for a grinder!). He is also a sailmaker and he played a key role in the team's sail loft.

Andrew Taylor was another grinder. "Meat" was the only sailor on board *Black Magic* who had been in every New Zealand America's Cup effort since the first. A boatbuilder by trade, he was responsible for all the winches and the maintenance of all the hardware used to trim the sails. Perhaps most important, he personified the spirit of the entire team. He was our cheerleader, a loyal, nationalistic, humorous guy to whom we always looked for a word of "inspiration" when we felt we needed a lift.

Give Meaty a job and it's guaranteed to be done to absolute perfection, although it might take a little longer than expected. Peter Blake once gave him the task of building a table for the Whitbread boat *Lion New Zealand*. Five months later, when the boat was ready to be launched, the table was not quite finished. It looked like a work of art, but it wasn't ready to be installed in the boat!

Jeremy Scantlebury was in the pit and he acted as the main co-ordinator between the sailors and the boatbuilders as far as making sure the right equipment was ordered and placed correctly on the boat. "Horse" also had overall responsibility for making sure the boats were ready for each day of sailing. He procured and oversaw the installation of all the hardware for the two black boats. He had sailed on *KZ-7* and on the Whitbread maxi *NZI Enterprise*. Horse, like many pitmen, can have selective hearing when the helmsman calls out an instruction which he may have a different idea about.

Our primary trimmer was Simon Daubney. We operated with only one trimmer upwind and one trimmer downwind and Simon trimmed upwind. "The Nose", appropriately named because of his unusually large beak, was responsible for developing the headsail shapes and designs. He also played the key role in designing our testing programme, which he mapped out on a computer.

Daubsey is a three-time Olympian and two-time match-racing world champion. He was a trimmer on *KZ-7* and has been a valuable addition to many entries in major international regattas.

There was some concern voiced over Simon's contributing to our design effort. For reasons beyond my understanding, Daubsey has claimed responsibility for the world-famous Daubsey range of yachts. These are generally asymmetric in shape, have a tortured sheerline, have forward mast rake, float nowhere near their lines, if they float at all, are painted the most inappropriate colours and look more like a caravan than a yacht. Daubsey is most proud of the "Oh my god, take a good look at yourself in the mirror" range of boats, most likely found with proud owners in places like Lymington, England.

He was also behind setting up the basketball hoop in the San Diego compound. Before the boat was permitted to leave the dock on race days, Daubsey insisted on shooting three pointers. He considered his making these baskets as our good luck charm. I suppose we were fortunate that he got his shot down fairly early in the campaign. Otherwise we might never have made it to the race course.

Robbie Naismith was the other headsail trimmer/tailer upwind. He'd tail the jib in and then Simon would take over and trim. We called him "Battler" because he is a fierce competitor and he never leaves a job undone, no matter how difficult or unpleasant. Battler has become one of the most sought-after trimmers in the world because of his talent and his attitude towards hard work. Yet in the years before his reputation spread internationally, there were a few rumours around that Robbie helped his image a bit by spicing up his resume. We've never been exactly sure how many times Battler has won the America's Cup or has sailed around the world!

Robbie and Ross Halcrow were the guys who maintained the sail programme. They ensured that our test and race sails were modified and reshaped to achieve the desired shapes. Roscoe was the downwind trimmer and was instrumental in the development of our gennaker shapes and designs. He has won the One Ton Cup, the Admiral's Cup and was part of Ed Baird's 1995 world championship match-racing crew.

Warwick Fleury was on the mainsail, responsible for the development of the mainsail design and the batten programme. He also helped organise the weather programme, which we felt needed a complete re-haul if we were going to be competitive. Warwick (or "Fluoride", as Meaty named him after a particularly intense brainstorm) did a lot of the early thinking behind who should be hired, what equipment was needed and how the programme should be set up – a side of the campaign that became one of our real strengths. Warwick is also one of those guys who is a winner. He has been on more than 30 boats that achieved first places in a variety of regattas all over the world during the past few years.

Richard Dodson was one of the strategists in the back of the boat, was also responsible for the runners and shared some of the driving duties when we were testing. Rick was an absolute master at translating all the data given to him about the daily conditions and, working in with Murray Jones, giving me a clear and concise tactical analysis. Rick has won the One Ton Cup, Admiral's Cup, the world OK Dinghy championships three times and many other international regattas. He is an owner of North Sails New Zealand and, with his brother Tom, has formed some formidable sailing campaigns. They are known as the "Shark Brothers".

Murray's job description was similar to Rick's. He also had a key role in the spar designs and the systems that go with it. That side of things, in my opinion, was done superbly and was a major reason the boat performed so well. I've always considered Murray one of the best yachtsmen to come out of New Zealand in modern times. "The Captain" represented our country in four Olympics and is one of the most versatile performers in small and big boats I've known. He was dubbed "The Captain" because of the commando approach he took to various tasks he attacked, particularly those on shore.

Brad Butterworth was our tactician and also helped keep an eye on our overall strategy. This was a key job as anyone who knows America's Cup history can tell you that a lot of the battle is fought on land. Brad was always a step ahead on that score and kept us out of trouble so we could focus on what we were doing on the water.

We called him "Billy" because of a favourite cartoon character he enjoyed. He used to pick up so much information on the opposition that we referred to his department as "the BIA – Billy's Intelligence Agency". During the *KZ-7* campaign, he was one of the crewmen who took a personality test supposed to give a reading on everyone's psychological and personality make-up. Billy scored a perfect 100% in the area of shrewdness.

While there are many attributes Billy brought to the programme, a high energy level concerning work probably wouldn't be one too many teammates would list. On maintenance days, he could usually be found at home watching a video with a supply of potato chips in hand. Yet his laid-back, extremely relaxed attitude was a real asset in high pressure situations, particularly when we needed his very accurate tactical assessments on the water.

Tom Schnackenberg, design co-ordinator and navigator, basically oversaw the design of everything – sails, spars, boat, keels and so on. He was also responsible for most of the budgeting involved in those areas as well. I've often said that although every person on Team New Zealand was extremely talented, all of us could have been exchanged for someone else and the result probably would have been the same. All of us except for Schnack. In my view, he was absolutely indispensable.

Tom has the ability to see things from both sides. If an object is black, Tom can come up with an argument that it could actually be seen as white. While he may have a brain the size of a planet, while using it he is often amusing to listen to. One time when he was sailing as tactician for Rod Davis the breeze was particularly shifty; so difficult some might say impossible to predict. There was no doubt a million computations going through Tom's brain, and he may well have simultaneously been mentally re-designing the sails while considering the tactical ploys, all in the thick of a strategic battle. Rod apparently asked him, "Tom, which side is favoured?"

Tom's response was, "Well, maybe the left looks better, but I could see how the right could also be just as good."

Rod asked again, "Yes, but which side is favoured?"

Tom thought for a minute before responding, "Well, that's an unreasonable question really." Vintage Schnackenberg!

It didn't make much sense to have the guy who was responsible for the overall programme, who was in charge of allocating the budget, and who had to answer to the sponsors, to be sitting behind a desk while we were sailing. I asked Peter Blake to be on board not only because he could more than fulfil the obligations of trimming the traveller and grinding the mainsheet, but because I thought it necessary for him to be a part of the sailing team, to see first hand what was happening at sea and to be part of every on-board decision. This was another big difference from '92. Peter wasn't on board and during those critical races in the Louis Vuitton Cup finals against *Il Moro* he had to make the decision to replace Rod with me from the shore. I've always wondered if he would have done the same thing had he been part of the action and witnessed exactly what was happening.

In all areas we were backed up by excellent reserves. Kevin Shoebridge, or "Shoeb", was a trimmer on *KZ-7*, a watch captain on *Steinlager Two* and on *New Zealand Endeavour*. On racing days, Shoeb was situated upwind in a weather boat gauging the strength and direction of the wind. Simon found his advice invaluable as he checked sail selection just before entering the pre-start.

Mike Quilter, known as "Low Life", is one of the most successful offshore navigators in the game today. Name a major regatta or long distance race, mention Whitbread or America's Cup, and Mike has been in them all.

Tony Rae, or "Tray", is an experienced mainsail trimmer who could also fill in for us in almost any position. He was working the traveller the day Blakie wasn't on the boat.

Nick Heron, who sailed with me a great deal on the match-racing circuit as the bowman, winning the 1993 World Championships, was a great source of support and encouragement to Joe and Dino throughout the campaign. He also ran the rigging shop.

Mike Spanhake was a reserve sail trimmer but also brought a huge amount of experience from many successful New Zealand and international campaigns to our sail programme.

Chris Ward and Jamie Gale were younger guys chosen from the 1992 team to help in a number of areas. They were being groomed for future America's Cup action.

Those are the soldiers and reservists with whom Team New Zealand went to war. I suppose like any group we had our share of personality conflicts, but I truly don't remember any of them. What I do remember is that we did work together very well and every one of these sailors performed his job better than expected. We also put a precedent on enjoying the experience and we did just that.

With the design and sailing teams now assembled and the first boat in the oven so to speak, there wasn't much for us to do except wait. Several of the guys were preparing for the 1993/94 Whitbread and I'd decided to take some of the others back on the match-racing circuit to keep us sharp. Already the rumours were circulating: "Team New Zealand is running out of money, they'll never make it to San Diego"; "I hear a bunch of the sailors have already quit"; "There are lots of arguments going on at Team New Zealand."

How we reacted to the word on the street was another difference between Team New Zealand and the previous challenges. Rumours are part of the America's Cup. They are a by-product of the secrecy with which all syndicates seem to surround themselves and since there is no way to eliminate them, you either have to try to make them work to your advantage as we did with "slow as dogs" talk or just ignore them. By now we'd been through this and we simply paid no attention to what anyone outside the team was saying. Actually, we went a step beyond ignoring it. We laughed at all the nonsense.

One reason so many rumours began cropping up was that we now had a competing New Zealand syndicate. Chris Dickson had put together a Whitbread team which would then evolve into an America's Cup syndicate. He was challenging through the Tutukaka Yacht Club, a small Northland club. The Tutukaka theme often used phrases like: "We're the people's campaign. Team New Zealand represents the establishment, corporate New Zealand. They've got all the money. They're trying to win the Cup for business – we're going to win it for the people of New Zealand."

Chris Dickson, the perceived rebel of New Zealand yachting, was back, and at his best. Behind the hype was the message that Chris had been shunned by Michael Fay, had been forced to sail for another country in 1992. New Zealand is a small country and there is not an abundance of money to go around. He pretty much had to take a different tack from Team New Zealand and accentuate the perceived differences to attract whatever "dissident" support and money he could.

Full marks to Chris and his team. They had a mountain to climb just to get to San Diego and they stretched every dollar and used innovative strategies to create a one-boat programme that made it to the semi-finals in the Louis Vuitton Cup and almost beyond. Once again Chris Dickson's talent and tenacity was put on display for the world to see.

I remember having a beer one evening with Peter Scott of Lion Breweries and Ross Blackman and Warwick Fleury of Team New Zealand. We were discussing the Cup in general and our new boat in particular. The original plan was to paint the boat green as we wanted New Zealand Tourism to benefit from the America's Cup exposure and green was the predominant colour of their new marketing brand, New Zealand Way.

Warwick, who was formerly a graphic artist, asked, "What would happen if Dickson paints his boat black, in New Zealand colours? Which boat do you think Kiwis will back? Shouldn't we be the first to have a black boat?"

We all thought about that for a minute. Our boat was almost ready to be launched. Dickson's, for all we knew, wasn't even on the drawing board yet. Warwick made a good point. Chris would be seeking every advantage he could. I said it might be smart to counter his PR efforts. He was already talking about what he perceived to be the radically different philosophies of the two groups and I suspected he would try to associate his success with the first New Zealand challenge to his new effort. After all, it was on board *Kiwi Magic* that he gained national recognition.

"I think Warwick has a point," I said. "I think we should paint the boat black and call it *Black Magic*. We'll beat Chris to the punch." The black boat wasn't an entirely new idea. We'd mentioned the possibility a couple of times in 1992, but it never took hold. This time around, for a variety of reasons, it garnered a lot of support.

A few days later I attended a sponsors' meeting during which I brought up the colour and name ideas. At first the group seemed indifferent at best, but Peter Scott had become a strong proponent and we got the go-ahead to look into changing our original paint scheme.

We had a model painted in green, then produced another painted black. The guys loved it. Andrew Taylor began his own campaign: "We have to have a black boat. Black and silver, New Zealand colours. Everyone in the world knows the All Blacks. We've got to have a black boat. Who wants a green boat? Paint it black!"

Simon Daubney and I are big fans of the Rolling Stones and one of their songs was "Paint it Black". I played that particular tune quite a bit in those days as I contemplated what effect the black boat would have on our campaign. Later, in San Diego, I'd have the Stones on the car radio most mornings as I made my way from Coronado to the compound. They became part of my good luck ritual, something that superstitious sailors subconsciously adopt and don't want to change.

The problem with painting the boat black was that it is something of a boatbuilder's nightmare. We were told that black retains heat which might soften the resin and weaken the structure. As well, because it's so shiny, it shows all the imperfections. We took that to work in our favour as the boatbuilders would have to do a perfect job of faring the hull.

Looking into the heat problem, Simon collected information from several experts, including roofers, about the difference in heating between black and other colours, such as the red New Zealand Challenge had adopted last time. He discovered there wasn't much. Our technical experts checked with resin companies and they were able to put together a plan that was acceptable to our boatbuilders, sponsors and sailors. *NZL-32* and *NZL-38* were painted black and almost immediately were referred to as *Black Magic I* and *Black Magic II*, although the boats were never called that officially. The name on their bows was simply *New Zealand*.

After the launching, some "experts" associated with other syndicates implied the black boats would melt. I found that interesting as many of the carbon-fibre and resin masts used in 1992 were black, including those on the boat that won! David Egan suggested we should call the United States military and inform them that their Stealth bombers were in danger of melting if they were left in the sun too long.

There was one other decorative feature that adorned both the boats. A large silver fern, national symbol of New Zealand, the same symbol worn by all Kiwi Olympians and our most prestigious sports team, the All Blacks, was painted on the hull.

NZL-32 was launched in September of 1993 at the Auckland Viaduct. There were perhaps a thousand invited guests present, including Prime Minister Jim Bolger and his wife, and representatives of the five sponsoring companies gave speeches. Douglas Myers from Lion Nathan, Bob Fields of Toyota New Zealand, Joe Pope from Enza, David Bale from the Lotteries Commission and Brent Harman from TVNZ all wished us well. The ceremony was covered live on national television. I was impressed by the amount of power behind the challenge. For a country the size of New Zealand to have five of the largest companies in the South Pacific behind a yachting endeavour said to me that corporate New Zealand believed in us, believed we'd bring home the Cup. Doug Myers let us know in no uncertain terms that his only interest was in us winning the America's Cup. Second place wouldn't do.

When we pulled the covers off the boat, revealing her sleek lines, black facade and the silver fern, the crowd was visibly and audibly impressed. Almost in unison, a thousand people drew in their breath at the sight in front of them. It was an emotional moment for the team.

Not all of the boat was visible. It's long been a practice for designers to acquire photographs of opponent's boats, especially when they are launched, digitise the photographs, reproduce the design and run it through VPPs to estimate the performance. Therefore we kept the boat's undersides skirted, hiding her waterline length and beam. We also pulled the forestay forward a little, shifted the gooseneck some, and made a few other changes that might lead spying eyes to conclude that the boat didn't rate, that she didn't comply with the IACC rule.

I wondered if anyone would fall for our tricks. Much later in the campaign a prominent New Zealand designer was understood to have suggested to the media that we would never race *NZL-32*. The reason given was that she didn't measure! When news of that story was related to Team New Zealand during a meeting, the entire room broke into spontaneous laughter. It was yet another piece of misinformation that we went out of our way to encourage belief in by those who wanted to believe it. In actual fact, the boat floated to within one millimetre of her designed flotation. Her lines were perfectly built to plan and the weight studies were as accurately performed as any yacht with which I've been involved.

It's no secret sailors are a superstitious lot. We tend to take lucky charms to sea, wear the same hat or shirt in which we won the last race, follow the same routine of a current victory. We also tend to perhaps read more than necessary into certain things that happen, things we might suspect are signs of bad luck.

In the early days of *NZL-32*, I began to wonder if the boat might somehow be cursed. While I never mentioned it and it was never discussed, I think the same thought was recurrent among a number of my teammates. There were a few minor incidents like the christening bottle not breaking on the bow until the third blow, despite the creation of an elaborate contraption to prevent misfires. But more serious incidents were when we almost lost the boat and when the front arm of the cradle on which the boat was sitting broke and *NZL-32* almost slid off.

The day the boat was completed at the McMullen & Wing yard, she was put on a trailer with the intention to transfer her to a barge. As the transfer was taking place, with the truck halfway on the barge, there was so much force from the weight of the trailer and boat that the barge pulled a piling it was tied to clear out of the water and took off. The truck fell off the barge and the boat began to tilt, looking for all the world like she was about to go her own way.

I guess you can read the situation either as a near disaster that came close to ending her sailing days before she ever reached the water, or you can choose to see the incident as proof that the boat's eventual success was destined to be. Yet, at the moment it happened, such rationalisation did nothing to calm our anxiety!

Another time we had been working on the boat, getting it ready to be launched and eventually sailed, when the breeze came up and we decided to put the boat back on its cradle and review our options after the wind calmed down. As we were having a cup of coffee, all of a sudden we heard this enormous crashing sound. The front arm of the cradle had fallen and the boat was suspended on the trailer with no front support. With the rig up, the boat could have easily caught a gust of wind and fallen off the side of the wharf, ruining her.

However, we survived these calamities, and a few other start-up glitches, and by the time we had *NZL-32* in the water she surprised us once again. It's one thing to make models, perform tests, read results and believe you're on to something; it's an entirely different matter to sail the real thing under real conditions. The history of the America's Cup is littered with "mistakes" that looked like world beaters on paper but couldn't get out of their own way on the race course. We didn't know how well the new boat would perform until we took her on to the Waitemata Harbour and lined her up against *NZL-20*.

We'd split the sailors between the two boats and for perhaps an hour or two we sailed independently of each other as we tuned, adjusted and prepared *NZL-32* for her first real-life test. In that time I remember thinking this boat feels good, seems right, looks good; but I confess, even after more than 25 years of sailing, I really can't tell the speed of a boat unless I'm next to another.

So it was with both excitement and a bit of trepidation that we lined up this black racer next to the '92 challenger. Over the VHF we radioed to Ed Baird, who was driving *Black Magic*, what we wanted to do, what we wanted them to do, and we were ready. I looked around at the faces of the guys who had waited for months for this day, some of whom I'm sure at times wondered if this would really happen. We were all eager to see if our ideas, our discussions, our decisions, as interpreted by Schnack, Dougie and Laurie, would pan out.

In the first few tests the trim tab and the hydraulics on the genoa sheeting system on *NZL-32* were not working. But we'd been waiting a long time for this moment and decided to line up the boats anyway. *NZL-32* was measured as sailing lower but faster than *20*, with the overall result netting out about the same.

After a few more tests, the tab and genoa system became operational and it was as if we had turned on an engine and *NZL-20* had thrown out an anchor. Our new boat sailed much higher and much faster. The look on those faces which just minutes before had been creased in tension now displayed elation and wonderment. We all had a sense that each of us was a part of something grand, something truly new. The design team hadn't missed a trick. Narrow she might have been, but a rocket ship she was. Even in smooth water, where *NZL-20* is at her best, she was no match for *32*. It was like sailing a fifty-footer against a one-tonner.

Peter Lester, a tactician with Chris Dickson, came out to watch us a few days later when we were taking scientific measurements. Unknown to Peter, there were wires, sensors, tape and measuring devices of all descriptions hanging from the bottom of the yacht, her keel and rudder. *NZL-20* looked pretty competitive against the spaghetti-entangled *32* that day. In fact, the performances were quite even.

Coincidence or not, the next day a new round of stories about the trouble Team New Zealand was in began to circulate. Mick Cookson and Gary Lock, two guys involved in building Chris' boat, were sitting outside a bar near the end of our wharf looking at us with huge grins on their faces as we docked the boat the day after the tests. I must admit, I enjoyed having the last laugh in 1995.

While testing against the older *NZL-20* proved our designers had hit all the marks, we still didn't know for sure exactly how fast the new boat was in comparison to the new boats the other 1995 Cup syndicates would take to San Diego. We suspected that because *America³* was the most narrow boat in the 1992 races and she emerged the victor, most teams would go as narrow as they thought prudent, or at least test the concept. That's not to say that simply making *NZL-32* a narrow boat was the secret to her speed advantage. It was no doubt a part of the success, but without the perfect balance achieved by the exact specifications and characteristics of all the other components – the keel, the wings, the rudder, the sails, the mast, the boom and so on – the hull shape alone would not account for the boat's overall performance.

Certainly we were not the only America's Cup group that knew that. The other teams were filled with talented designers who were pretty familiar with the opportunities in the IACC formula and the San Diego conditions. We had all studied each other's boats in 1992 and we had all learned from how each of us conducted our campaigns. We all cribbed from Bill Koch and his ever-burgeoning design team. So while we now thought we had something special in our new boat, we really wouldn't know until we lined up against the other contenders off Point Loma.

We also knew Chris Dickson was working with Bruce Farr. While Farr's services had not been contracted by Team New Zealand, we knew the designer had all the data from 1992, had been in the thick of things during that regatta, and there was no doubt he'd come up with a fast boat for Chris. Just because we had gone well beyond Farr's 1992 design was no guarantee the designer wouldn't do the same.

For all those reasons, we were cautious. We impressed upon each other that, yes, we've got a rocket ship but it's early days and we don't know what everyone else has, so let's keep what's happening on the water to ourselves.

Shoreside talk, especially if anyone outside the team is listening, is that the boat hasn't shown us anything yet.

As the misinformation campaign began to take hold, not a lot of international attention was paid to us. Across the Tasman, Bertrand and gang were taking a different tack. Everything out of their mouths was enough to make you believe the Americans might as well give them the Cup right now. The press lapped it up. Of course, it fitted right in with the story they so desperately wanted to report – the re-match between the only non-American to win the Cup and the only American to lose it: Bertrand versus Conner, a dozen years later.

We were particularly pleased when Gary Jobson, a commentator for ESPN, the American all-sports network with an international reach, was quoted as saying he believed the finals would come down to Pact 95 and Chris Dickson. A lot of sailing scribes are influenced by Gary and that statement served Team New Zealand well.

By the time *NZL-32* was on the water (*NZL-38* was launched three months after *32*), the 1992/93 Whitbread had concluded and our full sailing team was assembled. We began the long and often arduous practice of testing; testing appendages and sails and gear and sailors. We were on the water often before daylight to take advantage of the lighter early morning winds, and on a good day we sailed through to dark. They were sometimes tough days at the office, but we all knew it was a necessary process. And it was a process during which we built confidence in our boats and in each other. The team culture was much in evidence during those days. It's perhaps trite to say, but true, we became a family out there on the Waitemata Harbour.

The long days of testing served their purpose, but I felt the need for real competition. The match-racing circuit was still going strong and most of the top guns, even those who were in the middle of Cup programmes, made as many regattas as possible.

We hadn't competed much on the circuit in the first half of 1994 as we concentrated on our America's Cup programme and some invitational regattas were staged in Auckland, the Bay of Islands and Wellington. Rod Davis had signed up with oneAustralia and he and John Bertrand had returned to the circuit to get a feel for each other in real competition. John had "retired" from racing after his historic America's Cup victory, but now that he was back in the game he wanted to remove some of his match-racing rust.

Davis won the Australia Cup for the second year in a row, but fell to Chris Law in the final of the Congressional Cup. Law backed up with a win at the Royal Lymington Cup, raising his profile as one of the top helmsmen in the world. Chris was looking for an America's Cup position and, with dual citizenship from the UK and Australia, he was eligible to race for Syd Fischer's Sydney group. Syd did end up hiring Chris, which generated the establishment of numerous betting pools as to how long the two would work together. Both men have strong personalities. Syd is a veteran of several Cup campaigns and his choice of Chris was probably the best one he could make. Chris can perform brilliantly but, by his own admission, he can also stink up the joint. Predictably, his tenure with Sydney '95 lasted only through the first round robin in San Diego. Chris won two of the six races he was in, and some measure of his skills can be made by the fact that, after he left, *Sydney '95* won only three of the next 18 races.

Success on the match-racing circuit also provided American Ed Baird with an America's Cup position. I'd raced against Ed over the years and had noted his abilities. In 1991, he was ranked 42; two years later he had risen to number three in the world. He'd been a tough opponent for us in the finals of the 1993 World Championship, where one of the races was declared a dead-heat. Ed and I had discussed the possibility of his joining Team New Zealand as a trial helmsman and I'd talked it over with a number of the sailors on the team. I felt he would not only provide tough competition during our testing, but would be an overall addition to the programme. He brought with him an American perspective on the Cup, one which would be valuable if we made it to the America's Cup match. I thought it would be important for the Kiwis to work alongside an American, see the way he operates, the way he thinks.

Every other winner on the 1994 Omega Grand Prix was in San Diego when the first races for the Louis Vuitton and Citizen Cups began. Paul Cayard won in France, Peter Gilmour took the money in Sweden and Croatia, Rod Davis won in Bermuda and Frenchman Bertrand Pacé won the world championship.

We didn't make it to the Worlds that year as Cup responsibilities kept us in Auckland. Our absence set off a string of rumours, most of which were based on a theory that the only thing that would keep Coutts from defending his back-to-back world championships would be Team New Zealand having serious doubts about their performance in the black boats.

Of course, just the opposite was happening. We were achieving a lot and still getting design information to our designers that would help with future keels, wings and sails that were on the design table and about to be manufactured. Schnack had helped build our own wind tunnel and had tested fifty million shapes . . . well, it seemed like that many as the old wizard stood in front of giant fans day after day, week after week, testing gennakers and spinnakers.

In October 1994 we disassembled the boats and loaded them on a ship headed for Los Angeles. With the boats and team in transit, I headed for a last shot at the circuit. Five members of Team New Zealand joined me for the last two regattas of 1994. Brad Butterworth was on board as tactician, a particularly good move to strengthen our communication skills. We headed to Hayama, Japan, for the Nippon Cup where we beat Peter Gilmour in the finals. Back in Auckland, we finished the year with a win over Ed Baird in the Steinlager-Logan Cup. The victories gave us a psychological boost going into the Cup.

As the boats were making their way to San Diego, a number of us flew to California to watch the IACC Worlds. We had decided that racing in this regatta would not be any more beneficial to our overall plan than our testing programme, so we declined to enter *NZL-32*. Most of the teams that did enter, with the exception of oneAustralia and Nippon, were racing '92 vintage boats. We figured the Australians would win the regatta pretty easily and they did win, but not exactly easy. Something of a surprise was the performance of Bill Koch's all-women team. Although they were racing on the 1992 winner, most observers believed the yacht's speed would not be enough to make up for their lack of experience. However, they performed pretty well, winning one of the races and out-performing some of their male counterparts.

With their victory, the Aussies continued to tell the world how good they were and how well prepared they were for the Cup. Again, it deflected attention from us. We tended to agree with the Aussies – they would be a force to reckon with during the trials. We anticipated they would be our strongest opponent, but there was nothing we could do about them until we met on the race course. We heard that during much of December the oneAustralia group had discussed how they could "sand bag", or slow down, their boat, so as not to give other syndicates a look at how strong they really were. Our priority was to concentrate on our own programme, continue to test, continue to improve.

Shortly after the IACC Worlds, planeloads of Kiwis began to arrive in San Diego. The question of housing had been discussed early in the game and we determined that each team member should have the freedom to choose their own accommodation. This was a departure from the previous New Zealand challenges when we were assigned housing that more resembled military camps than family quarters. It was part of the de-regimentation process we established early in the campaign. Things had changed for New Zealand Cup yachties over the past decade. As a team, our average age wasn't 23 any more. We weren't new to America's Cup rigours. Most of us had been in a hundred cities around the world. Some of us had sailed around the world. We felt it was time to loosen the controls and emphasise the maturity we expected from everyone. In the end, there was really only one rule – everyone was expected to be on the boat or at their shoreside station at dock-off time.

Actually, Blakie tried to enforce another rule, which I think was a result of my cracking my ribs in 1991. We were told not to go skiing, but no one paid much attention. Those of us who did slide off to the slopes on occasion preferred to be guided by that part of our vision statement that exulted us to have fun. We felt it was more important to enjoy ourselves than protect ourselves from the slight risk of injury. Still, caution remained a priority and no one returned to sea level with a cast or even a strain.

Another factor in having everyone find their own housing was to prevent the fairly unpleasant situation we had experienced in the previous campaigns. There had been the endless round of complaints in the past over where we lived and how we were being treated more like soldiers than sailors. This way, there could be no grounds for complaint. The old saying of "you made your bed, you've got to sleep in it" was very *apropos*.

With the potential problems of housing complaints and unhappiness over pay defused from the beginning, the team was better able to focus on the job at hand. The approach paid off. Our programme during the first two weeks in San Diego progressed at a rapid rate. Everything came together with relative ease. At the end of 14 days, we had improved the speed of both boats by more than a minute around the course. We had also established that *NZL-32* looked a little better than her stablemate.

As the first round robin approached, we discussed which boat to enter and how to configure her. The question was whether we should come out with all guns blazing – our fastest boat with the fastest appendages and sails – or set up more conservatively so as to not divulge too much too soon. The America's Cup has often been compared to a marathon race. The first round robin races in the Louis Vuitton Cup began on January 14. The first day of the America's Cup match began on May 6. The four months between the trials and the Cup itself offered a great deal of time in which almost anything could happen. Those teams which felt their boat was off the pace could do a lot of changing, and many of them did. Some of the changes worked, a lot of them didn't.

We viewed the early round robins more or less as practice rounds, which was generally the consensus among most syndicates. Points allotted to each victory were 1, 2, 4 and 5, reflecting the relative importance of each round. The early races were generally considered a feeling-out process, a time during which all of us tried to learn as much as possible about everyone else's strengths and weaknesses while revealing as little as possible about our own attributes and flaws.

Doug Peterson thought our decision to race what we then considered our slower boat, *NZL-38*, in her less-than-fastest configuration bordered on the insane. "This is the America's Cup, guys," said our designer. "I know you think we have work to do on *NZL-32*. But we just don't know what everyone else has. We should go with what we think is our best boat and set her up with the fastest appendages and sails."

His point was well taken, but our decision was based on the prevailing philosophy that had been established long before the boats ever entered the design stage. We'd looked at a calendar and had counted the days, even the hours, we had from the time the first boat was launched to the first day of the America's Cup match. We felt our best chance to get to the starting line on May 6 was to develop and follow a continuous testing programme. Our sailors knew how to sail, they knew their jobs. It benefited neither the individual nor the team to spend time tacking or gybing or practising our high fives. The puzzle that is the America's Cup is probably best solved by continuous development of your boat. With *NZL-38* racing in round robin one, we were able to continue work on *NZL-32*. This allowed us to establish a benchmark with the newer boat, a benchmark from which we could gauge any and all changes to the older boat.

And if we had drastically miscalculated, if we were badly mistaken about how our boats would compare to the other six challengers, then we were probably in big trouble anyway.

So, as January 14 approached, we'd sealed our fate for round robin one. More than two years of planning, training, development and "Team Think" would be accompanying us to the starting line against *Rioja de España*, sail number ESP-42, out of the yacht club Bayona-Valencia, the Spanish team known as CADE '95. Finally, all our decisions would be tested and judged on the water.

10

Two Boats or Three

Iawoke to a bank of fog on the morning of our first race in the Louis Vuitton Cup. There's a song by an American group that has a line "It never rains in Southern California" – the lyricist must have been from Mexico. He sure wasn't in San Diego during the three days leading up to the first race of round robin one. It poured. Heavy rain drenched the streets of this city as it prepared for the opening challenger and defender rounds of the 1995 America's Cup.

Although the rain made the last-minute preparations around Team New Zealand a bit difficult, they didn't seem to dampen the enthusiasm of either participants or spectators who were in California for the races. While the best way to describe the mood around our compound is probably cautious optimism mixed with pent-up anxiety, there was an almost tangible feeling of excitement in the streets and watering holes of San Diego. It had been three years since the previous America's Cup, and to yacht enthusiasts around the world the regatta was the equivalent of the Rugby World Cup, the Super Bowl and the World Series all rolled into one.

So neither the rain nor the first day's fog did much to lower the excitement level. As I took my customary run along the beach in Coronado on the morning of the first day's racing, I think that my most prevalent emotion was one of relief; relief that after all the time spent preparing and working and training and testing we were now ready to see some action.

As it turned out, our concerns were soon dismissed. We finished the round undefeated and in first place, followed by *Tag Heuer* with five points, and

Nippon and *oneAustralia* with 3. The surprises were that *oneAustralia* hadn't performed better and that France had only one victory.

Our design team had done an excellent job. So far, so good!

Although it was much too early to make any real assessment of our opponents, we did feel the first couple of races pointed towards a few conclusions. We felt oneAustralia was clearly not as advanced as we'd earlier thought they would be. In our second race we were racing *Tag Heuer* in the match behind *oneAustralia*, starting a full 10 minutes after them. By the last mark, we had almost caught up and passed them and we rounded only half a length behind. After our spinnaker was set, we started to gain even more and had to alter course to avoid running into the back of them! This was totally absurd and actually quite difficult to accept. To start 10 minutes behind and gain time is one thing, but to almost pass them is a totally different matter.

There was considerable excitement on *Black Magic II*. Joe Allen couldn't contain himself and from the bow of our yacht he yelled out to the Australians, "Will you get that dog out of our way, we are racing."

Although embarrassed by Joe's comment, most of us couldn't help but be amused. Brad Butterworth had tried to arrange some practice races with the Australians before the series, using *NZL-32*, but the Australians refused, unless we brought out what they thought was our best, i.e. newest, boat. I suppose they didn't want to waste their time with the 'older Black Dog'. What a pleasant surprise awaited them!

Then there were the French. They had gone in the opposite direction to most of the syndicates on the "how narrow can we go" issue. Their boat was very wide. In our race against them, the breeze filled in early to a solid 15 knots, much stronger than normal and favouring a wider boat, if wide was the way to go. The French got a better start and lined up above us, but the test was all too obvious after a very short time. As Doug Peterson put it, using his American descriptives, "we were hauling ass".

I talked to Phillipe Briand, the designer of the French boat, after the Cup was all over, and he told me that when he had seen *NZL-38* in that first match-up, in 15 knots of wind, he knew at once that their design philosophy was horribly wrong.

We were quite impressed with Chris Dickson's Bruce Farr-designed boat in its first outing against us. Widely thought to be the most narrow and most radical yacht in San Diego, it performed reasonably well, but the overall performance was betrayed by poor spinnaker work.

In our early discussions with Bruce for the 1995 campaign, he told us his philosophy was to produce one boat very late, spend the greatest amount of money on research and design, and bring the sailors into San Diego at the last possible moment, just before racing began. This didn't align itself with the philosophy of Team New Zealand, but we still had a huge amount of respect for Bruce's design talents and of course deeply respected Dickson's sailing abilities. Bruce had all the data and research from 1992 and therefore had a head start on many syndicates there. We clearly had not seen the full potential of this team yet.

Nippon was quite impressive, pushing us hard and beating *oneAustralia* in their first outing. Their boat had been in the shed for well over a month and when it appeared it looked so different, it was a new boat in many people's eyes. Their original boat seemed to share a lot of the concepts of *NZL-20* and was predictably well thrashed in the October World Championships. The new boat looked to be very similar to *America³* and the oneAustralia boat. Yet it still must have been a surprise for the confident Australians when *Nippon* appeared for their first race, the crew still bolting fittings on as they towed out, and proceeded to soundly beat them by 1:06.

With a touch of sentimentality, I regretted the low opinion of "the other" Australian team. Syd Fischer had been something of a fixture on the international yachting and America's Cup scenes for several decades and although he was part maverick, part irascible curmudgeon and part showman, he had made many contributions to the Cup over the years and I was pulling for his team to be more competitive. Syd is extremely wealthy yet very tough. When I heard that he had a boat designed by Fluid Thinking and had the benefit of the tuning and testing that was done in Southport, Australia, prior to coming to San Diego, I thought that he may have finally got his Cup efforts together.

Peter Gilmour once told me a Syd story which gives an insight into the man. It was during the Fastnet race, in very rough conditions on the second night out, and already food supplies were running low. The conditions were miserable as seems normal in many of Syd's programmes as there aren't a lot of additional comforts around to make the journey any more pleasant. Syd poked his head out of the hatch and surprised everyone by asking who would like a chocolate biscuit. Most were surprised by the offer, given that the usual diet was Syd's personally made sandwiches, which were considered the most economical solution to the provision problem.

After most of the sailors had answered "Yes please," Syd replied, "Too bad we haven't got any."

The Spaniards were just too late into the game. An argument could be made that their timing was not appreciably different from the *Tag Heuer* challenge, but there were several significant differences: helmsman, designer and team. Chris Dickson, in almost everyone's book, was in the top echelon of international skippers. The team he put together was filled with experienced, highly rated sailors. And the designer, Mr Farr of whom I've had a bit to say, knew the game as well as anyone working.

The first round robin in the Citizen Cup, the defender races from which one of the three American teams would advance to the America's Cup match, were of mild interest to us; but again, it was so early in the game that the result meant little. However, Team New Zealand was as surprised as the rest of the world when, in the very first race of America's Cup 1995, the all-women team of America³ beat the experienced, heavily-favoured Stars & Stripes team led by Dennis Conner. The victory garnered headlines around the world and was a huge boost for the sport.

The race was won during the pre-start when JJ Isler, the starting helmsman, forced Conner into a classic port-starboard situation in which Dennis had to give way. The on-the-water umpires penalised *Stars & Stripes* for not giving enough room when the two boats closed upon each other and, after the start, the men had to complete a 270-degree penalty turn. From that point, Leslie Egnot, a New Zealander who routinely took over the helm after the start, steered a near-flawless race for the victory. The rest of the round didn't go as well for the women, but the win no doubt boosted their confidence.

Learning a lesson from our previous three America's Cup campaigns, we decided to avoid the controversies and contentiousness that had played such a part in creating an image among the international competitors and media that didn't reflect our own self-image. However, prior to and during round robin one, there were already enough controversies to keep the America's Cup traditionalists more than satisfied.

The two-boat rule which was new to the 1995 America's Cup was ripe for debate before the ink describing it had dried. The rule was born of good intentions. Costs during 1992 had got out of hand and if some sort of restrictions weren't implemented, the sailing contest had the potential to become a contest of who could raise and spend the most money.

But just as the Deed of Gift doesn't cover all eventualities of running an America's Cup regatta, the two-boat rule had more holes in it than a ton of Swiss cheese. Interpretations varied widely.

Even before the 1995 Cup began, there were questions about the March 1994 announcement that oneAustralia and Syd Fischer's syndicate had agreed to a co-operative joint venture in which they would share certain design help from a company called Fluid Thinking Pty Ltd. A majority of the challengers, as well as all the defenders, objected, saying this breached the "spirit and intent" clause of the rule.

In the early stages of our programme, Team New Zealand was thinking of doing a similar thing, and seriously considered building a test yacht. But after asking for an opinion from John Doerr, who was later appointed as head of the jury, we were convinced that the "spirit and intent" clause could, and most likely would, be very powerful. The advice given was it would be seen as a way of circumventing the two-boat rule and wasn't worth the risk. The rules in yachting for the most part do not have any provision for consideration of "spirit and intent". Interpretation is applied according to the written meaning of the words used in any particular rule.

But this new rule contained a "spirit and intent" clause, the intention being to cut off any attempts to circumvent the rule. Consider a hypothetical situation in which Team New Zealand wanted to build a third boat as an early test yacht or prototype for future development. I could imagine building such a boat, then giving or selling it to another local yacht club and having a secret arrangement to sail it against one of our "official" yachts as a trial horse. Perhaps that boat might just happen to be in the same piece of water at the same time as our yacht and just happen to be sailing in the same general direction.

Of course such a situation would be a clear breach of the spirit and intent of the two-boat rule. Team New Zealand would be getting the benefit of three boats as compared with other syndicates that would have only two.

In the Australian case, the heart of the argument was that Fluid Thinking was designing one boat for Syd Fischer and a further two boats for John Bertrand. Syd's boat would be tested against Bertrand's first boat before a second boat from Fluid Thinking was designed. Therefore, it was thought that Bertrand in particular would effectively have the benefit of a three-boat campaign.

As with so many issues in the America's Cup, this one turned political and dragged on for more than nine months as it seemed no one wanted to take responsibility for ruling on the guilt or innocence of the two Aussie teams.

The basic problem was that so much was at stake that no appointed body wanted to be responsible for making a ruling that may well have ended up in court, with some of the parties claiming potential damages and personal suits against the jury members as a result of their decision.

The situation was ludicrous. Imagine a rugby test where the referee is scared to make a wrong decision, or, for that matter, any decision, because of the threat of being sued.

Originally, the organising committee for the Cup, known as "America's Cup '95", heard the first complaints and then decided the proper body to decide the matter was the America's Cup Trustees' Committee, made up of the three yacht clubs which had won the Cup in the past – New York Yacht Club, Royal Perth Yacht Club and San Diego Yacht Club. The Trustees' Committee hired a special investigator to gather all evidence and substantiate the allegations made against the Bertrand and Fischer syndicates. The investigation lasted more than two months. After the findings were submitted to the Trustees' Committee, they decided the proper body to decide on the findings was the international jury.

By this time Bertrand was already well into construction of the third boat designed by Fluid Thinking and thus, if the jury ruled against them, it would have rendered this expensive new IACC yacht useless. On the other hand, if they allowed it to happen and oneAustralia ended up gaining an advantage, then all other syndicates with boats in San Diego could quite possibly claim their efforts had been compromised.

In the end, the jury elected to give what many considered was the "politically correct" ruling that allowed the Australians to use their new boat. I was very disappointed with John Doerr and the jury, feeling that the situation was precisely the type of stuff that the public at large couldn't understand, and frankly it gave the sport a black eye.

While that storm died out before the Cup racing began, it was only the start of things to come. The Nippon Challenge were very actively against the Australians at the beginning of the two-boat issue, yet after the World Championships, when their first new boat was severely thrashed, even by the

1992 winner, they appeared to take a less than enthusiastic position towards the resolution of the two-boat issue.

The Japanese were the first syndicate to arrive in San Diego with new boats and they had been training in Cup waters longer than any other team. As our compound was next to the one Nippon occupied, we naturally were aware of some of the things happening on each other's property.

For days on end we heard the continuous noise of reconstruction going on in their shed and carbon fibre dust was omnipresent. Substantial changes were being made. Of that, we were sure.

Then one day we received a telephone call from a woman in New Zealand who said she had been in Los Angeles on business, representing a marine supply company, and happened upon "what looks like two halves of an America's Cup yacht being built".

The plot thickened when two large portions of what looked like an IACC yacht arrived in darkness and were moved into the Nippon compound. If we thought reconstruction was intense before, it was nothing like what occurred over the next few days. Finally they wheeled out the boat, ready for measurement. Even under the covers, a knowledgeable observer could tell this was a completely different boat. The members initially refused to measure the yacht. However, they were told they did not have the right to refuse to measure the boat. If Nippon had breached a rule, it was a rule concerning mutual consent and was not a measurement rule as such.

Therefore the measurers were told the issue would have to be decided by John Doerr and the panel of international judges. Once again the jury faced a tough call. Major modifications were to many people against the spirit and intent of the two-boat rule. Such major changes to a yacht are not cheap and, in fact, could conceivably end up costing more than starting from scratch and building a completely new yacht.

All of this was discussed within our compound and we made a unanimous decision to protest the Japanese team for infringing the two-boat rule. The question came down to just how much refinement can be done before an "old" boat becomes a "new" boat. While changing a keel or wings or a rudder seemed perfectly within the rules, wasn't changing the bow, the hull and the stern really making a new boat? When our protest was made public and subsequently discussed in several press conferences, Bruce Farr stated the heart of the matter most succinctly. "It must be decided," he said, "when a modified boat becomes a new boat. Otherwise, you can jack up the windex and shove a new boat under it."

Although taken to extremes, that was exactly the issue we wanted resolved. While the judges were attempting to resolve the problem, several comments were made at press conferences which illustrated how contentious the issue had become. Peter Blake referred to the matter as the "Nippon Clip-On". That infuriated Peter Gilmour, who had already been the target of a nationality protest and a protest over his presence on the racing boat as the 17th man.

"The Japanese team," he said, "have really been offended by Peter Blake's comments referring to 'Nippon Clip-On'. We think it is completely unnecessary to be making statements that are just derogatory about another competitor."

While tempers flared, the international jury finally ruled, in so many words, that competitors could change their boats as much as they wanted. To me, this was saying the two-boat rule didn't even exist. In the end, the rule wasn't worth the paper it was written on. I felt it was a disappointing cop-out on the part of the jury.

The other contentious issue in round robin one concerned Team New Zealand's use of Murray Jones, hoisted up the mast to look for the long-term wind. We had worked extensively on this system and considered that we had an advantage because Murray was excellent at not only spotting the breeze lines on the horizon but at applying the best tactical strategies to what he could see. From his vantage point, some 30 metres above sea level, he could see the wind on the water beyond the top end of the course and we could plan our strategy around that. Murray would communicate the strategy to Richard Dodson, using an intercom system, then Richard would pass on the information and ask more questions. The system worked so well that Murray was effectively calling all the tactics from his position up the mast.

Not only that, but we found that he had a better perspective of judging the starting line than the bowman, and would therefore determine how close our yacht was to the starting line, particularly if our view from on board was obstructed by the other yacht.

Murray was well accustomed to being aloft as he is a mast manufacturer by trade and thus there was no doubt that Team New Zealand had a "secret" weapon superior to all other syndicates. That's when the politics and lobbying from the opposition syndicates started. Was having a man up the mast safe? What would happen to the person up the rig if the mast fell down? Would the jury itself be liable for an injury or fatality if, after a protest hearing, they allowed such a practice to continue?

These and other arguments were no doubt put forward by the syndicates which realised they didn't have a Murray Jones. After all, not everyone has the stomach to sail an entire leg of a race hoisted 30 metres up, at the tip of a violently moving pendulum. And those who do are not usually among the top bracket of tactical sailors.

I remember when ex-All Black prop Steve McDowell was hoisted to the top of an IACC rig in 1992. All Black props are, of course, famous for their toughness, yet McDowell appeared as though he required an urgent peel to a new set of underwear after the experience. As for Russell Coutts, I realise my limitations in this area and have never been past the second spreader. It is a lot higher and a lot more intimidating than it looks!

After our race with *oneAustralia* the press were all over the "man up the mast" issue. We treated the whole thing pretty lightly, perhaps a little too lightly as it turned out in the next round.

At the post-race press conference, Murray was asked why he was sent up and what he did up there.

"I'm the lightest person on the boat," he replied. "But I'm trying to eat as much as I can. I take my lunch box with me now."

I was also asked why we chose Murray as our pole sitter. "The problem is Murray talks too much on deck so we sent him up there and we just clean forgot all about him."

The media didn't seem to appreciate our humour and they took it that Team New Zealand was really trying to hide something. Some of the journalists after the conference were asking, "Why don't you tell us the real reason he is up the rig, which is to look for wind?"

I couldn't help but wonder why they asked the question, if it was that obvious!

Nippon was the first to file a technical protest, claiming that we infringed the communications rules. Just as in many sports it is illegal to receive outside communications during the game, so it is in yachting. Further, it is illegal to carry equipment capable of receiving outside assistance. The jury inspected our equipment and found no fault. The Nippon protest was seen by us as a reaction to our protest against them over the two-boat issue, but it got them nowhere.

In round robin two, John Bertrand and our friends from the oneAustralia group were a little more imaginative. They actually went into the rule book and then went to the jury, saying we infringed IACC rule 41.2. Rule 41.2 states that "no crew member shall station any part of his torso outside a vertical line through the sheerline in a heeled or level condition except when necessary to perform a task, and then only temporarily".

The rule originally came about to prevent crew hiking out or trapezing off halyards to increase stability, thereby gaining an advantage. However, when we hoisted a person up the rig, and with the rig swinging to leeward as it always does, the weight of the person decreases stability! Therefore, considering the yacht's straight-line performance, having a person up the rig is in fact a slight disadvantage.

The jury ruled that while the tasks of kicking the battens through on tacks and gybes, clearing the gennaker and performing structural checks on the rig and halyards were tasks that could only be performed up the rig, looking for wind and watching for obstructions were "not of necessity performed aloft on the yacht". The result was disqualification from the race for us and two points for oneAustralia.

The argument thus became: Is it necessary to be up the rig to see the long-term wind? From the deck of an IACC yacht, even from the first spreader, it is not possible to get enough depth perception when reading the wind on the water two or three miles up the course. I don't dispute that you can see the wind on the water maybe a mile up the course from deck level. I couldn't help but wonder if some of the jury members should be tacticians on the boats because perhaps they can see things that sailors simply can't. My argument was that you should be permitted to see the wind on the water for the entire race course, and if, by choice of the crew, that means being able to view the course area from 30 metres up the rig then that should be the choice of the professionals racing the yachts.

It was also interesting that under the jury's new interpretation, before performing a light-air gybe, we would have to frantically winch our bowman up the rig to kick the battens over and then immediately lower him after it was completed. If anything was dangerous, this was surely the most likely situation to cause injury. If the bowman was unfortunate enough to get a limb stuck in the rigging on the way up, the winch would probably win out and the crewman would suffer a breakage or worse.

The interpretation was confusing and should have had an impact on a number of other areas. Team New Zealand asked for an interpretation of the words "necessary to perform a task", citing the common manoeuvre of sending a bowman out to the end of a spinnaker pole to perform a spinnaker peel or a change to another spinnaker. For this task, it is very clear that the crewman would definitely be outside the sheerline. Although it would no doubt slow the boat down to perform the peel within the confines of the sheerline it could be done by simply letting the spinnaker pole swing back inside the sheerline where a crew member standing on the deck could perform the change. Given their previous ruling, we felt that it was obvious that it is not necessary to perform this task outside the sheerline.

The jury ruled that this task was okay to be performed outside the sheerline, even though it wasn't necessary to do so! I struggled to see how they could justify such a ruling. It was frustrating to witness such a lack of consistency, yet at least we had the most important areas right. We didn't have to rely on the jury to try and win us the America's Cup, and if we had to I'm not sure I would have been very confident.

We had fast boats, we were winning races and we were improving our best boat, *NZL-32*, each time we tested her between rounds. Regardless of Team New Zealand losing that protest, it was obvious the Australians were in trouble.

Recognising this, oneAustralia sent a lone David Barnes out to keep a watchful eye on the two black boats during the next test session.

After a few days of continuous shadowing, several of our guys took exception to the fact that Barnes was trying to gain information to assist our Australian competitors.

Our chase boat was called alongside *NZL-38* and unbeknown to Barnes, retaliation measures were being planned. Seven crew secretly hid under sails in our chase boat in preparation for a commando raid on the Australian target. After a few minutes, the chase boat slowly steered over to the *oneAustralia* tender and took up station alongside. Phillip Jameson began a conversation with Barnes, choosing a time when he was suitably distracted to give the signal for the troops to rush the Australian informer. Within seconds, Barnes was stripped naked and his clothes were delivered back to *NZL-38* where a few items were hoisted as victory flags. An hour or so later, as darkness approached, Barnes began a desperate plea for mercy. "Come on you guys, at least give me my wallet back". Of course, the team on *Black Magic II* struggled to feel sympathy for their fourmer teammate from 1992.

Meaty instead elected to call the Australian dock and advise them to be prepared to welcome home their loyal informer, who seems to have been adversely affected by a long day in the sun. It was the last time we would be followed by David Barnes.

Regardless of the extra attention we were now receiving, the reaction by our opponents puzzled me. It seemed that at the end of a round many rushed their boats into the worksheds and began modifications to their hulls and appendages.

But no one really realised the significance of our rig and how it was contributing to our upwind performance. The way we had set up our rigging and the position in which we flew sails was, to me, different from our opponents. Again, this one aspect of our programme was not the "big secret" to our success, but it has always puzzled me why the other teams didn't pay more attention to what we were doing. Perhaps their emphasis on hull shapes and appendages was a function of the widely held belief among many designers that "the wing's the thing". This, of course, grew out of the Australians' victory in 1983. Since then, it seems like everyone has spent a lot of time experimenting with the underwater parts of the boat, perhaps to the neglect of the total picture.

I remember reading a quote in a local paper made by Bill Trenkle, operations manager for Team Dennis Conner, when asked about the changes being made to the yachts after the first round of racing. "The boats are much more similar this time than the last Cup and the appendages play a much more important part. There are all kinds of foils, bulbs, fins, ringlets and rudders."

When I read that it occurred to me how intrusive this part of design had become. People were always asking Cup sailors what kind of wings we had, what did our keels look like. There was great anticipation over the common declaration day – brought about by another new rule which stated all syndicates would display their entire boat in mid-April.

At the conclusion of round robin two we still led the pack, but not by much. We ended the round credited with 16 points, oneAustralia and Tag Heuer nipping at our heels with 13. Nippon and the French were within striking distance with 10 and 7 respectively, and Sydney '95 and the Spanish brought up the rear with 4 and 0.

Winning all the races in round robins one and two was certainly better than losing them all, but it had very little effect on our overall programme. We considered these rounds little more than practice and an opportunity to get some idea of what stage of progress our competitors were at. However, we realised that if we weren't racing our fastest boat in her fastest mode, other syndicates might be playing the same game as well.

Round robins three and four, with their four and five points for each win, would determine which of the seven boats would meet the American defender in May. The racing was about to get serious.

11

That Sinking Feeling

E ven though we had had a couple of good, competitive races in the first two round robins, the general consensus around Team New Zealand was that we were still learning more from our own two-boat programme than from the trials. During the break between rounds two and three, we took the two black boats back out on the ocean and continued to test them against each other. Once again we discovered that some of the changes we'd made to *NZL-32* while she was in dry dock had improved her speed.

As we approached round robin three, the question most discussed was whether to bring *32* into action or keep racing with *38*. While *38*, *Black Magic II*, had not lost a race, we had only a three-point lead. And with third round victories worth four points each, that lead didn't seem too secure. On the other hand, we felt *Black Magic II* was still the boat to beat. Each of our competitors had made changes before round robin two in the hope of being more competitive with our boat, particularly on the upwind legs. A quick analysis tells the results.

In the first round, in every race, we led at every mark. In the second round, we were the second boat around six marks, three each in our races against Japan and Spain. But we had enough speed to come back and win both races.

We tossed around the idea of making a small, insignificant change to obtain a new rating certificate. We figured this would mean that we would still be able to guess and assess what changes the opposition had made during the break yet they would not know what we had changed and how that may have affected our performance. For the one-boat syndicates, the only real gauge they had was when they raced us.

France had brought in a new boat for the second round. We knew oneAustralia would be racing their new yacht in the upcoming third round. The general perception around San Diego was that *Black Magic II* was our faster boat. If that wasn't so, went the argument, why would we be foolish enough to race our slower boat . . . unless, perhaps, it didn't measure! It was just the perception we wanted to give. Also, we felt we had improved the speed of *Black Magic II* between the first two rounds and now, with what we had learned in our downwind sail testing, we could speed up our newer yacht and keep competitive with what awaited us in round robin three.

Although we fully realised the next two rounds were important, we also knew that four of the seven challengers would advance to the Louis Vuitton Cup semi-finals. Given that we had not lost a race on the water yet, the chances of dropping from first place to fifth seemed pretty slim.

So for all those reasons, we decided to race *Black Magic II* in the third round and continue to work on improving *NZL-32*. While we now had a better idea of how good our opponents were from first-hand experience, we still knew little more about the three American yachts than what we read in the papers and heard on the street. Their second round had been interesting as well.

After the first round of racing on the defender course, it appeared that Pact 95 and Team Dennis Conner would slug it out for the right to advance into the Cup match. America[3], the all-women team, seemed off the pace due to a three-year-old boat and a lack of experience. Within Team New Zealand, we rated the three boats in order, based strictly on speed, as *Young America*, *America*[3] and *Stars & Stripes*. However, when experience, sailing skills and intangible factors were considered, we all concluded any team headed by Dennis Conner could never be dismissed.

We also knew that America[3] was building a new boat and, because of our considerable respect for their design team, we expected it to be fast. The only question was when the boat would arrive and if there would be enough time to tune it up to speed.

The first day of racing in round robin three for the Louis Vuitton Cup was scheduled for February 14, but a frontal system passed over southern California, bringing with it heavy winds and gusts up to 30 knots. The race committee wisely called off racing for the day.

During the previous day, there was a brief press conference in which representatives from all the challengers expressed some thoughts about what this new round of racing meant to their teams. Some of the comments were particularly interesting.

Pedro Campos, helmsman for the 0–12 Spanish team, summed up his situation quite succinctly: "It's time to win."

Chris Dickson's analysis of round robin three was probably shared by most of the contenders: "Round one and round two were very much practice

Surrounded by guys like these, driving the boat was the easiest job on board. Here Ross Halcrow, Brad Butterworth, Jeremy Scantlebury, and Warwick Fleury are ready to give me plenty of advice.

Here's a rare photo on two counts: one is Brad is found on the bow and the other is that he's actually doing some work!

Design co-ordinator Tom Schnackenberg had a huge impact on most areas of the 1995 campaign.

Rob Tucker

Blakie and Meaty, trying to explain why they spend so much time at sea.

Peter Blake (in glasses) with Aran Hansen, the man whose 155kg weight meant he sank **Black Magic** *enough to give us more than an inch of additional waterline length!*

Doug Peterson (left of me) was a regular observer during our testing. Laurie and Doug's intuition was a huge part of **Black Magic's** *final concept.*

Andrew Taylor on the 'coffee grinder' with Simon Daubney and Brad Butterworth checking the sails. Andrew was a member of every New Zealand America's Cup challenge since 1986.

Craig Monk tosses me into the Pacific for a ceremonial dunking after we won the Louis Vuitton Cup. Hey, those are rocks right there!

*Grayson, my son, joined me on board **Black Magic** after the final race. Also seen is my nephew Carl and my mother and father.*

Brad Butterworth

We considered letting Roy Mason modify the trophy to hold more champagne.

NZ Herald

...eemed like all of New Zealand came out to welcome us home. Here the parade makes its way down Queen Street in ...ckland. We'd heard America's Cup fever had spread throughout the country, but we never expected anything like this. ...erleaf: The second event on the Brut Series in San Francisco. Here we are coming off the start with Alcatraz in the ...kground. Billy was moved onto the bow for this series. (Neil Rabinowitz)

The Brut Sailing Series Trophy is a Fabergé Egg, presented to us after winning three of the five 1996 Brut events. Simon joked that he may never have to fold sails again.

rounds to sort things out. Round three is reality."

Syd Fischer, standing at 2–10, gave a good appraisal of the obvious: "If we don't do well in this round robin, we're dead."

Peter Morris of oneAustralia, with tongue in cheek and recalling Mr Bertrand's misfortune in falling over the side of their yacht during his last race against us, told the audience: "We've put a running rail around the boat so that nobody leaves during a race."

The new boat oneAustralia raced for the first time in the third round was no doubt an improvement on their old boat. Except for our race, the Aussies also led at every mark in every race. We were anxious to see the new boat and to race against it. That happened on our fourth racing day after the Aussies had easily won against the Spanish, French and Japanese. The word along the docks was that *AUS-35* was a significant improvement over *AUS-31* and that the new boat would finally give us a real test.

Our day started with the usual weather briefing from Bob Rice and statistical analysis of the opposition from Ed Baird. Kiwis tend to be uncompromising with their black humour, often directed at their friends, and for those not brought up within the culture it can be quite unsettling. Ed was very popular with our team in San Diego and did a superb job but someone, in the form of Aran Hansen, noticed that Ed Baird's unusually steep forehead and his lack of hair made his profile closely resemble the forehead of the dolphin fish, commonly known as a mahi mahi. Unknown to Ed, he was given the nickname "Mahi Mahi", just as Simon Daubney was called "the Nose", or Meaty received comments on his ears, and as "Horse" was appropriately named for a physical attribute.

Ed's name had become so common that Aran and most of the team were ordering the "Baked Ed" from the menu at Fiddlers Green, Team New Zealand's adopted restaurant.

When Bob had finished his delivery, I asked, "Will there be any mahi mahi on the course area today?"

The place broke into uncontrolled laughter as Bob kept a straight face and proceeded to go into a lengthy dissertation about how there would in fact be mahi mahi on the course and they'd be hanging around our tender and generally critiquing the race with interest. That set the tone for the day, and although Ed left the meeting still puzzled about what all the humour was about, the team was in the normal frame of mind for the race against oneAustralia.

On the tow out the attitude remained relaxed. Meaty, by this stage receiving coaching on his speeches from Simon Daubney and Joe Allen, gave his usual team talk just before hoisting the sails. His drama coaches had suggested the mood was too laid-back and the advice was to pick things up a bit. Meaty responded in his speech by shaking a fist in the air and saying, "See this? This is what we need to give the Australians today. Let's hit them hard!" Raucous laughter erupted again as Meaty had successfully sent the group into an even more relaxed state, without even realising his own true usefulness.

By the time we got to the race course and sailed a few practice runs, we had become quite serious about the race, but the Australians were extremely keyed up. I don't think they ever envisioned going into the third round robin with five losses on the water. Nor do I think they took kindly to the fact that the Kiwis were undefeated. When we first encountered the Australians on the way to the race course, we could see the determination in their faces. They wanted to beat us and wanted it badly.

An incident that occurred before the start illustrates just how fired up they were. As we passed by *oneAustralia* for the first time, Brad gave a short wave to John Bertrand. Whether John saw only part of the motion or if he was surprised by the gesture I have no idea, but he later confronted Brad, apparently thinking our tactician had given him the international one-finger salute of disrespect. Someone in the press got wind of Bertrand's annoyance and questioned Brad about it during the after-race press conference. In his typically laconic, laid-back manner, Brad's answer was: "It's in the Royal New Zealand Yacht Squadron handbook . . . friendly wave of the hand to other yachtsmen as they go by."

Brad's words drew a laugh from the press and put an end to Bertrand's misinterpretation, but they by no means put an end to the Aussies' desire to stick it to the Kiwis. Over the next few days we made a point of having our entire crew give "a friendly wave" to the Australians, but the good-natured gesture drew no response from our South Pacific neighbours.

At the conclusion of the race, if it hadn't been apparent before, it was pretty clear to all observers that Team New Zealand had clearly set the standard for the 1995 America's Cup challengers. Although the race had been close, oneAustralia's new boat had been just a little slow off the starting line and hadn't been able to catch us throughout the entire race. Once again, our upwind speed got us to the first mark first, and even though they had gained some time at the first and second leeward marks, as well as on the last beat, it wasn't enough to get past us. Race to Team New Zealand by 26 seconds.

The victory may have been something of a dual-edged sword. On the one hand, we were of course happy to have won, but on the other, we knew we were now certainly the target of each of the other six challengers. As in most sports, the athlete or team at the top of the competition draws the most attention and all other competitors seem to rise to their best game in head-to-head contests.

So as soon as the race against the new *oneAustralia* was completed, Peter, Brad and I sat in the cockpit and discussed how we would deal publicly with what were sure to be numerous questions about our impressions of the Australian yacht. Privately, we didn't think it was the great breakthrough the Aussies were obviously hoping for. If we could stay ahead of her in *Black Magic II*, with old upwind sails, we were quite confident the faster boat, with all go-fast gear aboard, could keep ahead of her as well.

But that was not the message we wanted to relate. Instead, we concluded our strategy should be to try as hard as possible to set up *oneAustralia* as the favourite in the Louis Vuitton Cup. Despite their loss today, we felt we had the opportunity to implement part of that strategy at the press conference by extolling the virtues of the new boat and the Aussie team.

Brad and I represented Team New Zealand at the conference and I guess I got a little carried away. Here some of the things I had to say: "The boats are very, very close, and if anything maybe upwind they could have had the legs on us . . . It was a big-time technical battle out there . . . In New Zealand we regard Rod Davis as one of the best starting helmsmen in the world . . . We always knew the likes of oneAustralia would be tough competitors. They had quite a bit of a coup at the start of this regatta with the benefit of the three boats."

That last comment must have been the result of some of the residue left over from the two-boat rule that we felt the Australians had taken advantage of. I doubt if my words, or Brad's agreement on the virtues of the new boat, actually persuaded anyone that the undefeated team really thought the loser of six races was the favourite to win, but it was all part of what we call the "America's Cup head game".

Something else happened that day that helped to deflect attention from us and the race with oneAustralia. In the early evening, the French syndicate took their two boats, *France 2* and *France 3*, out to test a new quadrilateral mainsail. *France 2* suddenly lurched and capsized – for some unexplained reason, the keel, along with its 40,000-pound lead ballast bulb, had fallen off the hull. Eight of the twelve crew scrambled over the side of the boat as she turned, the others ended up in the water. All were soon rescued. Remarkably, the boat was saved when a harbour patrol vessel arrived and began a pumping operation which kept her afloat. Later, *France 2* was towed in on her side, with a chase boat and floats supporting the outer end of the mast.

Although the VHF radios were under water, Thierry Peponnet had a cellular telephone on him and was able to communicate with his compound as he and his 11 buddies clung to the side of the boat. I later heard the following story from both Thierry and designer Phillipe Briand, who was also on the boat. Apparently Thierry called into the compound and asked for Marc Pajot, the head of the syndicate.

"Allo, Allo, can I speak to Marc Pajot?"

"I'm sorry, Marc is very busy," said the receptionist. "Can you call back later?"

"No. This is extremely urgent. Can you please ask him to come to the phone?"

"I'm sorry," Thierry was told a few moments later, "Marc says he's too busy to come to the phone."

Thierry's reply was straight to the point: "Well then, tell him his boat has just capsized and it's beginning to sink." All Thierry could hear as he hung up was a loud gasp from the receptionist.

This was not the first catastrophe to befall the syndicate. On the day *France 2* was to have been put into the San Diego waters for the first time, a crane lifting the yacht dropped it onto a concrete roadway, pushing the keel up through the boat's deck. Repairs were lengthy and expensive.

My heart was always in my mouth when our own boats were lifted. Mike Drummond had made up a safety list which monitored the use of the lifting bolts and strops, including getting the equipment crack-tested, but accidents still happen no matter how careful you are. In fact, I was so nervous about the whole operation I used to find something else to do in another part of the compound so I wouldn't have to watch.

As the third round ended, Team New Zealand was at the top of the leader board with 40 points, followed by oneAustralia with 33 and Tag Heuer on 29. There was then a considerable drop to Nippon with 18, France at 15, Sydney '95 with 8, and Spain, which finally won a race, at 4.

The third round of the defender races proved little different from the second round – Pact 95 and Team Dennis Conner continued to share the lead after each won four of their six races. The women of America[3] had a tough go, winning only once.

As Team New Zealand prepared for the fourth and last round robin, there was very little discussion of which boat to enter. Barring some disaster, we were pretty much assured a spot in the semi-finals. Some of the guys worked out the various mathematical machinations of how many wins and losses everyone needed and who had to beat who, but I didn't pay much attention. Our charge was simple, sail as well as we could.

In truth, the performance of *Black Magic II* had been a little bit of a surprise to us. When we began with her back in January, I doubt any of us would have predicted she'd still be on the course in March. But it all came down to the old saying, "If it ain't broke, don't fix it." And *Black Magic II*, undefeated – on the water! – certainly wasn't broke.

I don't suppose there was anything in anyone's America's Cup experience that could have prepared us for the events of March 5, 1995.

March 3 and 4 were both grey, overcast days. The rain came on the morning of the fifth, accompanied by stronger than usual winds. As I drove from Coronado to the compound, I thought there was a better than even chance the races would be called off. The forecast was for continuing rain and winds gusting in the 20–25 knot range. Reserve days were built into the schedule and I assumed if the race committee was going to err, they would err on the side of caution. The safety of the boats and sailors, it seemed to me, should be the primary concern.

But when I got to the compound, all activity indicated the races were on. As the winds increased and the seas got sloppier, Blakie got on the radio to the race committee of the Louis Vuitton Cup regatta.

"Pat, the conditions seem marginal at best. Do you intend to race?"

"It's a fine day for racing," the response came back. "See you on the course."

Well, it might have been a fine day for sailing if we were in 12-metres or Whitbread boats, but we weren't. We were sailing 75-foot America's Cup boats built specifically for San Diego winds, which are almost always in the eight to 12 knot range. In these boats, it most certainly wasn't a fine day for sailing.

Pete got back on the radio: "We would like to register the fact that we consider the conditions marginal at best and you would be wise to consider a delay."

The response: "We considered that, thank you very much. We think it's a great day for sailing. See you out there."

There wasn't much more we could do at that moment so we boarded *Black Magic II* and headed towards the race course. As we were being towed, we realised the conditions were even worse than we'd anticipated. There was a consensus amongst the crew that the tow was only wasting our time. No way they'll race in this, we thought.

The shock loads on the boat as we crashed through the waves were extreme. Keep in mind the IACC boats carry a huge lead bulb and keel, weighing around 40,000 pounds, that drops off waves like a boulder off a cliff. The forces transferred to the light-weight carbon-fibre boats in such conditions are tremendous. We feared gear damage, but we were particularly troubled by the thought that if our mast broke, our two-boat programme would quickly be reduced to a one-boat programme. Masts run to about a half-million dollars each and although we had a spare, it wasn't really a good mast and wasn't meant for anything more than an emergency. We were very tight in terms of budget and cash flow and at that stage a broken mast would have taken four to five weeks to replace and ship to San Diego.

Soon oneAustralia and France 3 were on the radio to the regatta committee. They received the same stubborn response given to Team New Zealand earlier. I was astounded. The race committee was employed by the challengers to run races with the clear objective of establishing who the best challenger was, not which boat was the strongest in more than 20 knots of wind. I wondered why Pat Healy, the Louis Vuitton Cup regatta chairman, wasn't sailing one of these boats as he seemed to know more than the competitors about their capabilities.

At one point on board *Black Magic II* we discussed sailing over to *oneAustralia* and asking if they would join us in refusing to race. In retrospect, we were stupid to race, regardless of what the race committee said. It was the type of day that could have lost the America's Cup for us. The risk far outweighed the possible gain, which in the end was worth only five points.

But as the time approached for our start, the wind decreased slightly and we went ahead. After a bit of a sparring session in the pre-start manoeuvres, we had an even start and there soon began a spirited tacking duel up the first beat. There was no doubt that it was exciting on board as the boat cracked, bent and groaned under the huge loads. This was more like Fremantle than the normal conditions of San Diego. Again we managed to pull ahead a bit each time we came together and by the first mark we rounded several boatslengths in the lead. We added to that on the downwind leg, and then turned for the second beat. All the while the wind was increasing and the seas were building. On board it felt like we were inside a washing machine. The boat was charging through walls of water three to five feet high. The loads on the gear were enormous.

By now the intensity on board *Black Magic II* was at fever pitch. I was totally focused on the race, so much so that on the first run I told the guys to prepare a larger headsail for the next beat. I said I thought it would balance the boat better. But all it did was send us crashing through the waves, more loaded up and at a faster pace. It was insane and I was the chief crazy; the inmates were in charge of the asylum.

We hit one particular wave and the entire boat was awash. "Jesus Christ, guys, we're going down." This was my stab at humour, something to bring a little cheer to the crew. It was about one minute after that when someone said, "They've had a breakdown."

I whipped my head around and at first glance it looked like they'd broken their forestay or running backstay because the entire rig went slack.

"Looks like they've broken their forestay," Brad said. "No, no, they've broken their backstay."

Then Jeremy looked under our boom. "No, they've broken their boat! THEY'RE GOING TO SINK."

I looked again. Although the boat was in obvious distress, I couldn't come to grips with the notion that it was actually going to sink. I suppose anyone who has ever been to sea contemplates the possibility of a boat sinking, but contemplation is one thing and reality is another.

The officials claim the wind was at 16 knots when the accident happened, but I made it at well over 20 knots. Some of our guys had stopped sailing and stood transfixed at the side of the boat. Blakie suggested we back off and unload the boat. The race was over and we had little to prove. When someone like Blakie, a veteran of more than 500,000 miles at sea, starts talking about seamanship, it usually pays to listen. He's been in extreme conditions more than perhaps anyone else in the world. We slowed the boat down and then total silence swept over *Black Magic II*. All eyes were on *oneAustralia* as her crew abandoned ship, diving into the stormy sea. Chase boats circled the stricken vessel collecting the human jetsam. The boat had broken in the middle. As the ocean rushed in, attacking the exposed interior, the Pacific swallowed the yacht in less than three minutes. Three million dollars of high-tech racing machinery fell to the ocean floor some 500 feet below.

The scene, even as I replay it in my mind, seems so eerie, so unreal, that I sometimes have a hard time believing it really happened even though I was a witness to it.

The Whitbread guys were visibly shocked. They understood how little chance they would have if their boat sank that fast in the Southern Ocean.

Joe Allen, who had been packing a spinnaker below deck, came up and reasoned that we must be doing pretty well. "We're so far ahead of the Aussies I can't even see them," he said as he looked behind us.

When the shock began to subside, we collected our wits and decided to get ashore before something happened to us. No one argued. Blakie suggested it would be an act of good sportsmanship to withdraw.

We nursed the yacht into smoother water and felt a great relief when we got her to the dock. Once again luck had been with us. A careful inspection revealed that several of the rig's fittings had yielded and we were in real jeopardy of losing the mast.

Doug Peterson, as confident as ever, came down and pronounced, "That will never happen to our boats." Sailors are a superstitious lot and that kind of comment often comes back to haunt you. Doug was always confident in the boat, always said it would be the fastest, and he was right. We all liked his conviction, but on this occasion we didn't necessarily trust it.

Our structural team did a thorough check that night. Structural designer Mike Drummond had said, "It's extremely hard to design a boat for the shock loads experienced in a seaway. What wave spectrum do you design for? How much of a safety factor do you apply? Have all the carbon laminates bonded correctly? You never know for sure."

As for the Australians, perhaps John Bertrand's impressions of the event best tell the story. John is usually very articulate, but as the following excerpts from the transcript of the press conference that followed within hours of the sinking demonstrate, he was understandably still in shock:

"The boat broke in half and sank. That's what happened. We were sailing in about 20 knots of breeze with quite a severe lump. The boat came off a wave or series of waves at the bottom mark; we heard a crack, although these boats make a lot of noise anyway. We'd already blown the main drive shaft of our port main primary winch. So we were sheeting the genoa to the port runner winch. And the boat broke in half.

"She went down extremely quickly – I'm guessing one or two minutes. A sickening sound, of course, as the boat broke in two. It was obvious that a major disaster from our point of view was taking place. We all took off our boots and took to the water. We were picked up fairly quickly. We accounted for all the crew. We were concerned we were missing one, but we picked up all our 16 crew and 17th man.

"It's hard to know exactly what happened. It happened extremely quickly. We'll obviously be assessing the photographs and all the information we can get. All the focus is now into our first boat. We are having a team meeting tonight to update the organisation. It was obviously a huge blow to the programme.

"Through adversity people and organisations gain strength. I've personally faced adversity in previous years of sailing. I remember very clearly when we were 3–1 down against the American defender in 1983. We came back to fight another day. That's exactly how I feel right now.

"The boat appeared to break transversely behind the main primary winches. I believe we just completed a tack onto starboard and we were winding the sails. There was a lot of wind at the time. It was raining, a rain squall was going through. The seas were very difficult for this type of boat. My head was down at the time. The boat appeared to start to fold like a sheet of cardboard through the centre, and we heard this sickening sound as the boat was breaking apart. It was hard to know the full significance of what was unfolding in front of us at the time. It was all happening very quickly. These racing teams and myself are not conditioned for that sort of situation. We never rehearsed a boat breaking up underneath us, of course. The boat represents about 20,000 man hours of work, effort and emotion and to see that disappear so quickly . . .

"It became obvious that we were going to lose the boat. At that stage the boat was going down fairly rapidly. We were concerned also that the rig was going to collapse down on top of us and that could be extremely dangerous. So we told everyone to take off their boots and get the hell out of there, which we did. Half the crew went forward as the boat was folding through the centre and the remaining team went to the stern. The boat was unzipping in front of our eyes. We abandoned the yacht. About half of the team was still in the water being picked up by the chase boats, both oneAustralia and also Team New Zealand's chase boat. About half the team was still in the water when the tip of the mast disappeared. I remember watching the wind gear and the carbon fibre sensor at the top of the mast just disappear under the ocean. It was just unbelievable.

"Two of our guys, Billy Bates and Don McCracken, were down below when she started to break up. Billy had thought we lost the rig and was continuing to pack the spinnaker at the time. We let him know to get his arse out of there. He didn't need much encouraging. It was very important that we get our boots off and lighten up as much as we could. The water out there is very cold and the yacht was going down very quickly.

"I looked around when my head came out of the water. I dove in trying to get as far as I could away from the boat as fast as I could. At that stage only about half of the mainsail was in view.

"These boats are built light. We push the envelope in every area we can. The loads are extremely high. It's always a constant push to make them lighter, more high performance.

"We advised the race committee that we felt these conditions were unfit for these boats, as did Team New Zealand and the French. It was the race committee's option to conduct the races. The wind velocity generally was in the agreed conditions. At the time we were recording 20–24 knots of true wind.

"Rod Davis, the helmsman, said, 'I think we're going to sink.' Then he looked over to Iain Murray, one of our designers, to confirm. 'Big fellow, are we going to sink?' And the big fellow looked around and said, 'Yes, we're going to sink.' And Rod said, 'Shit, we're going to sink!'"

The story of the sinking made front-page headlines around the world. It was certainly an historic event. I still question the wisdom of the race committee for sending us out, and I still wonder how we could have been so stupid as to risk all our work and all our success for one boat race.

The conditions caused several other incidents as well. In the race between Spain and France, a titanium spreader-end fitting failed aboard *France 3* and the top of their mast broke. Two crewmen were thrown into the water but picked up quickly. It was a real blow to France's hope of making it into the semi-finals as they were leading at the time. And, as it turned out, they failed to make the semis by just three points.

Even after the sinking and the dismasting, neither the defender nor the challenger race committees called off racing. On the defender course, both *Stars & Stripes* and the new America[3] boat, *Mighty Mary*, lost the use of their mainsails due to broken gear. But both teams continued to race. *Stars & Stripes* bowman Greg Prussia tried to go aloft to clean up the mess, but understandably almost immediately became seasick as the 33-metre mast whipped around in response to the yacht pitching over the waves. The movements of a yacht are, of course, greatly magnified if you happen to be unfortunate enough to be picked to go up the mast . . . in a storm!

Prussia was brought down and bowman number two, Ralph Steitz, was sent up to have a go. When the yacht pitched over a particularly large wave, Ralph lost his grip. He was thrown away from the mast, swinging wildly around, and then battered back against the rig, where he was knocked unconscious. Now the problem was really serious. There was an unconscious person up the rig, swinging around like a haywire pendulum, now upside down in his harness and being further beaten about as he crashed and banged into the mast and rigging. The halyard could not be eased because more slack in the rope would make the situation worse. Prussia was sent up again, this time to get Steitz down.

Remarkably, other than a few scrapes and bruises, Steitz was generally uninjured.

Following the sinking, oneAustralia asked each of the challengers for a few days reprieve while the team attempted to bring their first yacht, *AUS-31*, up to speed. We didn't see any problem with that, but our race with oneAustralia was over, so we wouldn't have been affected either way. The vote among the seven challengers was 4 to 3 in favour of postponing the Australians' races for a day or two.

The jury allowed the substitution of the old boat and the race committee granted them a lay day. But then the French, who were scheduled to race oneAustralia the day after the sinking, protested. They believed that the postponement would materially prejudice them. Their argument was basically we're sorry about your boat, but we broke a mast and we're ready to race. The International Yachting Jury agreed with the French and upheld the protest, requiring the Australians to race. Since *AUS-31* wasn't ready for the race course, the French sailed the race by themselves and collected the five points, which put them right back into the battle with Nippon for the remaining slot in the semi-finals.

Along with the loss of the yacht, oneAustralia lost 11 sails. At this point in the regatta each team was allowed 30 sails, so in two minutes the Aussies lost more than a third of their allotted inventory. This would become an issue in the semi-finals.

A day or two after the sinking, I began to hear that Rod Davis had made some comments that he thought Team New Zealand had acted in an unsportsmanlike manner during the loss of their boat. I was absolutely dumbfounded. I couldn't imagine what he was talking about. It was our chase boat that raced to the scene to help pick up sailors. Our ground crew and maintenance people called the oneAustralia compound immediately to offer help in any way they could. Many of the sailors on our team had sailed with guys on *oneAustralia* in various Whitbread races. At one time or another, all of us had sailed in either a match race or a fleet regatta with the Australians.

At first I didn't believe Rod could have said something like that, but I called him and confronted him with what I had heard. Yes, he told me, he had said that. When I asked him why, I didn't get much of an answer. So I told him there were a lot of guys around Team New Zealand who would be pretty disappointed in his reaction. "I won't lose any sleep over that," was his reply.

To this day, I don't know what prompted Rod to make the comments. I'm willing to give him the benefit of the doubt and write it off to the fact that he was obviously disappointed over the entire sinking affair.

For several days after the boat went under, the talk of the sailing world was speculation about what caused the accident. Since the Australians concluded that salvaging the boat was unrealistic, I don't think we'll ever know for sure exactly what happened.

Engineers have calculated that the conditions experienced on March 5 on the America's Cup race course generated 60 to 65 tons of compression to be forced on the hull of *oneAustralia* by the mast and stays alone. Today's designers are well aware of the loads placed on boats, but the forces exerted on the hull in 20–22 knots of wind with three to five foot seas is a great deal different than those exerted by winds of eight to 12 knots in relatively calm seas.

We all "pushed the envelope" in 1995. With *AUS-35*, oneAustralia may have pushed a little harder than the rest of us. I think they made the hull as light as they possibly could and put the stabilising weight in their bulb. In a seaway, the bulb is thrown around with these accelerations, exerting additional forces on the hull. It appears that *oneAustralia* did not have enough strength longitudinally to accept these additional loads. It was a risk they took in search of better performance and, had they not encountered the conditions of March 5, it may have served them well.

A little harsher view was expressed by a fellow Kiwi who believed from the very beginning that the oneAustralia-Sydney '95 alliance was simply a smokescreen to circumvent the two-boat rule.

"This is God's way of punishing them for building three boats."

That's a hard way to look at it, but, given the absence of any real evidence, I suppose it's as good a speculation as my own.

The sinking of *oneAustralia* was obviously the big story of round robin four, if not the entire 1995 America's Cup. To say that we finished the round undefeated (with a DNF for the March 5 race) is anticlimactic. The leader board had Team New Zealand on top with 65 points, oneAustralia second on 53, Tag Heuer next with 49, Nippon on 28, followed by France, 25, Spain, 14, and Sydney '95, 13.

The format of the semi-finals was similar to that of the first four rounds in that we would all race each other. The difference, of course, is that now there were three fewer boats. A total of 12 races were scheduled for each team, so we were to race *oneAustralia*, *Tag Heuer* and *Nippon* four times. We knew they would all be gunning for us and they would be heading for the shed to make still more modifications in an effort to improve their speed, especially upwind. In the meantime, we had a major decision to make.

Once again, the question we discussed was whether to enter *NZL-32* or *NZL-38* in the semis. *Black Magic II* had certainly served us well during the first three months of the regatta, especially considering our original intent was to race her only in round robin one. But now we felt it was time to make the switch. There were three main reasons for the decision. One was that no matter how good our maintenance and shore teams were, and I'd put them in the great category, four rounds of racing had made *Black Magic II* race ready, yet *Black Magic I* was still very much rigged in test mode. The second reason was that although the boats were quite similar, we felt it was time to learn the idiosyncrasies of *Black Magic I*. We needed to sail her in race conditions to understand how to tune the boat to her full potential. The third reason was that there was no further need to hold back anything. The four teams in the semi-finals of the Louis Vuitton Cup had little time to react to what the opposition was doing and, if they had to, it would be a drastic last-gasp measure at best.

In a press conference on March 17, the day before the semi-finals began, Peter Blake announced the change. "We're using the old boat. We thought if it's good enough for the Australians, it's good enough for us. Our boats are fairly similar, and it's time to give this one a run."

Peter's statement sent the media scurrying to their typewriters and microphones. Generally, it was hard for most Cup followers to believe we'd switch at this stage. We still hadn't lost a race on the water, and it was apparent few people believed that we thought *NZL-32* was the faster boat. Conventional wisdom says the newer the boat, the faster the boat.

Blakie's mention of the change at oneAustralia was a nice little bit of gamesmanship. Although we've never discussed it, it seemed to me that he planted a little food for thought among our opponents. Australia didn't have a choice, but we did. And it may have appeared we were making a rash move, but I'm sure the other three teams concluded we wouldn't have done what we did unless we were absolutely sure *32* was the better boat.

So consider what kind of night our three foes had on the eve of the semi-finals. No one had been able to beat us in the boat we were racing, and now we were bringing in what must be an even better boat. Sounds like a sleepless night to me.

12

That Old Black Magic

ith *NZL-38* now retired during the break, *NZL-32* was prepared for her America's Cup racing debut. In many American sports, when great athletes retire, their numbers are also retired as a gesture of respect for their accomplishments. Battler suggested we do the same for the boat that had done so much for us. He thought it would be appropriate to cut out the 38 from the boat's mainsail and hang it above our basketball hoop. It was a great idea that everyone except the sailmakers supported!

We drew *Tag* in our first race of the semis and felt this would be a good test of *Black Magic I*. Although we believed oneAustralia would have *AUS-31* up to speed, we didn't feel that boat was as fast as the one at the bottom of the ocean. However, we were very impressed by the way the Australians had come back in the fourth round to win their last two races after the sinking.

In the pre-start against *Tag*, our weather team issued the instruction that this day was a "must win the left side" day. With 1:25 remaining before the start, we had a good position to secure that side, even though a right-hand shift was complicating things by biasing the right end of the start line. However, that situation would change with the anticipated larger left shift on the first leg of the course. Murray and Richard were very, very confident that would be the case.

Dickson was positioned for a run at the right-hand end of the line. His tacticians obviously had a different view about which side would be favoured and were perhaps basing that call on where the immediate advantage lay rather than the predictions for later. I wanted to start as close underneath and to the left of them as possible. We subsequently slowed *Black Magic* down, planning to wait for *Tag* to come back to us. Then we would time a run at the line that should place both boats near the right-hand end, thereby taking the bias advantage out of the line while still giving us the left. So far so good.

Then, with 50 seconds to the start, when we trimmed the sails to begin our final approach, the boat refused to accelerate. *Black Magic* had stalled, and the problem that would stay with us for the next series of races suddenly became evident.

During our break we had done very little, if any, pre-start practice, again chosing to concentrate on boatspeed only. We had experienced similar problems with *NZL-38* in some of the very early rounds, yet had convinced ourselves that we had gone a long way to solve those concerns. To avoid stalling in *NZL-38*, we had established a low-end speed which we tried never to go under. Yet as the countdown for the first semi-final race closed in, the new idiosyncricies of *Black Magic I* were suddenly being shown to us, in no uncertain terms.

We were late for the line and Dickson had the jump on us. Peter Montgomery on the TVNZ telecast described us as lethargic, but the truth of the matter was we were surprised by a difference in performance that we had not accounted for. We were forced to tack to the right and, fortunately, Dickson tacked with us. We immediately split tacks and tacked back to the left, while *Tag* chose to build speed before coming back on to starboard.

As both boats settled down for the drag race out to the left the speed difference became all too apparent for the guys on *Tag*. Within a few minutes, admittedly helped by the left shift, *Black Magic I* had blown *Tag* away in devastating fashion.

Chris had been critical of our boat switch leading into the semis and many of the journalists were talking about "the wheels falling off" the Team New Zealand effort, just as had happened with previous New Zealand efforts. Of course, in many ways this talk suited our game plan, yet, for two reasons, I found the suggestions amusing.

First, the competitors should surely by now have realised that we were not totally stupid. We had two boats. Better than anyone else, we should know the relative performance of those two boats. I could understand journalists being confused but I was astounded by the other sailors underestimating us.

Second, if comparisions were being made with the wheels falling off previous New Zealand efforts, then there was actually another New Zealand team in San Diego that had many key elements common to those previous efforts.

No doubt after the first few minutes of race one, as *Tag* moved to the usual position of aft of our stern, they may have finally realised that there were some areas where Team New Zealand might actually have made the right decisions. *Black Magic I* was clearly the class act of the 1995 America's Cup challengers.

The wind died before the first mark and the race was subsequently abandoned. So, back to the start we went. By the time we were ready for the second start, the winds had built to between seven and nine knots and the race was on. Chris came at us at the start from the buoy end on starboard, but he wasn't quite at full speed. We had the favoured side and we crossed a few seconds ahead. Then we put the old *Black Magic* into gear and simply sailed away from Chris and his guys. We gained an average of half a minute on every leg except the last to win by 2:15.

In the other semi-final, *oneAustralia* took out *Nippon* by more than two minutes. Although one race does not a regatta make, it was becoming obvious Team New Zealand and oneAustralia were the teams to beat.

The Tag team apparently came to the same conclusion as they put together a great effort on the second day to score a win over the Australians. It was also on that day that we showed just how fast *NZL-32* was. Our opponent was *Nippon*, the boat that had given us the most competitive races in the first four rounds. We had won each race, but they had been close, closer than the aggregate races against each of the other five boats. The final deltas were 1:00, 0:12, 1:34, and 0:57. In our first semi-final against them we won by 6:14. That result was a combination of our using a faster boat and Nippon miscalculating what changes to make to their boat between rounds. It soon became painfully obvious that they had slowed, rather than sped up, their yacht.

Judging from their performance, and from our knowledge of previous testing with wings, we suspected that Nippon was attempting to try something similar to what they believed we had underneath *NZL-38*. In fact, we had caught one of the Nippon designers with a tape measure, measuring the PVC frames that held the security skirts away from the wings as the boat was lifted and transported onto its cradle. The PVC frames were not exactly a detailed or scientific creation. Yet, if measured, they might indicate some rough parameters about the design of our wings.

The very next day, *Nippon* claimed to hit an object with their keel as they were being towed out of the harbour. Recall that Nippon was the first syndicate to base themselves in San Diego for their 1995 effort, yet it appeared they were still learning about the topography of the inner harbour. Of course, if they did have new wings, under the rules they would not be able to make changes to those until after the semi-final series . . . unless, somehow, they accidentally damaged them or even accidentally broke them off after running aground!

The jury was called to inspect *Nippon's* damage but, whatever the outcome was, it didn't make much of a difference to the Japanese America's Cup bid.

The *Tag Heuer-oneAustralia* match that day may have had some bitter overtones to it. As mentioned, the Australians had lost 11 sails to the bottom of the Pacific. Following the fourth round, they petitioned the International Jury and each of the challengers to replace those sails; on the surface, a fair remedy to the situation they found themselves in. On the other hand, rules are rules and every competitor racing in the 1995 America's Cup was subject to the sail limitation rule. For the rule to be changed, or an exception to be made, all of the defenders and challengers had to agree.

Team New Zealand remained silent on the issue when it first arose. We suspected that others would fight that battle and there was little point in our getting involved. Chris Dickson led the opposition, saying: "We are in favour of reviewing the rules for situations outside a team's control. The opportunity of gaining advantage from design and construction in these yachts is quite extensive, and those gains are not without risk. Different teams have approached the sail limitation rule tactically in different ways. Considering this, our position is that to give oneAustralia more sails than other teams would be an unfair advantage. We don't believe the situation that happened to *oneAustralia* was totally outside their control. We sympathise with them, but that's how we see it."

Chris made a fair point. If my interpretation is correct, what he was basically saying was that the Australians chose to gamble by pushing the envelope a bit too far in making their hull too light and they lost their bet. No one made them design and build the boat the way they did. They were in control of their destiny and they had to accept the consequences.

There were others who agreed with Dickson, but since only one dissenting vote was needed, the vote count became meaningless. Privately the Australians were seething, but publicly John Bertrand put the best spin he could on the decision.

"For a rule to be changed," said the skipper, "one needs unanimous support from defenders and challengers. Because oneAustralia has not received unanimous support for the proposed change, and therefore allowing the International Jury to make an impartial decision on what would be fair and equitable for oneAustralia, we are not taking the matter any further."

Tag's victory that day didn't surprise me a great deal. I thought it was a better boat at that particular time than *oneAustralia*. Full marks to the Aussies for bringing *AUS-31* back to life, but the boat wasn't as fast as it could have been nor was it as fast as it would be. If I had to choose between the two boats to race in the semi-finals, I would have chosen *Tag Heuer*.

Following the race, Chris was asked at the press conference if he had any thoughts about an all-New Zealand final in the Louis Vuitton Cup. The question amused me because there were 10 more races scheduled, but apparently Team New Zealand was already granted a spot in the finals, at least by one reporter. Actually, the talk in San Diego was that we would represent the challengers in the America's Cup come May. And, in truth, I'll admit we were already putting a few things in motion towards that end.

Dickson answered the reporter's question by saying, "The prospect of an all-New Zealand final is something all New Zealand is hoping for, as well as the two New Zealand teams."

In reality, it was clear what situation was about to develop. Team New Zealand, with the form boat, would technically be in a strong position to determine which of the other semi-finalists would proceed through to the Louis

Vuitton final. We could perhaps have chosen to let *Tag* beat us in some races and therefore knock the Australians out.

The press were no doubt figuring and perhaps even hoping that this scenario would develop. It would have pleased a section of the New Zealand public, yet it would have also given the Americans, the Australians and those journalists who enjoy controversy plenty of ammunition to fire at Team New Zealand.

There is also a fundamental entry in the first section of the yacht racing rule book that prohibits acts of bad sportsmanship. Although it may have been difficult to prove we intentionally lost a race, it would have been an issue ripe for debate. We were therefore reluctant to even consider such a possibility. Besides that, we had a new keel to test, and we now were more aware than ever that we had to resolve the stall problem that had surfaced on *NZL-32*.

An all-New Zealand final would have been terrific for the nation. It would have showcased the sailing talent and technological expertise that had become so prominent in the relatively tiny country in just over a decade. It also would have demonstrated how two different approaches to the America's Cup game could result in success. The *Tag Heuer* challenge was often described as being run on a shoestring. Chris Dickson and the syndicate managers did an excellent job of stretching that shoestring as far as possible. A lot of credit should be given to their operations manager, Laurent Esquier, the same man who helped us to learn what 12-metres were all about in Fremantle back in 1986.

But standing in the way of the all-New Zealand final was a group of very tenacious Australians who, despite one loss to *Tag*, weren't about to roll over. In fact, the loss made them even more determined to nail some New Zealand hide to their transom. As it happened, we were next on their schedule and our hide would suit them just fine.

After John Bertrand had skippered the 1983 Australian team to victory, he wrote a book in which he talked a good deal about the psychological aspects of competing. The team even hired a sports psychologist who taught them certain mind exercises that supposedly strengthened their will to win. John also talked a lot about how he received inspiration from the book *Jonathan Livingston Seagull*, a popular fable about a seagull dealing with some of life's obstacles.

Although John's book received criticism in some quarters, particularly from syndicate head Alan Bond, it was generally well received. However, in the yacht racing world the emphasis on the mind games was pretty much viewed as over the top. In New Zealand, we don't pay a lot of attention to trying to psych out our opponents and I doubt you'd find many Kiwis paying homage to a seagull.

Anyway, all of this is to say we began hearing a lot of talk and a lot of psychological discussion coming from the oneAustralia camp. "We can do it, we can do it," seemed to be a favourite chant. My view is you can say that all you want, but it doesn't do much good unless you can prove it. And if you can't, all the histrionics make you look pretty silly.

But on March 22, the men of oneAustralia came to the starting line determined to outsail us, not just out-psych us. They put together one of the best races they had sailed since January and we immediately recognised what may have been a skirmish or a battle in the past had now escalated to a full-blown war.

It was the type of day that draws people from all over to San Diego – cloudless sky, perfect temperature, seven to 11 knot breeze. Bright, sunny, and clear. On the tow out to the course, confidence aboard *Black Magic I* was in abundant supply. We weren't cocky, but after the devastating performance against *Nippon* and a three-month track record to rely on, we felt pretty good. Kiwis aren't by nature either braggarts or overly demonstrative, but I will attest to a quiet assurance aboard our boat that day.

We may have felt in control, but we were quickly reminded not all our problems had been solved and that, in sport, nothing should ever be taken for granted. As the saying goes, that's why they play the game. Rod Davis did a good job of keeping the pre-start action tight, and he convincingly won the start after I again mistimed the final approach.

As both boats came off the line, we were forced to tack but *oneAustralia* kept a close cover on us. Just as they had kept the action in the pre-start at a down-speed pace, their tactic was to keep the tacking duel at a slow speed by forcing us into frequent tacks. Apparently the Australians had realised two important facts. One was that if they allowed us any free space in which to use our boatspeed, we'd simply sail past them. The other was that, coming out of a tack, their boat actually accelerated faster than ours, but only if the boats were not at full speed.

For the first time in the entire regatta, we were unable to make an impression on our opponent. As we had anticipated, the wind shifts were to the left, but it was *oneAustralia* which was catching them. When the shift became big enough, they did let us get away from their cover and sailed off in the correct direction while we were forced to sail on the unfavoured tack. The Aussies were sailing flawlessly.

At the first mark we were 1:04 behind. While this situation was rare, it wasn't unique. We'd followed *Nippon* around the first and second marks back in round robin two, and we'd been behind Spain by more than two minutes in the same round. We'd come back to win with the slower boat, so there was no reason we couldn't do the same today in the faster *Black Magic I*.

On the first leeward leg, as we rounded the windward mark, *oneAustralia* gybed onto starboard as we continued on port. *oneAustralia* sailed a different run from us, which was both our hope and fear. We believed we had superior speed and felt they believed the same. Their only chance to add to their lead was to gamble on finding better wind and favourable windshifts on another section of the course. We, of course, felt that if the wind speeds and shifts were relatively equal we would gain.

That's exactly what happened. The Aussies didn't come back to cover us and by the time we got to the leeward mark we were only 37 seconds behind, a gain of 27 seconds.

Up the beat for the second time, we had *Black Magic I* flying. The official record indicates our average speed was 7.07 knots compared with 7.00 for *oneAustralia*. That may not look like a lot on paper, but it is significant on the water. Despite a problem with the leech in our mainsail and a miscue during a short tacking duel, we gained another 16 seconds to round the second weather mark just 21 seconds back. We peeled another 11 seconds off on the second run to head into the last beat a mere 10 seconds behind.

It must have been terribly discouraging on board *oneAustralia* to have sailed so well, established a big lead, and then watched as the black boat came closer and closer with every passing minute. If that was discouraging, then the final windward leg had to be downright depressing. In freshening winds, it must have seemed that we turned on an engine. The Australians had positioned themselves to windward and ahead as both boats set up near the starboard tack layline. I was cursing because, although we had closed on them, we had almost no positional options open and it looked like *oneAustralia* would lead us around the mark. Then the black boat must have decided she had had enough of the following position as she simply sailed around the Australians, took the lead, and rounded the top mark an amazing 44 seconds ahead. We had gained almost a full minute on the leg. Had it not been Australians we were racing, we would have been close to feeling embarrassed!

We sailed the final leg conservatively and won the race by 39 seconds. I searched the faces of the crew and it was as though this incredible come-from-behind victory was fully expected. We'd been asked throughout the regatta why we never seemed to get too excited with our wins. People didn't understand why we didn't jump up and down, throw high-fives at each other, and yell and scream. Part of it was because that's not the Kiwi way, and part of it is that we'd all been conditioned to the notion that we weren't in San Diego to just win a lot of races or even to just win the Louis Vuitton Cup. Nor were we there just to get into the America's Cup match. We were there for one reason and one reason only: to win the America's Cup.

Nevertheless, there was a show of emotion on board as we crossed the finish line that day. Brad Butterworth walked to the side of the boat, leaned over and patted the hull, saying for all to hear, "You are a beauty." Perhaps that's as much as one could expect from us at that point. The comment was picked up by the on-board microphones and Brad was asked about it at the press conference. His reply: "She's a good old girl." I guess that's his version of the high-five!

A serious analysis of the race pointed out a few key points to us. The first was that we had a massive speed edge and that the future strategy was to reinforce the tactics of low risk and avoid the big errors. The second point was that we had to address the downspeed acceleration problem. Perhaps this was our only weakness yet it had been exposed. It was incredibly difficult to judge the time it would take to accererate after a stall.

Regardless, we still tried to play down this fact as much as possible. I was saying publicly that I was going through a bad period, I was having timing problems in the final approach, I couldn't get my starting act together and I was working on my positioning after races.

There was no doubt that some of this was true, but openly stating the fact served another objective. That was to draw the attention away from detailing the exact speeds at which *Black Magic* was vunerable and get our competitors to focus on more general reasons for our problems. It was only in the downspeed state that we were compromised because, once *Black Magic* was up to speed, she could actually manoeuvre and accelerate better than the opposition.

We were particularly worried that our opposition would aggressively "dial us up" on starboard tack at the first cross in the pre-start. This is a common move in match racing where the starboard tack boat, at entry, forces the port tack boat to luff and tack resulting in both yachts sitting head to wind with their sails flapping. In many cases, the starboard tack boat loses out because she eventually has to tack out of the slow speed situation first, and the other yacht merely follows and ends up in the controlling position. In our case, once we were caught slow, the other boat could have easily controlled the action. When we tested the move in-house using *NZL-38* against *NZL-32*, our fears were confirmed.

After the race with the Australians, we speculated on what they would do, should they make it into the finals, to make their boat more competitive. It must have been incredibly demoralising when we passed them. At that stage they knew without a doubt they didn't have the boat to keep up with us and they must have had many discussions about how to change *AUS-31*. I'm quite sure they realised they couldn't just make a few small changes, they had to make a massive change.

That thinking must have been confirmed on our next race day when we met the Aussies again. This time we got the good start and then pulled ahead on every leg, winning by more than two minutes. It was now crystal clear that if oneAustralia was to get to the finals, the points would have to come from Tag and Nippon.

By the end of the sixth day of racing, halfway through the semi-finals, we remained undefeated. Nippon had yet to win a race in the series and Tag Heuer and oneAustralia were deadlocked at 3–3.

On March 27, Team New Zealand qualified for the final series of the Louis Vuitton Cup. On that day we beat *Tag Heuer* for our seventh consecutive victory in the semi-finals and even if we lost the final five scheduled races, we were assured of a spot in the finals. A number of decisions had to be made at that point, chief of which was to continue racing or devote our time and effort to further testing of our two boats. Several ideas to improve the speed of *NZL-32* had surfaced and we were eager to return to our testing procedures. We were keen to address our pre-start problems and come to an understanding of the precise cause for them. We also knew the remedy might entail changes that would take some time to properly manufacture.

As we docked the boat that night, there was a brief congratulatory celebration at the compound. Brief is an understatement and celebration is an overstatement. I don't want to give the impression we were totally immune to the emotions success generates, but all of us were still cognisant of our true goal. Perhaps Brad expressed it best at the afternoon press conference. "This is a fantastic achievement for us as a team and as a country," he said. "We are more than happy. But everyone was a bit quiet on the boat because we realise that we have quite a few tough races still to come. Getting past the next hurdle of the competition has always been a problem for us and we are aware of that."

KZ-7 had of course been the first New Zealand boat to stumble after this point and then *NZL-20* ended with a similar record in 1992.

Although we were assured of entry to the finals, we decided to contest two more races then concentrate on testing instead of racing the last three races against each of the other semi-final competitors. With one more loss, Nippon would be eliminated, leaving our opponent in the finals up to oneAustralia and Tag. Naturally we favoured Tag, but publicly we said we wanted to race whomever would give us the best race to prepare for the America's Cup. On the 28th, we defeated *Nippon* and *oneAustralia* beat *Tag*. That meant *Tag* had to win their final three matches and the Aussies had to lose all three. On March 31, *oneAustralia* crossed the finish line 2:41 ahead of *Nippon*, sealing their fate and that of Chris Dickson and his valiant challenge. We would meet the Australians in the best of nine finals for the right to race in the America's Cup match against the American defender.

Following the racing on the 31st, there was an emotional ceremony of sorts at the Louis Vuitton media centre on Shelter Island, not far from our compound. Every member of the Nippon and Tag Heuer challenges was introduced and the audience, made up of the media, team members' family and friends, various Cup officials and others, packed the room. Ernie Taylor, the chairman of the Challenger of Record Committee, thanked both teams for their great efforts and expressed what was on the minds of many observers when he said, "To Chris and the Tag Heuer team, what a great effort. I know that probably eight or nine months ago we didn't think they would make it. What a great job they did!" Judging from the applause, there was unanimous agreement.

Makoto Namba, the skipper of the Nippon challenge and one of the most genuinely nice guys in the game, choked back tears when he approached the microphone. "This is Japan's second America's Cup challenge," he said. "This event has been going on for 140 years, and we've only been involved for eight years. I will take this opportunity to thank chairman Yamasaki. I know he is a little disappointed, but we made the decisions which we believed in. I hope that he is still interested in sailing . . . we will come back. We're really proud to have competed against such a strong group of challengers. I'm sure that one of you guys will take the Cup."

I couldn't help but think back to the days before I heard about Team New Zealand when the Nippon offer was in front of me. Had Ross Blackman not driven two hours north to convince me the offer from Alan and Peter was genuine, I might well have been working alongside Makoto, Peter Gilmour, John Cutler and the rest of the Japanese team. Obviously I was happy that Ross had made the effort.

When Chris came to the microphone, he too was met with tremendous applause. He might be a bit of a controversial figure in the world of big league yachting, but in many ways that is why he has enjoyed tremendous support. Also, there are very few people who know the game who don't have respect and admiration for him. I think it's fair to say he and his team distinguished themselves during the 1995 Louis Vuitton Cup.

"We are only able to be here," he said, "because we had a team that were prepared to make a lot of sacrifices. We certainly wish we were going a little further but we also are very aware that in a short time, with a very small budget, we have come a long way.

"I'm not sure how we can help but we will now put all our support behind the Team New Zealand effort. Anything we can do to help them win the America's Cup we are happy to do. Whatever we have they are welcome to."

It was a classy gesture by a guy who, because of political and fundraising concerns, had once been fairly negative towards me and Team New Zealand.

The official results for the semi-finals show Team New Zealand with nine wins and three DNS (did not start), oneAustralia with seven wins and one DNS, Tag Heuer with six wins and one DNS, and Nippon with no wins and one DNS. It's difficult to explain the total collapse of Nippon. They gave us some of the most competitive races we had in the round robins, but the changes they made for the semi-finals obviously didn't work.

NZL-32 was clearly the dominant boat and that was the dilemma the Australians were facing going into the finals. They knew they had to make radical changes, to take some big risks. Their boat as it was simply could not withstand the onslaught of either of the *Black Magics*. That had been proven in every race since January and was painfully evident in the race in which they led by more than a minute and we came back to pass them as if they were sailing backwards.

So they had to gamble and reconfigure their boat. One advantage was that they now faced only one boat. They could therefore choose to optimise their yacht for extreme conditions, either lighter than the expected winds or stronger. Then, if they were lucky, they could get more days that were unusual and therefore be competitive. It wouldn't matter that they would lose big on the other days. A loss is a loss.

In many ways, this is what happened to *KZ-7* in Fremantle. Dennis Conner optimised for the extreme windy conditions, knowing that he couldn't beat the Kiwis across the wind range. Fortunately for him, it was the windiest February on record for Fremantle!

As we suspected, the Australians put their boat into the shed and began major work.

Two years before the Cup, in May of 1993, the Cup organising bodies, including the Challenger of Record Committee, signed what was officially known as the Common Declaration Decree, but was more popularly called the "Reveal Your Keel Day" document. It established April 9, 1995, as the day all Cup syndicates still involved in competition would put their boats on public display, with all keels, bulbs and wings visible for all to see. The powers that be made a lot of lofty comments about levelling the playing field and making the Cup more accessible to the public; from our perspective, it was hard to see this as anything more than a publicity stunt.

The mystique of the Australians' winged keel from more than a decade earlier was still with us, and it is true the public does like to speculate on what they can't see. Just how much interest the unveiling generated is debatable, but I will say there were some pretty large crowds at the compounds I visited and I admit to plenty of interest on my part.

I went to see all three American boats and *oneAustralia* with Tom Schnackenberg and a couple of other guys. I was most impressed by how differently each of the five syndicates approached the underwater appendage design puzzle. Yes, there were some apparent similarities, but it would be a stretch to say any two boats looked very much the same under the hull. Considering size, shape and placement of the major components of keel stem, keel, bulb, wings, trim tab and rudder, it's fair to say that the five teams went in five different directions.

The last compound we visited – oneAustralia – held the most interest for us. When the boat was uncovered, the result was a longer waterline hull, by several feet. A new bulb was added which was quite long and aggressively "squashed", both for upwind performance and for added stability. They had large wings, again for upwind performance, and a new, larger rudder for additional manoeuvrability. They had reduced sail area as a trade off for their additional length and had made changes to their rig, adopting a lot of the black boats' philosophies.

The changes all seemed sensible to us, given the Australians' predicament. The alterations seemed to be aimed at improving the boat's upwind performance and, because the boat was wider, they apparently hoped for a better performance in stronger winds.

Among the defenders, the most interesting feature I remember was the enormous rudder on the America[3] boat, *Mighty Mary*. The boat had been named after syndicate head Bill Koch's mother, who was reportedly quite a sportswoman in her own right. The boat's bulb was relatively short and other features signalled a focus on the downwind legs. The rudder to the contrary was very large and full-depth! It appeared to us that by going with the full-depth rudder, they were trying to distribute lift between the rudder and fin to reduce drag, but, with the type of bulb they had, it didn't quite add up to us. Other components seemed to indicate the America[3] designers and the Team New Zealand designers shared similar concepts.

But the rudder was the feature that stood out the most. It was absolutely huge and shaped like the rudder used by the Italians in 1992. As we were walking out of the compound, we encountered Buddy Melges, the great sailor who had spent the majority of time behind the wheel of the winning boat in the 1992 Cup. Buddy has an electric personality, always plugged into humour.

"Hey Buddy," we asked him, "did you design the rudder?"

"Yeah, sure did," he answered. "I had a dream about it one night and I woke up stuck to the sheets."

His allusion was pretty much how the rudder appeared to us as well.

The Pact 95 boat had its wings in the middle of the keel, and a dip on the top of the bulb. The concept behind the hollow area at the top of the bulb stems from wave effect caused by the intersection of the bulb and the fin. Both are curved surfaces, and if you can smooth out that intersection by producing a trough, theoretically you can reduce the interference effects of the intersection. The boat's design and construction seemed to us to be exceptionally well planned and executed. We felt that if we were to meet up with *Young America* in the Cup, we'd have a good match on our hands.

As I walked into the Team Dennis Conner compound with Brad Butterworth, he turned to me and said, "Listen to this, Dennis will bag the designers."

I had to laugh because, sure enough, Dennis was saying, "You'll notice that, of all the boats unveiled today, *Stars & Stripes* has much more topside flare than all the others. I guess the way to look at it is there are four right and one wrong or one right and four wrong." We concluded that Dennis wasn't overly happy with the design of his yacht.

Stars & Stripes also had the dip at the top of the bulb, but whereas *Young America*'s bulb was long and skinny, this one was short and fat. The wings looked like they'd just sort of been tagged on to the back of the bulb. The rudder was small. We felt the hull shape looked quite nice, but the detailing on the yacht looked pretty rough.

Why, you might ask, were there three defenders on display. That's a question we asked as well. The answer to it is that the organising committee for the defenders decided to allow three boats into the originally scheduled two-boat final. It was a perplexing solution to a rash of protests the three syndicates had filed against each other towards the end of their semi-finals.

At that stage, Pact 95 had secured a spot in the finals and Team Dennis Conner and America[3] were still shooting it out for the remaining slot. The women had now been joined by a man, tactician Dave Dellenbaugh, the starting helmsman and tactician from the 1992 team. The press had a field day with that move, calling the team "*Mighty Mary* . . . and Joseph", "the almost all-women's team" and "the mostly women's team". They called Dave "the bearded lady". Whatever they were called, they had improved their performance and were beginning to sail their new boat to her potential, pushing Dennis hard.

On the eve of the final race to determine whether *Stars & Stripes* or *Mighty Mary* would advance, the three defenders held a secret late-night meeting in which they devised the three-boat-in-the-finals plan. The plan was accepted by the organising committee before what would have been the determining race. The women put their hearts into the race, won it, and believed they had earned the right to meet Pact 95. Bill Koch had not told them of the deal. When they found out, they were understandably crushed.

The deal was incomprehensible to us and almost everyone else. Newspaper and magazine editorials shouted foul, decrying the changing of the rules mid-contest. The entire incident left a black eye on the event, providing fodder for critics who called the regatta a business deal more than a sporting event.

While we were amazed and irritated by the development, there was nothing we could do. The defenders ran their side of things and they could do anything they wanted in the name of finding the best boat and team to defend the America's Cup.

The reasoning from the three syndicates was amusing. John Marshall from Pact went into a long, involved explanation about how their mathematicians and scientists had calculated that letting Dennis back in actually increased their odds of winning. America³ gave a shorter explanation but basically said the same thing. Then Dennis responded, tongue in cheek, that, after his mathematicians had looked at it, they realised that he was better off alive than dead!

The first race of the Louis Vuitton Cup finals was sailed on April 11.

We brought *Black Magic I* onto the race course to meet the radically altered *oneAustralia* with some significant changes of our own. New sails, new wings, changes to the rig and a few other changes would bring us more speed, we hoped. Our changes to the boat since she was launched in Auckland so many months before didn't include changing her waterline, but they were perhaps as extensive over that period as *oneAustralia*'s were over the past 10 days. The difference was that our changes were the result of a planned programme, each one proven after a great many tests. The Australians, forced into accelerated action by disaster and circumstance, had to rely solely on the calculations and predictions of their designers.

To judge the success of the Aussies' modifications by the results of the first race is misleading. The fact that our victory is recorded at almost five minutes, the largest margin ever over *oneAustralia*, does not accurately reflect the destruction of two Aussie spinnakers on the final run. Still, *Black Magic* performed outstandingly well again and we gained on the Australians on all six legs.

The strategy of avoiding the tight circling and positioning ourselves for the side we wanted served us well. Winning the start wasn't our priority, and while we crossed the line after our opponent, we were about 100 metres to windward and sailing at full speed. When the wind gradually shifted 25 degrees in our favour, our positioning strategy proved useful and the race developed into a non-event.

The story of race one is best told in the speed differentials of the two boats. Statistics don't tell the whole story; then again, numbers don't lie. On the three upwind legs, our averages speeds were 6.01, 5.21 and 5.65 knots; those for the Australians 5.86, 5.11 and 5.56. The leeward legs were (with *oneAustralia*'s speeds in parentheses): 9.31 (9.18), 8.91 (8.74) and 8.97 (8.07). We simply ran away from them.

Races two and three were more of the same. With a victory of just under two minutes in race two and 2:26 in race three, we knew we had the Aussies on the ropes. Our upwind speed was just too superior and, with new downwind sails, our performance in that area was equally dominant.

It was after race two that Rod Davis exclaimed, "Our whole goal is to take a race off them. We won't go down without trying a knockout punch here. We'll just keep swinging and see where we end up."

Our strategy remained to be conservative in the starts, go for position rather than attempt to win the start outright, and then get to the side of the course we felt was favoured. Rod's statement confirmed what we thought was their only hope – gain a penalty on us at the start or even go for a collision.

Race four has been described at the beginning of this book. I stuffed up the start and although we had recovered from similar problems over the past four months, the Australians were not going to let us back in the race today. They sailed as near perfect a race as could be sailed and all we could say at the end was full marks to them.

Flush with their success at the starting line, *oneAustralia*'s brains trust had decided to make winning the start a high priority. Perhaps too much pressure was on Rod because he made an unforced error, crossing the line a full seven seconds before the gun, and by the time he re-crossed, we already had a half-minute jump on him. A little more than two hours later we won by almost four minutes.

The score was now 4–1 in our favour, meaning we needed just one more victory to advance to the America's Cup match. To be honest, we had anticipated that situation for quite some time, particularly after we won the first race in the finals against oneAustralia's re-worked yacht. In truth, we began paying a great deal of attention to what was happening on the defender's course.

You'll remember the Americans decided to race three boats in their two-boat final. I guess they were absent from school the day addition was taught. And it seems the folk at Pact 95 must have been absent through the entire semester of their logic courses. Pact 95 had established the best record through the round robins and semi-finals. They were in the driver's seat with what appeared the fastest boat and a strong sailing team. Before they consented to "The Deal", all they had to do was sit back and wait to see who would win the last race between Team Dennis Conner and America[3], secure in the knowledge they had beaten both teams with some consistency.

For reasons never explained, or at least never understood by me, Pact 95 chose to allow both boats into the finals in return for two bonus points. In a move that was obviously made to give the defender team sponsors' additional visibility, the finals became a 12-race round robin, just like the semi-finals. The winner of "the race of the century", as the final race between the mostly women team and Team Dennis Conner was billed, would receive one bonus point.

Pact 95 fell apart in the final series and the question of who would advance once again came down to a race between *Stars & Stripes* and *Mighty*

Mary. It is a race that will go down in yachting history as one of the most incredible comebacks ever. *Mighty Mary's* crew had outsailed the men on *Stars & Stripes* by so much that it was hard to believe. Each leg they pulled out more and more distance until they rounded the last mark with a seemingly insurmountable lead of some 44 lengths.

But in one of the most bizarre finishes ever witnessed, perhaps fitting for the eccentric way the defenders chose to run their regatta, *Stars & Stripes* rounded the mark and headed to the left side of the course while *Mighty Mary's* crew found themselves on the right side in a dying breeze. When the wind regained strength, it did so from the area of the course *Stars & Stripes* was sailing. They brought the wind down the leg with them and by the time the boat and the wind found *Mighty Mary*, the America³ team had lost their lead. I heard that as the guys on *Stars & Stripes* pulled alongside the Cubettes, genoa trimmer Steve Erickson called across the water to them, using his best Jack Nicholson impression, "Hi girls . . . we're back."

"Mr America's Cup" had pulled off his most incredible victory. The "comeback kid" had done it again.

So, once again, for the third time in the past four America's Cups, New Zealand would race Dennis Conner. In 1987 it was *Kiwi Magic* versus *Stars & Stripes*. In 1988 it was the big boat mismatched against the catamaran. In 1995 it would be *Black Magic* and *Stars & Stripes* racing for the America's Cup. At least, that's what we thought after Dennis had pulled his rabbit out of the hat. But we soon discovered there were still more surprises in store.

13

Clean Sweep

Winning the Louis Vuitton Cup was a special accomplishment for all of us, but it was only part of our overall goal. As Blakie had said throughout the campaign, winning the challenger trials wasn't what we were in San Diego for. The only reason we had travelled more than 7000 miles was to win the America's Cup. Anything less would be considered falling short of our goal.

It must have been a great disappointment to the oneAustralia team not to have advanced to the Cup match. They had come to San Diego as the pre-regatta favourite; filled with confidence. The dramatic loss of their boat was, of course, a huge setback, but the way they battled back from extreme adversity was impressive. Full marks to them. All of Team New Zealand felt the Aussies showed the world their mettle when they reworked their old boat, sailed near flawlessly, and advanced from the Louis Vuitton Cup semi-finals to the finals. I've always felt they improved in each race of the finals and had they made the same changes to the boat earlier, they would have been a great deal more competitive.

The question is often asked whether oneAustralia would have been able to beat us in the finals had *AUS-34* not sunk. While *34* was a faster boat than *31*, I don't think it was as good as *NZL-32*. And since their new boat was never able to beat *NZL-38*, which we considered to be our slower boat, it's difficult to make a case for their *34* beating our *32*. However, I do think that if the boat hadn't sunk and they had made the changes to it they made to their older boat, the finals would have been a great deal closer than they were.

Despite what must have been an emotional time for them, the oneAustralia team displayed true sportsmanship in word and deed following our last race. They saluted us on the water and as we brought our boats into the Southwestern Yacht Club immediately after the race for the Louis Vuitton Cup presentation, they came aboard *Black Magic* and congratulated us man to man.

During the ceremony, Craig Monk got hold of me and tossed me into the water, the traditional celebratory salute following a regatta victory. It was one of the most enjoyable dunkings I've ever had!

Although champagne corks popped and there was a good deal of partying going on among the spectators, we approached the celebrations in a fairly low key manner. Winning the Louis Vuitton Cup was nice, but it wasn't the reason we were in California.

At the press conference following the presentation, there were thanks and congratulations from many of the officials and sponsors who had played key roles over the previous four months. All the good words were appreciated, but perhaps John Bertrand's meant the most to our entire team. He had been in our position 12 years earlier and he knew exactly what it took to get there.

"Team New Zealand put together a fabulous campaign," said the oneAustralia leader. "Their attention to detail from the windex to the bottom of the keel throughout their sailing programme has been excellent. I think the opportunity for the challenger to win the America's Cup is very strong. The Americans will lift their game, but if you talk about pure boatspeed, then Team New Zealand would win the America's Cup tomorrow."

It was during this press conference that a reporter observed that we didn't seem too overjoyed. He said he didn't see any high-fives, hadn't heard any great shouts of exultation. This subject had come up before and we tried to explain that this isn't really the Kiwi way, but the American press made a big deal out of what they saw as our indifference to victory.

Of course, within Team New Zealand, we took all the flutter about this as total nonsense. I remember early in the round robins we were asked why we never high-fived. The next day, Joe Allen and Murray Jones started high-fiving at every opportunity they could find.

"Great hoist, mate," said Joe with his hand in the air.

"Couldn't have done it without you," said Murray, slapping his hand.

"Boat's moving well," ventured Murray, a few moments later, raising his hand.

"Very well," confirmed Joe, slapping the offered hand.

"Beautiful day." Slap, slap.

It was all done in humour, but we got the point early on. The two kept it up throughout the race until we crossed the finish line and Matthew Mason had heard enough. "That's it, you guys, you're going in."

Over the rail went both Joe and Murray, thrown in by most of the crew. It was then and there established that if you do the high-five, you're going to get deep-sixed.

The local paper, the *San Diego Union-Tribune*, ran a piece a few days before the Cup match trying to explain "the Kiwi way" to their readers. It generated a great deal of laughter inside the Team New Zealand compound.

The article pointed out that when *Stars & Stripes* crossed the finish line in front of *Mighty Mary* to win the Citizen Cup finals, the American crew "exploded in roars and hugs and high-fives and high-tens." The reporter asked Schnack to explain the difference in behaviour. "There are cultural differences," said Tom. "Americans typically are up front and direct. New Zealanders have a funny set of restraints, so more can be said with less. Somebody wrote a book once called *The Passionless People*, which said we were too withdrawn. But it's a young country, built with people whose roots were in farming, and a farmer's life is a lonely one. He whistles at his dog and growls at his wife."

Peter Blake alluded to a dog in his analysis of the Kiwi character on Team New Zealand. The reporter wanted to know why he kept hearing that the entire team was responsible for our success. "Why go out and get expertise and not use it?" asked Blakie. "There's no point in having a dog and barking yourself."

Whether the American reporters ever felt they understood us I'm not sure, but I do know the American public seemed to embrace us. Even though the problems of the past two Cups held in San Diego had not been completely forgotten and even though we were racing the home town boy representing the home town yacht club, we were treated very well from the day we arrived. If there had been any animosity between San Diego Yacht Club members and New Zealand officials, it was never mentioned. The SDYC membership seemed to go out of their way to extend us every courtesy. I guess the many controversies and problems that descended upon the club and the city with the winning of the America's Cup had been a strain on their good nature. We often got the feeling they'd be happy to see the trophy go.

Because the challenger finals were completed a few days before the defenders had finished, at that point we did not know who we would race in the America's Cup match. While publicly Team New Zealand claimed indifference to who we wanted to race, I'm sure we didn't fool anyone. "Dirty Den", as he was dubbed in the New Zealand press after his "cheating" comment of 1987, was the man every red-blooded Kiwi wanted to see opposite us on the race course. While I understand the New Zealand public was overjoyed when it turned out we all got our wish, in San Diego we played it down. But all of us on Team New Zealand knew what meeting, and beating, Dennis would mean to our national psyche.

But Dennis wasn't the only villain in the eyes of many New Zealanders back home. We expected to see Paul Cayard at the wheel, the same man who three years earlier had been behind the wheel of the Italian challenger, *Il Moro di Venezia*. The same man who, after going 4–1 down to New Zealand in the finals of the Louis Vuitton Cup, had taken the bowsprit issue to the jury room and won the infamous annulment decision. Conner and Cayard were the perfect duo to do battle with as far as most Kiwis were concerned.

It's true there were probably a few hard feelings left over from 1987, '88 and '92 but, for the most part, I think a lot of that was dredged up by the press to fill column inches. Some of our guys aboard *Black Magic* had raced with Dennis on the Whitbread and considered him a friend and a great sailor. Cayard had fought hard for what he considered right in 1992 and I don't think any of us around Team New Zealand felt he'd done anything untoward. The fact is, we had a great deal of respect for both Dennis and Paul.

It's hard not to. In 1995, Dennis was involved in his seventh America's Cup, the veteran of all time. Cayard was racing in his fourth Cup. Dennis has almost single-handedly changed the face of the modern America's Cup. Before he began running campaigns, there was no such thing as a two-boat test programme. Before he brought his intensity to the game, teams generally met a month or two before the event and practised a bit here and there. A one- or two-year sailing programme was unheard of, yet these are now staples of almost all defender and challenger campaigns.

None of us took Dennis and Paul or any of the American sailors for granted. We knew they would come to the starting line with the skills, expertise and experience of champions. They would also be very confident.

But knowing the sailors and knowing the boat were two different things. The great mystery of the America's Cup match is that no one really knows how the challenger and defender boats compare. Four months of racing against different opponents on different courses under sometimes very different conditions doesn't throw a great deal of light on how they'll match up against each other.

In this America's Cup we did, at least, have the opportunity to inspect each other's boats during the "Reveal Your Keel" day. Comparatively speaking, it seemed from the keels and appendages of each of the defenders we saw, and for example, from the position and angle of their wings, they were geared more for the downwind legs than we were.

It was an interesting difference. When considering how to mode an IACC boat, there are perhaps three major parts of the race that concern the designers, builders and sailors: pre-start, upwind legs and downwind legs. Statistically, in a match race the boat that wins the start usually controls the upwind leg. That advantage changes to the trailing, or attacking, boat on the downwind leg because of the tactic of blocking the wind of the leading boat. But that tactic only works if the trailing boat is close enough to make it work. Thus, logic would indicate that the faster you are on the upwind leg, the better off you're going to be.

In fact, at the end of both the Louis Vuitton and Citizen Cups, statistics were published that showed 86 percent of the boats rounding the first mark ahead won the race. It was no secret that we concentrated on upwind performance, so, on paper at least, it seemed like the challenger and the defender were bringing opposing philosophies to the race course.

So while we had a sense of the American sailors, we had little more than speculation about their boat on which to base any kind of a game plan. And all of that speculation changed radically when it was announced that Dennis had worked yet another deal. This time, he was going to abandon *Stars & Stripes*, the boat that got him into the America's Cup match, and he would sail Pact 95's *Young America* against us.

This didn't come as a total surprise to us. The ground work had begun to be laid by America's Cup '95, the event organiser, back in March. In years past, the challengers were required to declare which boat they would race before the trials began while the defender was afforded the luxury, and the great advantage, of waiting until the first day of the America's Cup match. Part of the reason for the common declaration date of April 9 was to level the playing field.

But the issue arose in early March when officials from America's Cup '95 informed Ernie Taylor, chief executive of the Challenger of Record Committee, that their interpretation of the common declaration agreement allowed them to select any boat competing in the defender finals they felt would prove the best boat to defend the America's Cup. Incensed, Taylor called the officials "cheaters and liars".

The defender interpretation was based on the fact that each challenger syndicate represented a different yacht club while each of the defender teams represented the San Diego Yacht Club. Therefore, to their way of thinking, the SDYC could choose whichever boat they wanted and still comply with the agreement, which read, in part, ". . . Yachts selected to compete in the America's Cup XXIX Match will be selected from those competing in the Final Series."

Taylor's answer to that was, "It was obvious to us that if we are to choose yachts, they will be the winners of the finals, even if it wasn't stated. Throughout the world, the winner of a final plays in the grand final. Only in San Diego is that different."

When we first heard about the boat switch, our official reaction was to remain silent until we were able to gather all the facts. We eventually asked the America's Cup Trustees Committee to rule on the legality of the switch and their decision was unanimous that it was legal.

Dennis had said that there was no way *Stars & Stripes* could beat *Black Magic*. We weren't going to argue with him, but it did seem to us his reasoning was somewhat questionable. *Stars & Stripes* had outperformed *Young America* in the Citizen Cup finals. The boat had also beaten *Mighty Mary*. While Dennis said this was a result of how well his crew had performed, we knew no matter how good a group of sailors you have, you can't make a slow yacht consistently outperform a faster boat. And no matter how good the men of Team Dennis Conner were, and we knew they were the most experienced Cup crew in San Diego, they would be racing a boat new to them and different from the boat they'd been on for four months. But it was Dennis' decision, he made it, the trustees had legitimised it, and that was that.

Now we knew we would be racing Dennis and Paul and "the Mermaid".

That knowledge didn't change anything around our compound. It was too late in the game to try to change things in reaction to our opponent. What we did do was continue with our two-boat testing programme and it paid off in a very dramatic way. We made the biggest leap in performance between the end of the Louis Vuitton Cup finals and the beginning of the America's Cup match that we had made during the entire time in San Diego.

Testing a concept that had been suggested several months previously, we discovered we had gained about a length-and-a-half in a 10-minute test. The changes we made mostly involved the appendages, but there were also improvements to the sails which played a significant part in our improvement.

You might think that after four months of racing, a boatload of very experienced sailors who have raced all around the world would be pretty used to making our way out to the race course once again. But I recall that on May 6, 1995, the morning of the first race of America's Cup XXIX, there was an electric excitement flowing through Team New Zealand.

As I arrived at the compound that morning, I noticed stacks of faxes, letters and telegrams, all wishing us good luck. The phone never stopped ringing. Crowds of spectators, many wearing the trademark red socks, gathered outside our docks and yelled encouragement. We knew that as many as a dozen planeloads of Kiwis had arrived in the past few days.

No, this wasn't your typical race day. This was why we were here. This was what we had planned for, worked for, waited for, for more than two years . . . this is what all of New Zealand had waited for since that day in 1984 when a small group got together and asked each other if there was any possibility our little nation could put together an America's Cup team.

On the tow out, we passed shore fronts lined with cheering people. All around us were boats headed for the race course. Overhead a plane flew by us streaming a banner behind reading: "Take it home, *Black Magic*, *NZL-32*." Boats loaded with New Zealand flags raced by us. Others had large cardboard cutouts of the kiwi pasted to their hulls. Everywhere we looked, we saw thousands of people waiting to witness this first race, waiting to see who had got it right.

Aside from excitement, we felt well prepared. We thought we had the boat at its fastest and, despite our 37–1 record compared with our opponent's 20 – 17 score, we were not overconfident. There were still enough memories of what happened in Fremantle against Dennis, when New Zealand had a similar record, to keep us in check.

When we got to the race course, the scene was unbelievable. Boats everywhere, horns blasting greetings and support, news and television helicopters circling above, press boats filled with photographers and cameramen circling us on the water.

Simon and I have long had a saying between us, whether we're in a great race or at an unusual social event or at a Rolling Stones concert. "Where would you rather be right now?" When the answer comes back "Nowhere," there's a good chance you are in the right place at the right time.

Looking around at the scene, checking out the wind, at that point registering about 15–17 knots, I said to the guys "Look at this scene, where would you rather be right now?" The question didn't need to be answered. There was no doubt in my mind that this is exactly where everyone wanted to be, exactly where I wanted to be.

My only concern was that the boat was pounding in pretty steep waves. The possibility of gear failure was high. We had a brand new heavy-air mainsail on board; when the breeze began blowing 17 knots, we changed to it. Having the sail on board was another indication of how prepared we were. This sail was designed to handle winds above 25 knots and although the boats certainly shouldn't be racing in that type of wind, we didn't know what we could expect from this race committee. We were no longer dealing with the challenger officials. The people running the America's Cup races were officials of the San Diego Yacht Club and their representative was our opponent.

The wind gusted to about 19 knots a few times well before the start of the race, but then dropped to below 15 and we changed back to our original main. I steered for the growing spectator fleet to sense some of the atmosphere and to get used to our surroundings. We were cheered everywhere we went, by the Kiwi faithful and Americans as well.

It was something of an odd sensation to find support from the Americans. I think some of it was a reaction to the controversy the Cup had brought to town coupled with the skulduggery of the defender series. The three boats in the two-boat finals had caused a great deal of consternation to the sport's observers and many American publications editorialised that such shenanigans were ruining the event.

We had drawn the port end of the line to enter the starting box, and, in this type of stiff breeze, I began thinking, "This isn't perfect." In a chop like we found ourselves in, our boat did not manoeuvre well and I thought we had to avoid downspeed tacking if we could. I was wondering if Cayard would try to dial us up at the start and try to push us into a downspeed situation.

I went through the pre-start for perhaps the twentieth time in my mind. Bob Rice and his team had told us that shortly after the start we should be prepared for the wind to move right. At this point, we never even thought about getting a second opinion. Bob and the gang had been spot on in almost every race we'd had, particularly over the past two months. There was just no question; if he said move right my only response was "how far?"

So we wanted to come off the start line to the right of the Americans and then go right when the breeze dictated. Being on port was okay, as long as we could get to the right without their using their starboard advantage to block us.

As we entered the starting area, we sailed past them and I noticed Paul behind the wheel staring at us as if he were in a trance. It was an unusual moment, one I can neither describe nor explain. I'm not sure if he was trying to psych us out or if he was psyched out by us. Rick Dodson was also surprised by the unusual behaviour and gave him something of a stare back.

I gave a slight wave as if to say "Isn't this great, the first race of the America's Cup," but there was no reaction. He just kept staring. But there was no time to give the snapshot much thought.

We circled a little bit, but avoided any tight manoeuvring. Dennis and his team had never raced this boat and they were playing it somewhat conservatively. When the gun went off, we had managed to get to the right of them and to windward, but we were closer to them than we wanted to be. We were a little further behind the line than them but, all in all, happy with the start. Starting so close to them in a windward position, we were expecting to be forced to tack off to the right. But the wind had already gone right a little and we decided to wait for a short time.

In less than a minute, the breeze started clocking further right, just as we'd been told. We went with it as did *Young America*. The two boats were sailing at about the same speed, but it was already evident we were sailing higher. Schnack looked under the boom and said, "Boy, this is going to be a quick America's Cup."

The wind shifted between 15 and 20 degrees in our favour and we began to stretch out a lead. But then the breeze settled down, so did the Americans, and they were going along just fine. Schnack took another range reading and said, "Well, maybe not as quick as I thought."

We got to the first mark in the lead by 31 seconds. As expected, our upwind speed had served us well once again. But we suspected we were racing a boat that had been set up for downwind speed. We were now about to see how successful she was.

We noticed immediately that there was a huge difference in the type and shape of spinnakers flying on the two boats. As we sailed down the first run, *Young America* came at us like a freight train. She kept coming and coming, closer and closer. I began thinking this could be a real concern. If they could keep close to us on the upwind legs, they would definitely threaten us downwind, and the final leg on the course was downwind.

As we approached the mark, we had trouble with the spinnaker pole during a couple of gybes. That may have left an opening for *Young America*. I started thinking this is not the time to be having spinnaker problems as we try to protect an inside overlap, coming into the bottom mark.

But a little luck came our way and we opened up just a little breathing space to get around the mark a couple of boat lengths in the lead. Our 31-second lead had been reduced to 12 seconds. We'd have to put together a good weather leg to stretch out enough so the next run wouldn't damage us too badly.

And then it all came together. All the work, all the testing, all the guessing, all our confidence in the boat. The breeze died a bit to come into the range in which *Black Magic* performed best, and we simply sailed away with the leg and the race. At the second windward mark we were 42 seconds ahead and then we gained on each following leg to win by 2:45. It was a tremendous performance.

Not too much was said on board as we crossed the line. There were some "well dones" and we shook hands, but we knew we needed four more wins to take possession of "the Auld Mug". But if we weren't saying much, after what had just happened, I doubt there was anyone on board *Black Magic* who didn't know in his heart of hearts that we were going to win this regatta. It was simple and it had just been proven: we had the faster boat.

Following the race the opposing camp made a few statements to the effect that they were hoping for lighter breezes and smoother seas. But when they made the switch from *Stars & Stripes* to *Young America*, they had said they had done so specifically because the Pact 95 boat was a stronger performer in the type of conditions we encountered in the first race.

The results of the race had to be extremely discouraging to the Americans. They obviously believed *Young America* was a better boat than the one which had got them to the dance, but once inside the party they had discovered not much more than the make-up was different on their new date. But with only six days to get to know her, we wondered how they could expect much more.

The press had reported that the Americans were having some trouble getting used to the new boat. It wasn't set up the same as *Stars & Stripes*; the boat was narrower, the boom was lower and the winches were in different places were only a few of the differences.

"It was a tough day when you really needed to know your boat," Paul Cayard was quoted as saying. "It was like two races in one. The first two legs it was really close and I thought, 'Terrific, it's going to be a great series.' Then the rest was a blowout. I saw some reasons why they got ahead, but I also saw some Kiwi speed. Maybe they were nervous in the beginning and then finally got it rolling."

Well, maybe. But maybe we just had a boat that sailed even faster once the conditions changed in the latter half of that race.

The following day was a scheduled lay day during which both teams were back on the ocean, testing. Race two was on a Monday, and the Americans left their dock in their new and different boat, with new and different uniforms to new and different send-off music. Dennis was big on thematic music. He loved the theme from the movie *Top Gun*, and in the days of the semi-finals and finals of the Citizen Cup, when he was clawing away to stay in the game, the send-off music was the Bee Gees' "Staying Alive".

This morning the tune wafting across San Diego Harbour was "I Still Believe". Apparently the new uniforms, white in colour instead of their traditional navy blue, were the result of a last-minute order that was filled incorrectly.

Neither the boat nor the uniforms nor the music made much difference. Nor did Dennis Conner taking over the wheel about two-thirds through the race. *Black Magic* was simply devastating. Perhaps our boat took exception to the Americans saying they were waiting for better conditions to do well, apparently the hopes of our opponent didn't sit well in either case. We were behind at the start, but Bob Rice and his team had once more given us the right weather information and, after catching the first shift to the right, we took the lead, added to it, and put together an incredible 4:14 thrashing of the boat that was claimed to do better in lighter and smoother conditions – just what was on the course today. We crossed the finish line some 42 lengths in front of the Americans. It was the worst defeat of a defender since 1871, when Britain's *Livonia* beat the US yacht *Columbia* by 15:10.

I don't suppose there was anyone who had observed the first two races of the 1995 America's Cup match who held out much hope for the defenders – there didn't even seem to be much hope among the defending team itself. Following the race, their navigator, Jim Brady, said at the press conference, "We thought we sailed the boat pretty close to its potential today."

Bill Trenkle, Dennis Conner's long-time operations manager, was quoted in a local paper as saying: "That was hard for our guys. We're not used to that kind of a stomping."

Paul Cayard was already thinking about the next America's Cup and looking towards the South Pacific. In an interview with Angus Phillips of the *Washington Post*, the American helmsman said: "Change is always good. The Kiwis have been at the top of the sport for ten years. They've won the Admiral's Cup and they've been at the top of this event. So it was long overdue for them to get into the Cup match. They'd be great hosts, very enthusiastic. The venue probably will be more exciting, with more variable weather conditions."

Inside our compound we were happy to read comments like these, but no one had handed us the trophy yet. If we were to prove Paul correct and be great hosts four and five years down the track, we had to win three more races.

It was apparent at the start of race three that the two teams had different views of where the better wind and wind shifts would be. We took the right side, they took the left and we crossed the line on split tacks. Almost immediately upon crossing, the wind came our way and so did *Young America*, quickly realising their mistake. At the first cross we tacked with our stern just clearing their bow, prompting them to raise a penalty flag claiming we had tacked too close. The on-the-water umpires didn't agree, signalling with a green flag that no rule had been infringed.

A short tacking duel followed until we decided to go for straight-line speed. I asked, "Which way do you want to break out of this guys?"

"Protect the right," was the call from Murray. I turned the wheel, pulled out of the duel, and drove straight up the course. We thought *Young America* might have been a little quicker in manoeuvring and we didn't want to be caught in a downspeed situation. The first two races had proven our boatspeed superior, so why play their game?

We turned the first mark ahead by 20 seconds and headed for the left side of the course. Cayard then rounded and ran to the right side. If we were racing by the book, we would have gybed over and covered them but in light, shifting winds, that strategy can be more risky than not covering at all. Murray and Rick were discussing the situation, watching the Americans, talking to me, looking back at our opponent, talking to each other. At this stage in the regatta, I had total confidence in the afterguard. I concentrated on steering the boat fast and following their advice on when to turn and where to take the boat.

"I like our chances on the left better," I heard one of them say.

"Me, too. If we gybe back at them now we will be out of phase. It's safe to keep on this course."

Some may have considered our tactics something of a gamble, but the decision paid off. We added a full minute to our lead and they never got closer. Race three to the Kiwis by 1:51. Two to go.

After the first two races, the papers were filled with speculation about whether Dennis made the right decision in changing boats. That story was getting old, but Tom Whidden threw some humour into the discussion after being asked at the press conference what they could do to stop us. With a straight face, the American tactician, one of the best in the world, answered: "I think the two big improvements made in the rules this time are that there are nine races instead of seven, which should work to our advantage. And the second rule is the one which says the defenders and challengers swap boats after every third race."

For a moment the room went silent while the press wondered how they could have missed this new dictum. Then the joke was realised and the room burst into laughter. Tom, still with a straight face, asked: "Oh, did I get that wrong?"

As the laughter died, I couldn't resist. I leaned into the microphone and asked a question of my own: "Don't you think you guys have swapped boats enough?"

That brought forth another round of laughter. Unique within the world of sports, press conferences at the America's Cup and on the match-racing circuit always have representatives of all teams on a single dais at the same time. In other sports, it's rare that two tennis players are in front of the same camera at the same time or two rugby coaches face each other in the press room. Our interviews almost always generate a provocative comment or some revelation or good humour, even in the face of defeat. Tom's wit was appreciated.

Race four may have exemplified the skills of Team New Zealand better than any of the previous 41 races we had entered during 1995. The routine of checking every piece of equipment before we left the dock had kept us relatively free of gear breakage. Our pre-race strategy meetings helped all of us understand what we would try to do out on the race course. The weather team, at this point, was close to being deified in all our eyes and we unquestionably followed their every word of advice.

So, in those respects, race four was not unlike all those that had come before. But it was a particular incident that illustrated to me why our afterguard was the best in the business and I attribute a large portion of our victory to them. *Young America* could have and probably should have led the race at the first mark.

We came off the starting line and went left. Our weather intelligence had predicted a shift to the left and we wanted to be in position to take advantage of it. It did indeed occur, but five minutes after it was predicted to do so. As we sailed further and further out towards the layline, the breeze was clocking more and more to the right, giving *Young America* the advantage. For the first time in our series, the Americans crossed ahead of us. This is just what Paul Cayard had been waiting for. Earlier, he had told the press that if he could just get ahead of us on the first leg, he stood a good chance of holding us off for the rest of the race.

While looking at *Young America*'s stern for the first time was new, the attitude remained calm aboard *Black Magic*. We'd followed other boats before and got past. All those experiences did was bring out more confidence in our team and in our boat.

We'd been told the wind would come left, and it did. We were getting closer and closer to the layline and the wind continued to move left but not enough for us to pass *Young America*. We wanted to avoid the situation where we'd get to the layline and they would tack to cover us and build on their lead. So we tacked towards them and the wind lifted us, which was not what we needed. That meant that when they tacked, they'd be in phase with the wind and they would force us out of phase.

That's just what happened. They tacked on top of us, forcing us to tack, and they put some more distance between the two boats. As soon as we got back to speed, we tacked again to take up position on their hip as they were on the favoured course and we didn't want to spend much time on the opposite tack. We needed to keep the race as close as we could. No gambles today.

A minute or so later, they tacked towards us and, just as the two yachts were about to meet, our guys in the cockpit picked up a big breeze on the left-hand side. This was the wind our weather team had predicted.

I turned to the afterguard of Jones, Dodson, Schnackenberg and Butterworth and said, "Now we're really in the cart. They're going to cross us, keep going to the breeze, tack, and they're gonna be gone. What do we do?"

I started thinking maybe we should tack underneath them, which would have kept us close to them but probably behind at the first mark.

"Keep going," I was told. The tactical minds of our strategists agreed with each other and I wasn't about to do anything but follow their advice.

What must have happened was that our guys saw the breeze just as we were approaching *Young America* and they figured the Americans may not have picked it up.

A lot is going on in the cockpit as two boats approach each other. Match racing has often been called a chess game on water in which you have to think several moves ahead. Their conversation on board at the time must have been focused on the impending cross and retaining the starboard tack advantage for the rest of the leg. Had they seen the new wind, the decision would have been easy – keep going.

But that's not what they did. They tacked on us, away from the new pressure, allowing us to immediately tack away towards where we saw the wind. As soon as we tacked, I looked at the afterguard, smiled, and said "We're ahead now." We weren't at that moment but we soon would be. They had made a brilliant call. They had stayed on station looking for breeze. They had not been distracted by what was happening at that very moment in the race. And, they had total trust in the weather team so they knew where to look. We caught the breeze, it lifted us towards the mark, and within minutes we had surged into a four or five boatlength lead. When we got to the mark, we turned with the biggest lead we'd had against *Young America* at that point, 1:09. Race over.

At the press conference the men representing the defenders looked and sounded beaten. Short of some massive catastrophe in which we lost both our boats, no one was believing the Americans could win five races before we won one more. Paul Cayard spoke for the team and probably best expressed their feeling of futility when he said: "I'm not to the point of crying, but I've never been in a race where I felt I had so little control over the outcome. I don't even feel like I'm in a sailboat race."

We knew from similar comments the defenders were reeling. Tom Whidden, who's been with Dennis for more than 20 years and has been calling tactics in America's Cup races longer than anyone, told a reporter: "This race was won five or six months ago. The Kiwis were focused when they arrived here last November and they've stayed at it. We never guessed the entire defence effort was so far off the pace. We can't even engage these guys in a race."

Before the start of the fifth race we had a slight scare when our starboard primary winch decided to go on strike and the Cunningham track pulled off the mast. Shore boss Tim Gurr, alias "the Rat" – who had not been out on the water in his whole time in San Diego – rushed out from the compound to personally make the repairs. As he worked furiously to fix the breakages, Joe Allen and Simon Daubney proceeded to give him a bit of stick. "Ratty, in case you didn't know, that boat over there is the American boat we are racing."

"Shut up you guys."

"And that point over there is Point Loma, and that's Mexico down there . . ."

"Shut up you guys."

"And this here is our America's Cup boat."

"SHUT THE —— UP!"

"Ratty, I was sailing off this coast in *Pendragon*, when you guys were boys, too young to be yachtsmen." *Pendragon* was a famous Laurie Davidson boat that won both the Three-quarter Ton Cup and the One Ton Cup. Joe and Daubs' behaviour did show that the attitude on board wasn't that tense on the final day of the America's Cup. The truth is, the Rat and the rest of the shore team had built a fantastic pair of boats and had detailed them perfectly. Joe, Simon and anyone else chipping in, enjoying giving the Rat some lip, were really saying thank you; proof that Kiwi teams are "culturally different".

This concluding race was not unlike our first encounter. In about 10 knots of wind and sloppy seas, *Young America* stayed close to us on the first upwind leg and we didn't add much on the first run. But then some bad luck for the Americans sent us on our way to collect the Cup. *Young America*'s jib halyard broke and the headsail crashed to the deck. By the time they got back to full speed, we were 59 seconds ahead and impossible to catch. We won the race by

1:50, completing a clean sweep.

This was also the race that Meaty was caught waving at the television monitor positioned just in front of the huge grinder. Daubs' was asking the big man to grind coming into the last mark and when nothing happened he looked over and noticed Meat directing a thumbs-up at the camera. "What the hell are you doing Meaty?" We later discovered that the faithful grinder from all our America's Cup efforts, had devised a hand signal to advise his wife that his lunch had been prepared just how he had wanted it on that last day!!

I've said throughout that statistics don't tell the full story, but perhaps these will give a more definitive picture of just how dominant *Black Magic* was.

Our 5–0 score was the greatest margin of victory in the 144-year history of the America's Cup. The rules were different in 1987 when Dennis Conner won 4–0 as a challenger against Australia, but his average margin of victory per race was 1:39 and he never won a race by more than two minutes. Our average victory in the Cup match was 2:52, with three of the races won by more than two minutes.

Against *Young America*, *Black Magic* led at all 30 marks, gaining time on 25 of the 30 legs. In more than 13 hours of sailing, the black boat followed the Mermaid for less than half an hour. There were only two occasions in the entire series that *Young America* crossed in front of us.

Our 42–1 overall record was the best ever posted by any America's Cup team. Our average margin of victory in all our races was 3:06.

We gained time over the opposition in 77 percent of the 260 legs we raced. We were in the lead on 93 percent of those 260 legs.

We spent approximately $US15 million on our two-boat programme. The three United States syndicates spent some $US55 million.

The population of San Diego county is twice the total population of New Zealand.

Not one member of Team New Zealand left the programme.

And so the fourth time was a charm. Team New Zealand built on what Michael Fay and Chris Dickson and Roy Dickson and Laurent Esquier and Rod Davis and Bruce Farr and David Barnes and a thousand others on board and ashore had done over the past 11 or so years and we accomplished the goal every Kiwi challenge had had since 1984. We did it because of what came before us, because of what collectively we'd learned on the oceans and in the design rooms and tank testing facilities and sail lofts of the world. We did it because we put the team first and we learned to trust each other totally. We did it because we all had a say in what we thought would make the boat go fast. We did it because we'd been to Admiral's Cups and One Ton Cups and dinghy world championships and the Olympics and the match-racing circuit and the Whitbread Round-the-World races and races on Auckland's Waitemata Harbour. We did it because we had an entire nation behind us. And most of all, we did it because two black boats were faster than anything any other nation could come up with.

Pure magic? No. Team magic? Probably. A magic time? Most definitely.

14

Aftermath

While our victory was made all the sweeter by beating Dennis Conner, "Mr America's Cup" was gracious in defeat. It could not have been easy for him to lose the trophy his name has become synonymous with in his own hometown. And yet I believe he viewed our campaign with great respect and had a true appreciation of the hard work and sacrifices made by everyone connected to Team New Zealand. He had to, because he's been through it so many times before.

With tears in his eyes, Dennis told the world, "If the Cup had to leave San Diego, there could be no better home for it than Auckland, New Zealand. It's a just reward, and congratulations to all those who are in New Zealand – you can be justifiably proud of your heroes."

In truth, the days following that final race are pretty much a blur. The media that for so long had wondered if Kiwis ever showed emotion and celebrated got a full dose of just how much this victory meant to us. Champagne flowed for days, the parties never stopped, the celebrations never ended, the noise still rings in my ears.

Immediately following the race, we turned *Black Magic* towards the San Diego Yacht Club where thousands of cheering spectators were waiting to watch the informal transfer of the Cup. All across the waters on which we had raced for almost five months spectator boats blew their horns in a deafening cacophony of congratulations. Our chase boat arrived packed with joyous Kiwis, one of whom was my son Grayson. This was a surprise to me and I was elated. I put him behind the wheel and he looked as if he was in a dream.

Another boat arrived, carrying Bill Koch, head of America³, the 1992 champion. In one of his typical generous gestures, he unloaded several cases of expensive champagne onto the black boat and came aboard to personally shake our hands. I remembered back to our meeting during the very first days of Team New Zealand and to how open he was to share information, particularly his philosophy of team. He came up to me and, speaking about the team, said, "You've taken the America's Cup to a new level." His words meant a lot to me.

By the time we got to the club, we'd made a huge dent in Mr Koch's stores and again what sounded like a million air horns greeted our arrival. Music blared, flags waved, cheers flooded the waters. Soon after we arrived, *Young America*, filled with the sailors and their families and friends and syndicate members, pulled up alongside and the next thing I knew I was swimming, courtesy of Mr Cayard. Blakie was already in the water, and before long most of the crew was wet.

Back on board, we were met by what seemed like most of San Diego, a long parade of former competitors, Cup teams, media reps working and non-working, and a thousand well-wishers.

Then the America's Cup trophy appeared and Peter and I raised it above our heads for all to see. It was an exhilarating moment.

I'm not sure I will ever be able to justly describe the emotions I felt and those I saw on the faces of my teammates. Perhaps Meaty should be called upon once more for a few words of wisdom, this time dead serious. Andrew Taylor had been the only sailor on board *Black Magic* who had sailed aboard every boat entered in the America's Cup by the four New Zealand challenges. His words no doubt echo the sentiments of all the men and women who played a part in each of those challenges.

"Over all these years," said the big man, tears freely rolling down his face, "I never felt like giving up the fight for this Cup. It is great to be bringing it back to a nation which will really appreciate it."

I do recall Blakie and I appearing at the media conference after several hours of celebrating at the San Diego Yacht Club. Peter addressed the over-filled room and, in his typical fashion, laid it straight on the line: "I really can't tell you much of anything because I'm not fit to speak." A champagne-induced grin spread across his face as appreciative laughter met his honesty. Peter was good to his word – he didn't say anything else.

I was in no better shape and people tell me I had a few things to say, none of which made much sense I'm sure and certainly none of which I remember.

I can remember the trip back to our compound in a small rubber raft. We were accompanied by the trophy we had just won, which was in turn accompanied by the guard who had protected it for the past eight years. He didn't take too kindly to our handing it back and forth, drinking fine vintage champagne from it, and holding it over our heads for people on shore to see. I think it was even suggested that we should get Roy Mason to modify the trophy to allow for a greater volume of champagne. Of course we were feeling no pain, but the same could not be said for the guard. He was absolutely terrified.

But we arrived at the compound safe and sound, only to discover thousands more people outside the gates. The one disappointment on the day is that we couldn't let everyone into the compound for our party. It was just physically impossible to accommodate everyone. So there were security guards outside politely attempting to restrain the crowds.

I had stepped outside for a moment to chat with an old university friend and when I appeared at the front gate to get back in, the guard said, "Who are you?"

"Well, I'm a team member," I told him, which brought a round of laughter from the crowd around us.

"No you're not," said the guard. "You're just trying to get in."

"No, I promise you, I'm part of the team," I pleaded.

By now, the scene had attracted a lot of bystanders, all of whom thought this was great fun. One of my fellow teammates yelled "Don't let him in. He's trying to con you." Someone else yelled, "He drove the boat, guard, let him in."

That statement was confirmed by a number of the others and the guard finally let me in.

Later I heard both Rupert Murdoch and Dennis Conner came by, but the guards wouldn't let them in. I considered myself lucky that someone backed up my story!

There was a formal ceremony two days later in which the Cup was officially handed over to Royal New Zealand Yacht Squadron Commodore Peter Hay. After packing up the boats and most of the equipment, the team was flown to the east coast of the United States for more celebrations in New York and Washington.

We arrived in New Zealand on May 24 with Cup in hand. We had heard the victory inspired our countrymen and women to great joy, but we in no way expected what awaited us in Auckland. The first suggestions of what our nation had in store for us were evident at the airport. We stepped off the chartered Air New Zealand jet (the Cup had its own first-class seat) onto a red carpet, lined with cheering airport employees. After a brief press conference, we boarded buses for the trip into the city, where we heard "something of a celebration" had been planned.

The entire way from the airport into the city, some 12 miles, was lined with New Zealanders – babies, kids, parents, grandparents. By the time we got to Queen Street, we were absolutely overwhelmed. People said this was the biggest outpouring of support in the history of the country. Sir Edmund Hillary came to meet us and give his congradualtions. I'll always remember the ice pick someone sent me in 1992 when we were backed up against the wall. The pick had the words Hillary on it. Sir Edmund being there meant a lot to me.

An estimated 500,000 turned out. The next day, the scene was repeated in Wellington, where some 400,000 people came to cheer us. Similar scenes followed in Christchurch and Dunedin. As the streamers fell like rain and the shouts of joy surrounded us, we came to understand the reception was something that none of us can do justice to in words. I'll have to leave it at simply saying it was a once-in-a-lifetime experience.

Not long after the Cup racing was over, I remember Michael Fay telling me it would take me a long time to regain the desire to focus on top-flight competition. He predicted a period of "America's Cup burn-out" and estimated it would take a year for the emotions and sensations of winning the Cup to wear off.

He was not far off. I participated in a few fleet races and match-race regattas throughout the rest of 1995, but I admit my heart wasn't in it and the results were painfully obvious that was the case.

But during the early part of 1996, I had some time to myself away from sailing and was able to recharge the batteries somewhat. There was also a pretty big incentive to get back into match racing.

In March of 1995, in the midst of the America's Cup challenger trials, a press conference was held at the San Diego Yacht Club to announce a new sponsor on the match-racing circuit. The American fragrance and toiletries company Brut was coming into the sport in a big way. In addition to sponsoring five of the most prestigious events on the circuit, they offered a challenge to all skippers. Anyone who could win three of the five events in one year would take home $US250,000. In addition to the quarter-million, the lucky skipper would also take possession of the Brut Sailing Series trophy, a Fabergé Egg.

The specially commissioned Sailing Series Egg, created by the Victor Mayer Co in Pforzheim, Germany, is 18-carat gold turned and enamelled with the guilloche technique made famous more than a hundred years ago by master craftsman Peter Carl Fabergé.

During the first year of the Brut Series in 1995, Dutchman Roy Heiner won the Brut Cup of San Francisco and the Brut Cup of New York, setting up the possibility of winning the grand prize in Bermuda. Unfortunately for Roy, he didn't make it.

I raced in only the New York and Bermuda events in 1995 and didn't do very well. But there was a lot of talk about the quarter-million among the match-racing sailors and I admit I became intrigued by the idea. So I asked Brad Butterworth, Warwick Fleury and Simon Daubney, all members of my match racing team on and off for years, to join me in a run for the money.

The first event of the 1996 Brut Sailing Series was in Lymington, England. Apparently the break had done us all good as we were undefeated in 13 races and beat Chris Law in the final. We were one-third of the way to the cash and the Egg, but we knew the next event, in San Francisco, would present a real challenge.

Although I had been living in San Francisco for a while, as the California location is a little more central than New Zealand to the many venues I attend, it takes many years of sailing to understand the currents and winds just off the famous St Francis Yacht Club. The event was also filled with one of the most competitive fields in recent memory. We struggled with some of our spinnaker handling, but we were able to sail well enough in the critical races to make it to the finals. I was particularly pleased to see Morgan Larson, a relative newcomer to the circuit, make it to the finals as well.

We beat him in a hard-fought series and headed for Sete, France, hoping our luck in French events of past years would stay with us one more time. Despite the fact that this was the third event in three different venues in three different types of boats, we handled the conditions fairly well until we came up against Peter Gilmour in the semi-finals.

Gilly wanted to be our spoiler and he came very, very close to doing so. In strong winds, the Australian took the first two races off us and needed only one more to send us home. As in San Francisco, we were having problems handling the spinnaker, but then the French luck we had hoped for kicked in. The winds moderated enough to where we got the boat and sails under control. We were able to tie up the series before the racing was called for the day because of darkness.

The next morning, in lighter breezes than the day before, we got by Gilly and then went on to face Frenchman Marc Bouet. By now we were a little more used to the boats and we felt we were ready to take on the 1994 match-racing world champion in his home waters. And, in truth, we had a little more incentive to win than he.

We did win the event and the grand prize of the money and the Egg. It was a great thrill for all of us. On a personal level, I'd have to say winning the Olympic gold medal, the America's Cup and the Brut Sailing Series Trophy have been the three greatest moments in my sailing career.

Now, as I look towards the America's Cup of 1999/2000, to be held in Auckland, I anticipate one of the most exciting and competitive regattas in the history of that storied event. I believe the world will be amazed to see the number of spectator boats surrounding the race course. I also think we'll host more challengers than in any previous America's Cup. It will be interesting to see which team can plot their successful course to victory.

Career Highlights

1981   Winner of the Single Handed IYRU World Youth Championships

1984   Gold Medallist at the Olympics

1984, 1993, 1995   New Zealand Sailor/Team of the Year

1985   Awarded MBE for his contribution to Yachting

1986   Completed his Bachelor of Engineering degree,
University of Auckland

1989–1996   Helmsman winning 21 International Grade One Match Race
events, worldwide

1992–1993   Two-time World Match Racing Champion

1992, 1993–1995, 1996

             Helmsman of World Number One ranked Match Racing Team,
22 months straight and over 35 months total

1993   Tactician with the One Ton Cup winner *Pinta* for the German
team

             Winner of the Admirals Cup, with the German team

1994   Awarded the National Award, The Silberne Lorbeerlatt,
with a similar status to the CBE

1995   Winner with Team New Zealand Louis Vuitton Cup,
37–1 victories

             Winner with Team New Zealand America's Cup

             Awarded CBE

             Sperry World Sailor of the Year Award

             Awarded the Halberg trophy with Team New Zealand

1996   Helmsman for the winning team, Team Magic, in the Brut
Sailing Series Trophy, The Fabergé Egg

             Awarded the World Trophy for Oceania on behalf of
Team New Zealand